FEDERALIST & REGENCY
COSTUME: 1790-1819

FEDERALIST & REGENCY
COSTUME: 1790-1819

by R.L. Shep

R.L. SHEP
MENDOCINO

Copyright © 1998 by R.L. Shep
ISBN 0-914046-25-X
Library of Congress #97-30321
Printed in the United States of America
Published by: Distributed by
    R.L. Shep   R.L. Shep Publications
    Box 668   P.O. Box 2706
    Mendocino, CA   Fort Bragg, CA
        95460   95437

Library of Congress Cataloging-in-Publication Data

Shep, R. L., 1933-
    Federalist & Regency costume : 1790-1819 / by R.L. Shep.
        p.   cm.
    "Contains the complete text of the tailor's complete guide by the
Society of Adepts, 1796.
    Includes bibliographical references.
    ISBN 0-914046-25-X
    1. Costume--England--History--19th century. 2. Costume--United
States--History--19th century. 3. Costume--France--History--19th
century. 4. Tailoring--England--History--18th century.   I. Title.
GT737.S53   1998
391'.009'033--dc21   97-30321
                                                               CIP

Contents

1814 - French *Journal des Dames et des Modes*
Chapeau à bord plat. Gilet de Casimir. Pantalon de Tricot.

Notes on Fashion and Tailoring

FASHION

We have a tendency to think of the words "French" and "fashion" in the same breath. And it is true that France was the leader of fashion and, in terms of women's clothes at least, is now a leader of fashion. In the world of the 18th century Louis XIV made all the aristocracy of France attend him at Versailles. There they all wore fancy court dress, complete with ruffles, embroidery, and fashions that looked backwards - not forwards.

Meanwhile, In England, all this had changed as the court was not the center of social life and the aristocracy did not spend their time at court. They spent their time on their estates, in the country, and they dressed accordingly. Men appeared at court in what might be called "country fashions" and even if women, when being presented at court, had to dress more fancifully, they too had altered their dress to suit their lives on their country estates.

The upshot of this was that after the French Revolution when it was dangerous, if anything, to wear French finery, people started to adopt English styles of dress. One only has to look at some of the names of the styles... "Robes-Redingotes," "Spencer," "Robe dite a l'Anglaise," "Lévite a l'Anglaise," "Frac a l'Anglaise," to realise this. Mila Contini says: "The Revolution had from the start declared war against all the fetters and chains imposed by the tyranny of fashion... A uniform dress was created that would be the same for all, drawing no distinctions between the classes: for men the bourgeois fashion, and for women extreme simplicity, influenced by English fashion. Since the time of Colbert in the 17th century, France had had unchallenged supremacy in the world of fashion, just as Italy had in the 16th century. In the last decade of the 18th century France, preoccupied with political problems, left the field to England."

Even though France and England were at war during a good deal of this time, the French fashions were influenced by what they called "l'anglomania" and the fashions turned right around and came back to the English magazines as French fashions. Laver puts this very well: "It is one of the curiosities of social history that the French, so completely convinced that there is no culture but French culture, so chauvinistic, so provincial even, in their estimate of what goes on outside France, should yet suffer from recurring bouts of what they themselves recognize, by the name they give it, as a kind of madness, namely anglomania. It raged in the 1790s, in the *Directoire* period, and the fact that the two countries were at war for nearly twenty years seems to have made no difference to the admiration which Frenchmen felt for the Englishman's clothes. When contact was re-established in 1814, and again in 1815, after the brief interlude of 'the Hundred Days', it became plain that if English women decided, once for all, to adopt French fashions, French men were equally determined from then on to dress *à l'anglaise,* with the nagging suspicion that, try as they would, they were not quite managing to do so."

Uzanne, a noted French writer on fashion, says: "Anglomania raged, swaying fashion and habits just as powerfully as the mania for the antique. In the eyes of certain fashionable ladies, nothing that was not in vogue in London could be either pretty or in good taste. So much so that certain French tradeswomen crossed the Channel, so as to be sure of giving satisfaction to their customers."

If the English and European writers see things in this light, many American writers of college texts do not. They have somehow come to the conclusion that the people in Jane Austin's novels, who were after all English, wore *Directoire* fashions!

Be that as it may, there is no doubt that Fashion went through some extreme changes between the French Revolution and the end of the Regency. The scope can be seen in the contrast between the illustrations of both male and female fashions of the 18th century, taken from Planche (please note that this is not a primary source as they were done in the late 1800s), and the fashion illustrations from 1818 — the man is French and the women English. Even when one takes into account the stylizations, etc., it is apparent that these fashions represent completely different worlds. If the late 18th century was a time of revolution, both in the United States and in France; then, certainly the early 19th century was an era of progress and scientific discovery and is often called the Age of Enlightenment. So too in fashions, Nora Waugh says: "Whereas the 18th century was characterized by its attention to cut, the 19th was notable for its concentration on fit." and Claudia Kidwell says: "By the early 19th

Gentlemen of the reigns of Queen Anne, George I. and II., from Jeffrey's collection, published in 1757.

a, 1700-15; b, 1735; c, 1745; d, 1755.

Planche - men's costume
of the 18th century

1818 - French

Journal des Dames et des Modes

Habit à Collet de Velours et Boutons de soie. Pantalon de Nankin.

Ladies of the reign of George II., from Jeffrey's collection.
a, 1735; *b*, 1745; *c*, 1755.

Planche - women's costume
of the 18th century

1818 - English

Walking & Evening Dresses for July 1818.

century, men's suit coats had become sculptural forms created more by their cut than by the drape of the textile. Increasingly, a gentleman's figure was the product of his tailor's art rather than his parent's genes."

This might also be called the era of the last flowering of male fashions, or the male as a bird of colorful plumage. This too is the time when Dandyism and Beau Brummel were in full force. The Dandy was not a show-off (as some people think), but dressed impeccably. Beau Brummel said: "If John Bull [the English public] turns round to look at you, you are not well dressed; but either too stiff, to tight, or too fashionable." This last flowering of male fashion lasted until the Victorian Era and then became codified and somber and has never fully recovered. In fact you can look at a typical Victorian frock coat and imagine it full of embroidery and lace and that it could possibly be acceptable in the French court of that late 18th century. Although that might be a far stretch of the imagination, it is easy to see that the long skirts in front and the closed nature of the costume is a far cry from the elegance of the Regency period.

Giles, writing in 1887 about male fashions in the Victorian Era said: "The general character of costume has not undergone any change during this reign." Dandyism, however, in one form or another has survived in its way. The male fashions of the Carnaby Street Era come to mind. For a closer look at Dandyism and its effects on men's fashions see: "Dandyism & English Tailoring" in *Late Georgian Costume.*

In terms of women's fashions we are fortunate to have detailed descriptions, as well as many illustrations, from contemporary magazines of the type garment that would be made by a mantua-maker, or dressmaker. These have been included after the tailoring systems. Tailors did make some women's garments and these can be found in the tailoring manuals. Books about women's dressmaking do not appear in this period.

In the United States there is ample evidence that Americans were not all simple backwoodsmen who, as parodied in Yankee Doodle Dandy, just stuck a feather in their cap and called themselves Macaronis. The Macaroni, unlike the Dandy, was an over-dressed, effete, member of a club in London who made a spectacle of themselves in terms of fashion. As Laver says: "The Macaronis of the 1770s and early 1780s were not dandies: their style of dress might be described as the last flourish of eighteenth-century artificiality before the dandy revolution."

Americans were very interested in fashionable dress. It is said that

Washington kept his measurements on file with a London tailor so that he could order clothing in the latest style and have it sent over by fast packet. Kidwell gives a quote from the early 19th century: "There was no fashion in London but in 3 or 4 months it is to be seen at Boston." And again from Annapolis in 1771: "The quick importation of fashion from the Mother country is really astonishing, I am almost inclined to believe that a new fashion is adopted earlier by the polished and affluent Americans than by many opulent persons in the great metropolis..." [i.e. London]. Ready to wear shops appeared in American by 1800, and tailors often made up extra stock to sell over the counter. In fact, Brooks Brothers was started in 1818. What Kidwell calls the difference between "Made for somebody, and made for anybody." The tailoring manuals refer to jackets made for anybody as "slop jackets."

It is little wonder then that Queen and Lapsley took this tailoring manual of 1796, adapted it to the fashions that were prevailing in 1809, made what they felt were necessary changes, and reprinted it to serve the needs of the growing number of tailors in the United States.

For those of you who are not particularly interested in tailoring systems and do not feel that you need to read this one, we would point out that there is much to be learned about the fashions of the times, as well as attitudes. Here are a couple of interesting items — in the 1809 version we find the following statement regarding breeches: "Remember, that if the party must have linings (we always recommend drawers, as they can be occasionally washed,)..." We trust this will give you some ideas regarding the hygiene of the time. Another item you might find of interest from the 1796 version is the following comment about the fitting of a Ladies' Riding Habit: "this fault was, the coat would not hang down straight before, but rose up on the belly, which totally disfigured the Lady, and shewed her in front in a situation which circumstances had not in the least entitled her to;..." presumably this made her look pregnant, which they could not bring themselves to say. For the serious costume researcher there is a lot to be learned from this text, even if you do not ever intend to make any of the garments.

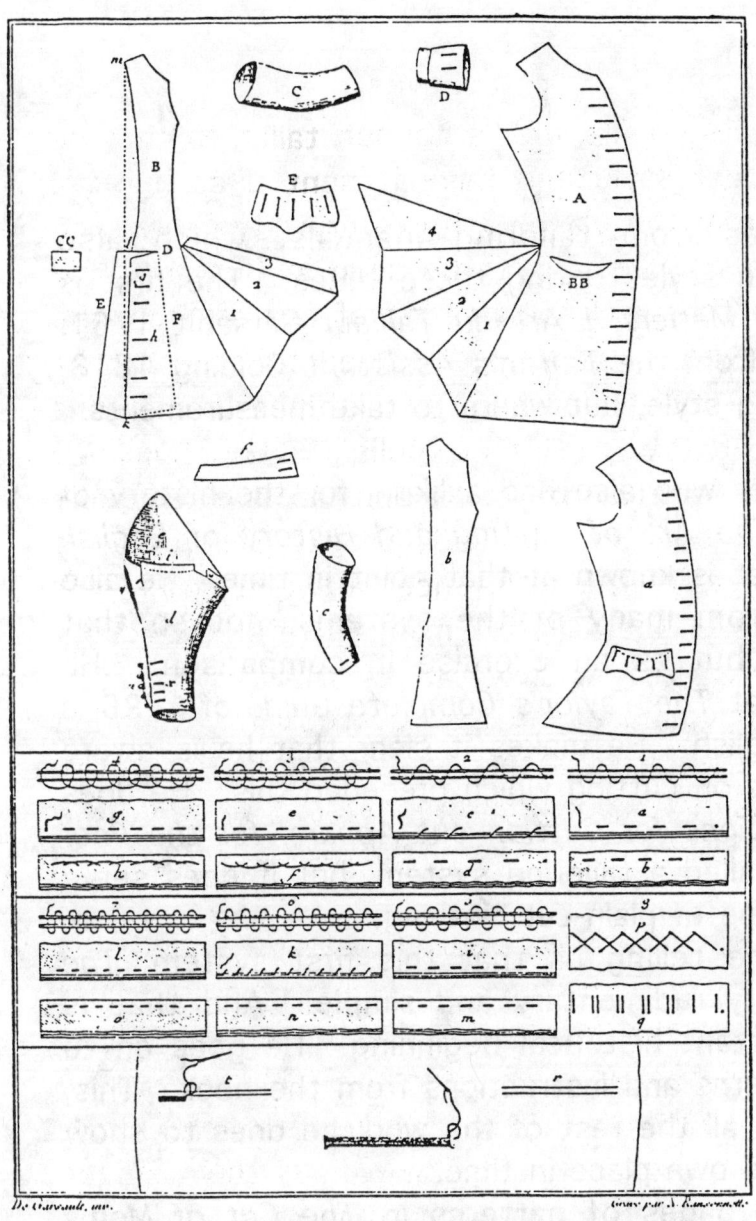

1761 - Garsault. *L'Art du Taileur*

1817

frontispiece from Golding's
The Tailor's Assistant

11

TAILORING

We are showing two examples from tailoring manuals, which also illustrate the extreme change in styles during these times. The first is French, *Description des Arts et Métiers, L'Art du Tailleur* Garsault 1761. The second is the frontispiece from the *Tailor's Assistant* Golding 1818, and shows not only the prevailing style, but where to take measurements.

Edward Giles was a master tailor who also had a liking for the history of tailoring. In 1887 he wrote *The Art of Cutting and History of English Costume* in which he traces what is known at that point in time. He also gives excerpts and patterns from many of the systems, not so that garments can be reproduced, but as an exercise in comparison. He contends, as many people do, that *The Taylor's Complete Guide* of 1796 is the first tailoring system in English. He makes it clear that he is aware of the Spanish and French works on cutting which preceded this. He does not seem to be aware of *Instructions for Cutting out Apparel for the Poor* of 1789, which can hardly be called a tailoring system, but it does serve as a useful reference for this type of plain-cut clothing.

Giles spends a lot of time telling us that this first system, *The Taylor's Complete Guide,* is very rudimentary and simple. And that is indeed true. But it is an important historical beginning. He goes on to reproduce a number of the patterns and instructions from the book. This, in a way, becomes the basis for all the rest of the work he does to show how tailoring developed up to his own place in time.

Nora Waugh reproduced 2 pages of patterns in *The Cut of Men's Clothes* with no instructions and does not even identify the various pieces of the patterns. Again, in *The Cut of Women's Clothes,* she reproduced patterns for the bodice part of a Ladies' Riding Habit "without the usual seams." Here too the parts of the pattern are not identified, there are no instructions, and it is not even made clear that this is part of a habit.

But there has never been an attempt made before this to completely show this system and compare it to the supposed U.S. reprint of 1809: *The Tailor's Instructor.* Giles mentions this latter book in passing. Claudia Kidwell, on the other hand, writing from the standpoint of American tailoring in *Cutting a Fashionable Fit,* has a much better understanding of the value of it. We have given the full text of the work of 1796 and compared it to that of 1809, showing the additions, deletions and changes. In doing this we find that there are two chapters in the 1809 work that don't even appear in that of 1796. But even more important to the study of fashion, the styles in 1809 were different, which is reflected in those plates.

Betty Williams, who was one of the most knowledgeable costumers I have ever known (especially in the area of men's historical tailoring) has helped identify the various pieces of the patterns, where possible, for both texts. She also said: "I compared the coats in Q & L with the coats in Golding and Wyatt and they are remarkably similar. It can be made to work right up to 1830, which seems to me a good useful range." Essentially what she is saying is that she compared the patterns in Queen & Lapsley's *The Tailor's Instructor* of 1809 with Golding's *Tailor's Assistant* of 1818, and Wyatt's *The Tailor's Friendly Instructor* of 1822 (this is included in *Late Georgian Costume*), and that she felt that the patterns of 1809 are similar enough to be used until 1830. She was speaking as a knowledgeable costumer, of course, and realised that the basic lines were the same but changes would have to be made in small ways, such as collars, etc.

ACKNOWLEDGEMENTS

I have had a lot of help with this project and want to thank: Betty Williams (deceased) who was an expert in historical men's tailoring, amongst other things. She kept pushing me to publish the system and tried to identify the parts of the patterns in the plates. Kathy Hammel, who amongst other things, is an expert on Regency women's fashions and writes articles on this subject; she has given me invaluable help over the course of the last year. Mike McAffee, Curator of History, West Point Museum, and Bill Brown, of the National Park Service at Harpers Ferry, for their help with the military uniforms. Bob Trump, historical tailor, for his help in reviewing the glossary, and Fred Struthers.

I also want to thank the following: Irene Joshi, Librarian: the University of Washington; Kathleen Kannik of Kannik's Korner; Alan Stein, curator: Morristown National Historical Park; Gail Cariou, costume curator: Canadian Parks Service; Mimi Sherman, curator: Old Merchant's House Museum; Carol Hall, Associate Director of Interpretation: Old Salem; Edward L. Praxmarer; and Janet Rigby;

Practical Information on the Tailoring Systems

The entire text of *The Taylor's Complete Guide* of 1796, by a Society of Adepts in the Profession, has been transcribed and retained here. This is said to be the oldest tailoring system in the English language and was published in London. The only changes have been to render the older style of "f" to "s" where appropriate. In this way words like "fatin" become "satin" and "cafe" becomes "case".

In 1809 *The Taylor's Instructor*, by James Queen and William Lapsley, was published in Philadelphia. This work has often been referred to as just a reprint of the earlier one from England. This is not entirely true. In the first place the plates (and thus the styles) are different. A certain amount of the text is different, and each work has chapters that are not in the other work. On the other hand it is true that Queen & Lapsley did use the earlier text for the majority of what appears in their book, they even admit to this.

The text of *The Taylor's Complete Guide* (hereafter referred to as "Taylor's") appears on the right-hand pages and the deletions, changes, additions, etc., that are in *The Taylor's Instructor* (hereafter referred to as "Queen & Lapsley" or "Q&L") appears on the left-hand page. The additional parts of Q&L appear as separate chapters at the end.

Taylor's had three oversized plates, only. These are shown in the original binding instructions. We have reduced each plate for an over-all view and then enlarged them to two pages for a better view. The text often refers to numbers and letters which do not show up on these plates (due to their age, or whatever). Also the plates were never marked to show which patterns went with which garment. We have tried to remedy this with the help of Betty Williams, who was an expert in historical men's tailoring. Also, to make matters even worse, the text often refers to "Plate D" - there never was a plate D. At this point they are talking about "Coats" and they appear on Plate C.

Q&L has five plates and we have attempted to put them as near as possible to the garments that they refer to. Betty Williams has also attempted to identify the parts of the garments shown on these plates.

Aside from all this, Queen and Lapsley, when they laid out their book of 1809, decided to change the order of the book entirely. They started with "Coats" — where Taylor's starts with Breeches". We have preserved the order shown in Taylor's and at the beginning of each chapter have indicated the page on which the corresponding information appears in Q&L.

THE

TAYLOR's COMPLETE GUIDE;

OR,

A Comprehensive Analysis of
BEAUTY and ELEGANCE in DRESS.

Containing Rules for cutting out

GARMENTS OF EVERY KIND,

And fitting any Person with the greatest ACCURACY and PRECISION, adapted to all Sizes.

Pointing out, in the clearest Manner,

The former Errors in the Profession, and the Method of rectifying what may have been done amiss.

Rendered plain and easy to the meanest Capacity.

ILLUSTRATED WITH COPPER-PLATES.

To which is added,

A Description to cut out and make the

PATENT ELASTIC HABITS and CLOATHS,

Without the usual Seams,

Now in the highest Estimation with the Nobility and Gentry,

According to a Patent granted by His Majesty.

The Whole Concerted and Devised

By a Society of ADEPTS in the PROFESSION.

LONDON:

PRINTED FOR ALLEN AND WEST, 15, PATERNOSTER-ROW.

Price 10s. 6d.

1796

DEDICATION (Q & L)

To the Master Taylors, Journeymen and Apprentices, and the whole Body Corporate of the Trade in the *United States*

THE following work will no doubt, produce in your minds a degree of curiosity, as it is the first of the kind that has made its appearance in the United States, and we believe the second ever known in the English Language. The first was published in London, in the year 1796, and received the liberal patronage of the Trade in general, not only for its novelty, but for the interesting and useful instructions contained therein. The one following was more judiciously executed, being an improvement on the first, and exhibited one of the briefest compends of instruction, both in cutting and making up work of different kinds; so that from the Master Taylor, down to the youngest apprentice it proved interesting and useful.

We propose to follow the London copy in its most prominent features, comprising what is really beneficial, in the present state of improvement at which the trade has arrived. We sincerely wish we may be found clear in our communication in detail, as we are conscious of the motives which have induced us to dedicate a few leisure hours to oblige our fellow labourers in the profession. It has been our great aim to lead the ignorant and unexperienced, whose want of practice, as well as opportunity, could never enable them to compass the merits of the business.

That we have strictly adhered to this, every one will find, who will take the trouble to revise our labours, and study the maxims we have laid down. It is our sincere wish that the trade may be enlightened, and human nature receive its proper embellishment, by the improvement of graceful dress, and complete fitting. We sincerely hope we have given satisfaction, under which grateful sense, we humbly dedicate our endeavours to the trade, and mankind in general, wishing to be permitted to subscribe ourselves,

Gentlemen,

Your humble Servants,

THE AUTHORS.

DEDICATION

To all the Master Taylors, Journeymen, Apprentices, and the Parents of Apprentices, and the whole Body Corporate of the Trade.

The following Treatise may in some measure claim your Patronage; as it was concerted and undertaken for the Benefit of the Trade in general; and to alleviate the Difficulty that may arise through Want of Experience. We sincerely wish we may be found as clear in our Communications in Detail, as we are conscious of the Motives which induced us to dedicate a few Leisure Hours to oblige our Fellow Labourers, whose Want of Practice, as well as Opportunity, could never enable them to compass the Merits of the business. It has been our chief Study to lead the Ignorant and Inexperienced Taylor into the Road of prosperity and Happiness.

That we have strictly adhered to this, the Trade will find, who will take the Trouble to revise our Labours, and study the Maxims we have laid down. It is our sincere Wish, that the Trade may be enlightened, and Human Nature receive its proper Embellishment, by the Improvement of the graceful Dress, and compleat Fitting. We sincerely hope we have given Satisfaction, under which grateful Sense, we humbly dedicate our Endeavours to he Trade, and Mankind in general, sincerely begging we maybe permitted to subscribe ourselves, with Respect,

Gentlemen,

Your most humble, most obedient,

And very dutiful Servants,

THE AUTHORS.

Re. PREFACE

Q&L - this is essentially the same except that some of it has been paraphrased in Q&L.

Verbose, they put down the tailoring trade in general. Interesting comments on slop-made coats and working from patterns instead of measuring.

Maxims: a general or proverbial truth

PREFACE.

We know not how the Connoisseurs and Judges of Literature may receive this Work. It is our first Essay; and being but superficial Judges of logical Disquisitions, and other Embellishments of Diction we shall beg Leave most humbly to shield ourselves under the Banner of good Intent. Our chief Motive in this Undertaking is to improve the Trade, remove the Barbarism from the general Mode of Practice, establish a Criterion to avoid Error, and leave a lasting Monitor to all succeeding Generations.

It has been by the Dint of great Application and much Practice, that we have arrived at the perfect Standard we mean to define to the Trade in the following Sheets; for as every Effect has its primeval Cause, we shall point out such certain Rules, which if properly adhered to, will prevent Error in the Application, and the Learner will gain Credit by filling his Employer well on his first Effort.

It has long been to the great Disgrace of the greatest City in the World, where the Arts and Sciences are so liberally courted, and the Palm so nearly won, that clothing Human Nature should remain a Secret as to Certainty; for by observing the grotesque Figures we daily meet in the Streets to whom Nature has been extremely bountiful, you plainly perceive by the Distortion and cutting of the Garments, that the whole is erroneous, and void of Design as of Method. We remember a Taylor in the Country, whose chief Boast was his great Experience, having made Clothes for three succeeding Generations. Being interrogated by a new Rector of the Parish, touching his Skill in fitting, he made Answer, that knowing all the newest Fashion, which he progressively learned from a Friend in London, and fitting People like Skin upon their Backs, by which he had got all his Reputation and vast Custom. The Divine being satisfied by this feasible Assertion, unfortunately put his French superfine black Cloth into his Hand; but alas! when he received his Coat from the Taylor, he too fatally found he had been gulled; for one of the Sleeves was an Inch and a half too short; the Elbow of the other was cut two Inches above the Bend of the Arm, too low in the Neck, the Waist too short, the Skirts lower before than behind; and what was worse, it was not wide enough in the Waist by five inches. The Rector asked him what he meant by deceiving him in a Matter of such material Consequence: The Taylor told him he could not see how it could happen to fit so badly, for he had made it by the blue Pattern, which he never knew to fail before.

This Method of working by Patterns, we are afraid, is too much followed by the Trade; instead of working by their Lengths, and following Nature in every existing Circumstance. Patterns can be but of little Service to any but Slop-makers where they have them from the smallest Size to the largest Figure upon proportionable Scales; but where Nature has a little sported with the Formation of a Figure, a Person would be as ridiculous in one of those slop-made Coats, (though perhaps not very outré in the Length or Width) as the poor disappointed Rector was in his Coat made by the blue Pattern.

To arrive at Certainty is the Perfection of Art, which we hope clearly to elucidate to the Satisfaction of the Trade; therefore hope no Practitioner will think his Time and Labour lost, by endeavoring to acquire a Knowledge of the Maxims in the following Sheets; for surely, no Situation can be more distressing than that of a Taylor, who having cut and mutilated his own or his Employer's

Re. INTRODUCTION

Q&L - some slight paraphrasing in Q&L.

Verbose and doesn't say much.

Cloth, wasted his Trimmings and Labour, which will frequently be the Case, when a Man has nothing to depend upon but the poor bankrupt Resource of Chance or Hope that his Clothes will fit. Much depends on Practice, although you are positively in possession of the Theory, which we shall clearly detail in every Stage and Circumstance.

THE TAYLOR'S GUIDE

INTRODUCTION.

One of the first things to be acquired in order to the improvement of arts and the enlarging of our ideas, is for a time to step out of the beaten way of common practice; and by a prudent reserve and charitable modesty, make such strict and judicious enquiries into the matter you would fathom, before you make any anti-conclusions to the theme in question.

We are not unapprized what objections may be made to the bold assertion of arriving at the Ne Plus Ultra in any art.

Science is the knowledge of things in their causes, and the way to arrive at it, is by consequence and deduction. We must own our best knowledge is sometimes imperfect and fallacious: After all our confidence, it is possible, things may be otherwise. This must be when demonstrations are raised from false principle, but when genuine Effects, produced by natural Rudiments, and proportionate Systems appear from Efficient Causes, and when the Object is within the Boundaries of our own Intellects, we must pronounce the axiom incontrovertible; upon these Principles we build our Superstructure — these are the criterions of our Propositions, and we hope the Trade will assent to them as soon as they compass their meaning, and conclude the System true. The blind hypothesis of certainly, we own, may be alleged as full of difficulty and doubt, especially in so abstruse and complex an Art as the variegated Maxims of Cutting Cloths, when the least Error of appropriating or uniting the most trifling separation of any of the Parts, would overturn our boasted System; this we may allow, but this could not happen where the Practice is coincident with the Theory, and both conjoin to display their reasonable Efforts together; it is enough for our Theory to know, that we possess such principles of Art, sanctioned by long Experience; which we hope clearly to define both by Precept and Example, and which the Trade must assent to when there is not the most distant Shadow of occasion to doubt the truth of either. We hope our Maxims will be Universal; that every one may know and practice, if they will but give themselves Time for application, and move modestly on till they arrive at the beautiful Temple of Certainty, where their Business will be conceived, as soon as premised, and executed with Pleasure, Ease, and Satisfaction — not subject to the opinions, whims, fancies, and foolish humours of mistaken Men; but a certainly all the World over averred by conclusions, clearly and distinctly perceived by every Artist in the Trade, and that they are peremptorily established. If we may not be thought too sanguine in the Cause we have espoused, we think we may with veracity say, that a Treatise of this kind has been long wanted. Why nobody has explored the unbeaten Path to its

Re. OF FASHION

Q&L -the same.

Philosophical views on fashion and the need for moderation and taking the figure of the person into account instead of blindly following an extreme fashion full extent, we are at a loss to say, for certainly if it was ever known, the Possessor of the Art suffered the secret to die with him; for nothing we have seen has the least resemblance of that which we mean to possess the Trade with.

That all the world may be improved, and human nature receive its pristine Grace and Elegance, is the principal object of our ambition; and by administering to the general good, and conferring an obligation upon industrous Individuals, our ultimate end will be answered.

OF FASHION.

When the Boundaries of an Art is properly defined, we proceed to shew and garnish the fancy with every Grace that is excellent in that Art; we conclude that Science is confirmed of the truth which enlivens the Imagination, and we modestly look forward for Incidents to facilitate the Mind with what is most congenial to the Subject, for an embellishment of Taste, Fashion, and Elegance — in this, the Eye has its correspondence in all that is just and beautiful; it acquires a kind of habitual nicety, and answers every genuine Impression which results from ocular Demonstration; the Eye will soon discriminate between Grace and Affection, between the Elegant Contour and Dress of a complete Gentleman, and the extravagant whimsies of a City Fop — there are great considerations in the article of dress, the former being the result of Grace, Sensibility, and refined experience, the later the extravagance of folly, under the sanction of the Whim of Fashion; though we would have all our Brothers of the Trade understand us right, in this great particular; although we may in these Sheets have occasion to criminate the Luxury of the Whim to shew what is opposite to Grace and Elegance, we by no means discountenance the Votaries of Fashion; for we are well convinced of its Use and Benefits. The novelty of Fashion is the Nursery of Trade, the propagator of the Arts, and Field of great Employment. By Fashions our fancies are constantly amused, by the brilliancy of every newly engendered Improvement, and our Minds become respondent for every Change, — in the gradation our understandings are passive till we arrive at the very summit of Excess, and having there regaled ourselves upon the very top, and apex of our fancies, we grow tired with the sameness of the Scene, 'till the fluctuating Goddess takes a retrospective view of the variegated steps by which she ascended; she then modestly returns to the medium from which we started, nearly by the same progression, and when we are seated there, and in possession of all the proportions of Symmetry that can give graceful effect to Drapery, we are still unsatisfied; the Mind is not at Ease, still Fancy leads us by the same meanders, till we are seduced to the opposite extreme.

Thus are the Arts encouraged, Trade supported, and Mankind made happy by their Industry and Endeavors for the benefit of Society and the general good; so much advantage does Trade receive from Fashion; but we must have the Reader understand, that though this fickle Goddess is so beneficial and necessary, she by no means holds an arbitrary station in our Theory — for it is but of little consequence to a complete Taylor, what the Fashions are; his business is to fit the body, that no constriction or unnatural compression may be felt in any part, that freedom without contraction, and liberty without redundancy, may be the source and Theme of his Practice.

It matters not whether narrow or broad Backs are the Rage of Fashion, Stand-up or turn-down Collars, short or long Waists, or whatever turn the cut of the Skirts may take, the ultimate end is to cut and fit well, taking care to harmonize the prevalence of the Whim, by assimilating the Parts with Prudence and Ease, having the following Maxim in view, That the very Pride of Elegance is Collective Neatness.

Never strive to hurry on excesses, let them move gradually as Custom sanctions the prevalence, and remember that all Fashions are most bearable upon well-turned figures; for observe, when Clothes of broad Backs, long Skirts, and heavy Sleeves are the *Ton*, how preposterous it would be to go to the very extreme with a light small figure; such a Person, under such a circumstance, must be almost immersed in Cloth, — on the other extreme, how truly ridiculous did a heavy athletic Man look a few seasons ago, with a back to his Coat not more than three inches broad, skewered up like one of the new raised infantry, without front or Skirt to cover his Body or Breech. So much we mean as a hint to the learner, that he may devise a happy medium on every occasion, and never exceed the dictates of Reason.

If your Employer should be an over strenuous advocate for the reigning Fashions of the Times, endeavor to point out the happy medium you would aim at, and shew him what is repugnant to Elegance and graceful-seeming; if rational, it may perhaps excite him to moderation, which when properly understood, will reflect great credit both upon your Wisdom and Practice.

Notwithstanding what we have urged here as a bar to excesses, we must allow that Fashions in many Cases are very captivating; for things that are new raise a kind of pleasure in the Fancy, surprise as it were the Imagination, and gratify the curiosity with things it did not possess before.

If it were not for the unstable fluctuation of Fashions, People would be too familiar with one set of objects, and wearied out with the dull repetition of the same thing. Therefore we must allow whatever is new or uncommon, adds to the pleasurable variety of human Taste; it serves us as a kind-of refreshment — yet we must return to our former opinion, that nothing strikes so forcibly upon the mind as beauty in Perfection — that is the Seat of Satisfaction; when we once attain that, the Imagination is at rest, and the Faculties are in their meridian of Enjoyment, beholding the Picture of Ease united with Simplicity in Elegance and Splendor.

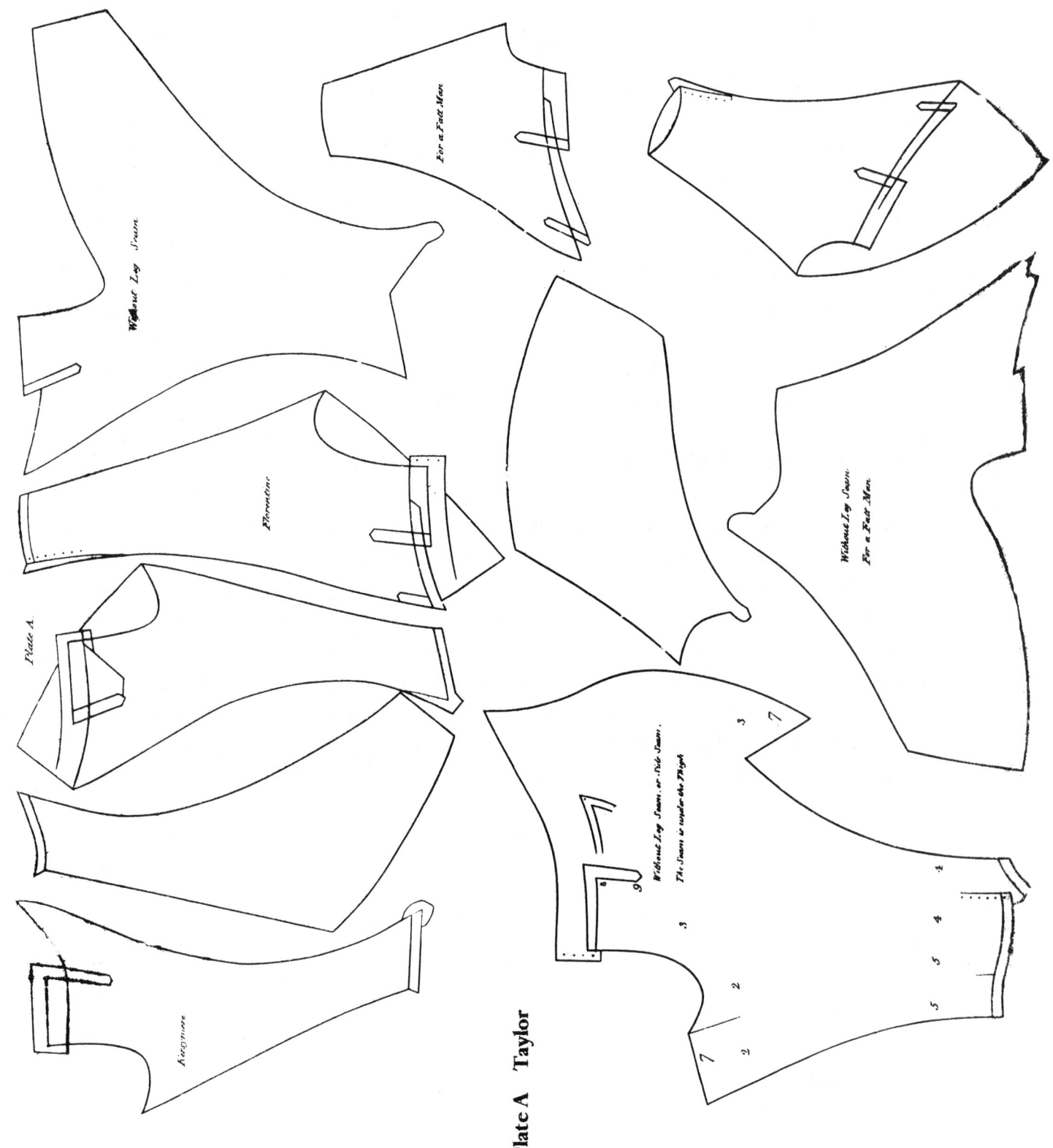

Plate A   Taylor

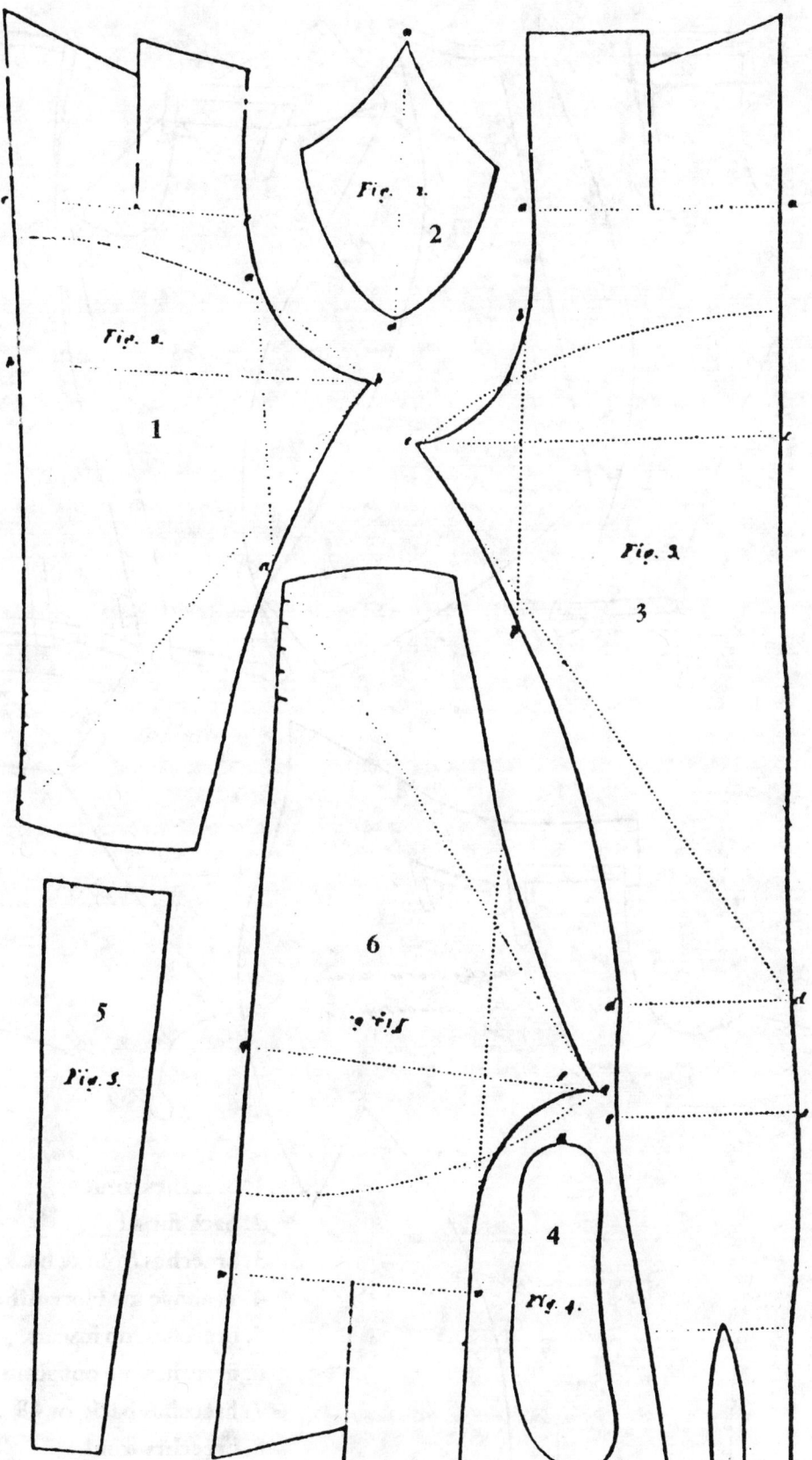

Plate VI   Q&L

Breeches & Pantaloons

1. tongue for feet
2. breeches
3. pantaloons
4. sole of foot
5. waist band
6. breeches

N.B. #6 is longer and
    slimmer in the leg
    than #2.

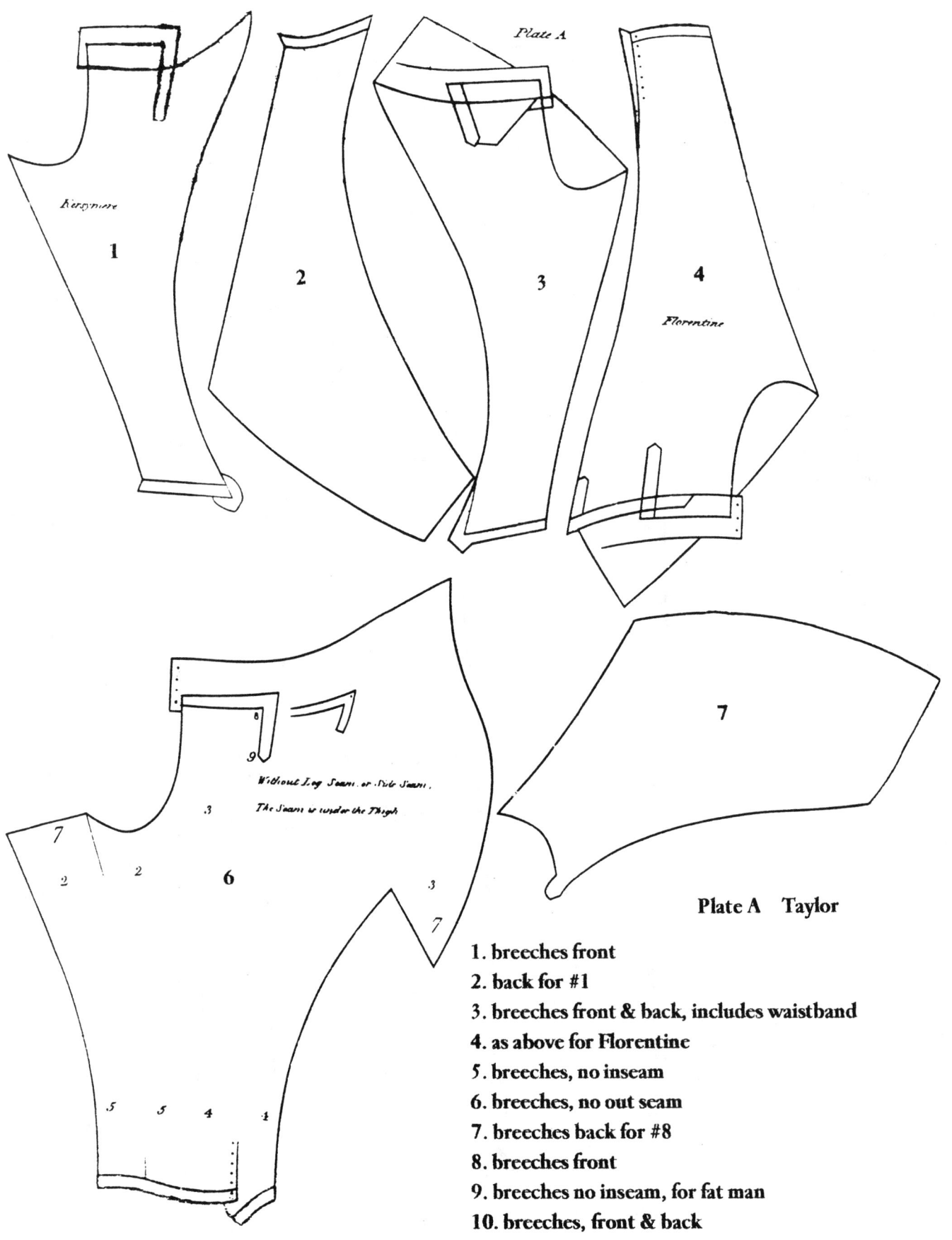

Plate A

Kersymere

1

2

3

Florentine

4

Without Leg Seam, or Side Seam.

The Seam is under the Thigh

8

9

6

7

7

Plate A   Taylor

1. breeches front
2. back for #1
3. breeches front & back, includes waistband
4. as above for Florentine
5. breeches, no inseam
6. breeches, no out seam
7. breeches back for #8
8. breeches front
9. breeches no inseam, for fat man
10. breeches, front & back

Please rely on garment name not necessarily #'s in text.

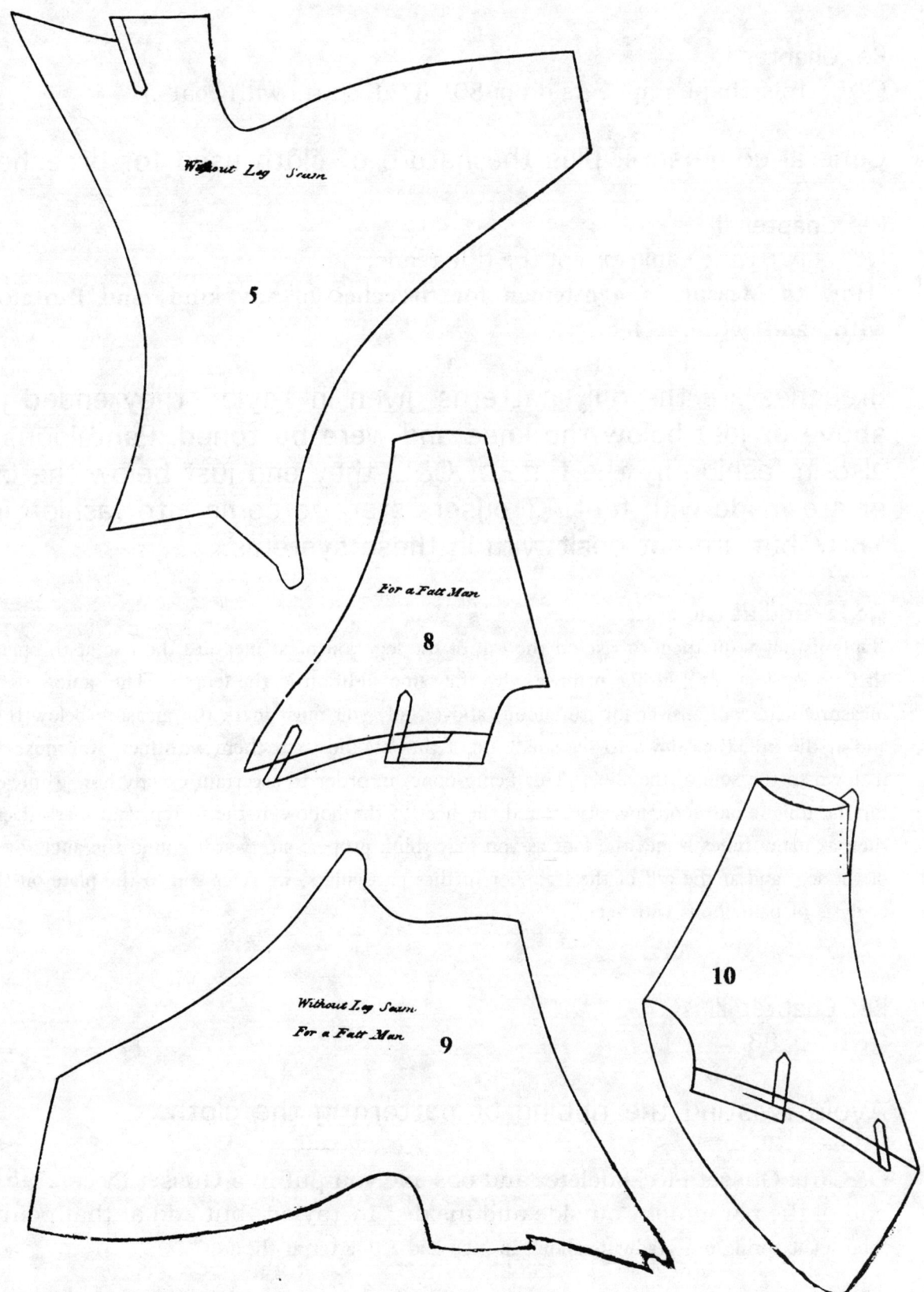

Without Leg Seam

5

For a Fatt Man

8

Without Leg Seam
For a Fatt Man

9

10

Re: Chapter I

Q&L - this chapter appears on p. 80. (Q&L starts with coats.)

General comments, plus the nature of cloth used for breeches.

Re: Chapter II

Q&L - p. 81.the same except the title reads:

"How to Measure a gentleman for Breeches of any kind, and Pantaloons, with, and without feet."

Breeches are the only patterns given in Taylor, they ended just above or just below the knee and were buttoned. Pantaloons are also in fashion by the time of Q&L, they end just below the calf or are made with feet. Trousers start to come into fashion in 1807 but are not dealt with in these systems.

Q&L - add at the end:

"Only if they want them to rise on the calf of the leg, you must measure the rise at the place they want them; and, in like manner, give the same addition in the length. The same measurements will answer for pantaloons above; only you must mark the measure below the knee and at the calf, then down to the small: or, if they should want them with feet, you must extend it down to the sole of the shoe. This being done, in order to ascertain exactly how to measure for the tongue and foot, measure round the heel to the hollow at the instep, and mark it exactly, then as many times round the foot as you may think proper; afterwards round the ancle or small of the leg, and at the calf of the leg. For further particulars, we refer you to the plate on the analysis of pantaloons with feet."

Re: Chapter III

Q&L - p. 83.

Avoid twisting the ribbing or pattern in the cloth.

Q&L (re: Gusset Piece) delete "and observe you put in a Gusset Piece..." to the end of the paragraph "outside and inside." in Taylor, but add at that point:

"and let it spring out gradually about an inch and a quarter at the top."

SECTION I.

Chapter I

Of the Theory and Practice of Breeches.

This delicate and necessary appendage to Dress requires more comments than the Trade would perhaps really imagine, chiefly owing to the great variety of materials of which they are composed for choice and approbation of various customers, and as they may suit the purposes of various occasions; for in all the changes and various textures of the different stuffs to be used in those matters, there is a serious difference both in the Theory and Practice, as will appear in their separate definitions — owing to the elasticity of some, and the turgidity of others, and repulsion of the rest: therefore till our Student has sifted and properly digested this matter, and availed himself of the different maxims of measure and making, and, as it were, screwed them to his Memory, we hope he will carefully read and follow the examples hereunto annexed, as they will prove to him in every respect a perfect justification of our precepts.

Chapter II

How to Measure Gentlemen for Worsted Stocking Breeches, Ribbed or Plain.

First lay the end of your Measure up a the Hip Bone, and extend the Measure down the Thigh to the bottom of the Cap of the Knee, and as much lower as the rage of Fashion may induce the Party to require it.

Secondly measure the Thigh very tight, also measure tight below the Knee, and likewise measure tight the hollow part above the Knee, next measure the thick part also tight as possible — then measure round the small part of the Body for the length of the Waistband, which is all that is necessary.*

Chapter III

Of Cutting and Making.

When at your Cutting Board, and have our Stocking Piece before you, observe the following maxim, which entirely results from the stretch or elasticity that there is in all Frame Work of this nature, and requires that the Breeches must be three Inches longer than the Measure. — But for more particulars we refer you to the Plates.

Lay your Measure upon the Piece within one Inch and half of the top, then extend it to the

Q&L (re: Knee Band) delete all the text after "let the Knee Band be cut" to the end of the chapter in Taylor, and replace it with:

"(let the kneeband be cut) exact, lining it with a piece of brown holland to the size. If they rise on the calf of the leg, cut the band one inch longer than your measure, and bear it on the ham in the under side, which need not be hollowed in the ham, as for short small-clothes. And in all stocking web, silk, or any other kind, you may bear on the waistband according to the length of them both — and not the breeches; which though diametrically opposite to the common practice in use for cassimere and all other kinds, yet we do affirm is positively right, and the true way, proved and justified by long experience, and which will convince every practitioner on his first essay, if he only strictly adhere to the rule here laid down, for making all kind of frame work.

Re: Chapter IV
Q&L - p. 86.

Cotton drawers require more stride.

Flannel is also called: Swan Skin.

intended place for the Knee, and mark it, and cut it longer an inch and a half below at the Knee; then for the width lay on the measure at the bottom of the Knee, and mark for cutting one inch narrower than the measure upon the Stuff in the double, and one inch less in gradation all the way up the Thigh, and be sure to abide by the following Example for the stride.

First make a deep fall down, and having laid your Finger upon the Measure at the bottom of the Knee, with the other Hand extend the Measure to the fork, and make the stride within three inches of the length of the Measure; this will give proper room for the elasticity of the materials,and ease and freedom to the Wearer.

Next cut your leg seam very straight, and not hollow as the common practice; and let your side seams be likewise straight from the Knee slit up to within four inches of the Hip; and * observe you put in a Gusset Piece from that place on the outside of the Hip two inches and a half wide at the top, and cut taper or bevelled down to a point five inches long, both of the outside and inside.

When this is done, and your Breeches are put on,you will find the Ribs go straight down the Thighs, which will avoid and provide against an abominable error in the Trade of twisting the Ribs across the Thighs, making them appear crooked, inwardly inclining which seems to the spectator (according to the old vulgar adage) as if people were ill shap'd or knap-knee'd. When you have got so far,cut your seat at the joining of the waistband, less by two inches double; and in making, let your * Knee Band be cut one inch longer than your Measure, and baste it on Lining, and sew it in with the Knee Band to the Breeches, this will keep them to the full size at the bottom, and make them lie agreeably, and rise to the springing of the Calf of the Leg, if required. Let both the Knee Bank and Waistband be beared on according to your length of them (both) and not the Breeches, which, though diametrically opposite to the common practice in use, we do affirm is positively right, and the true way proved and justified by long experience, and which will convince every practitioner on his first Essay, if he does but strictly adhere to the rule.

Chapter IV.

How to make Silk Frame Breeches.

The method of cutting, measuring, and making of Silk Frame Breeches, are the same in every respect as the worsted ones already defined, with this exception, that as the elasticity in Silk is more than that in Worsted, the true method is to cut them half an inch less in every place of the widths in the double, and three quarters of an inch longer in the lengths.

Note. If they are to be lined be sure only to fasten the Linings round the top to the Waistband, and leave them quite loose at the Knee, and for the Manner of cutting the Linings, take the following instructions.

Cut them one inch longer than the Measure, and half an inch double wider; give them plenty of stride up within one inch of the top of the Measure, after the same mode of practice you pursued in cutting the outside, and cut the seat two inches wider than the length of the Waistband, and bear it

Q&L - leave out the entire paragraph "If the Linings are to be of Flannel..." to the end "if the texture be very fine." in Taylor.

Re: Chapter V
Q&l - p. 88. the title differs:
"Rules for cutting frame Breeches for a corpulent man."

Many men were heavy so a lot of attention is paid to making clothes for them (for example George III and George IV).

Q&L delete the sentence starting with "In the next place" in Taylor, and substitute:
"In the next place, be sure to give them a good rising on the hip, as much as four inches higher than the top of the falldown;"

on in putting into the Breeches, that they may answer the elasticity of the outside. Cotton Drawers require more stride than any others in use, owing to the repulsion or contraction of the stuff.

* If the Linings are to be of Flannel, or what is called Swan Skin by the Trade, cut them half an inch less then the Measure, and even a diminution of that, less in regular proportion, if the texture be very fine.

If the Linings are of Dimity, follow the same example as in cutting the Cotton ones, which will answer the intended purpose.

Chapter V.

Rule for Cutting Stocking Breeches for a Fat Man.

When you measure a fat man, first lay your measure in the hollow of the groin, by the side of the fall down, and extend it to the inside of the Knee and to the bottom of the leg seam, and mark your measure.

Secondly, lay it as near the hip as possible and down to the string or buckle of the outside. Having made your mark, do not be ashamed of measuring this twice; for though there is no more difficulty in fitting a fat man than a thin one, if you are correct in taking your dimensions; but in this case, to be certain, it requires great circumspection. In taking your front length, be sure your measure goes up to the hollow under the belly, and not above that part in front; for it is a general complaint that fat men's breeches are mostly too long at the knees, chiefly owing to the weight and pressure of the belly which bears them down from the Hips.

Thirdly, for compassing the width, take your girth below the knee above at the knee slit, and as high up the thigh as possible.

Fourthly, observe well the length of the Waistband, as there are often gross errors committed in the particular.

Having proceeded so far, and your piece being laid before you, and the object in view, both in plate and person, lay on your measure to the different parts, and observe when cutting they must be one inch less that the measure (if Silk or Worsted Stocking) the length of the stride must be to the full length of the measure from the groin under the belly to the bottom of the leg seam; and also take notice that in laying on your measure in the place, you will find in the making that the sides of the Leg seams must be one inch longer than the bottom of the Knee Slit. This is necessary in all Breeches for fat men. * In the next place be sure to give them a good rising on the Hip, as much higher than in the groin by four inches, according to the plate. And in taking the length of the seat lay your measure on the point of the fork at the top of the Leg seam; keep your finger on that, whilst you extend it to the hip, and after run it up to the seat seam one inch longer to the hip than it is from the fork, which strictly adhered to will fully accomplish the intent of this awkward and difficult Practice.

Use care in cutting expensive materials, and use care in cutting to obtain a good fit.

Q&L (N.B.) add at the end of N.B.:
"and a quarter more, if they should rise very high."

Q&L (re: fear of ravelling) insert after "least fear of ravelling."
"If you cannot get gum, a little piece of bees' wax will answer the end. But take care and put but little on, as it is of a greasy nature. You must rub it on the exact length of the hole, with an iron, lapping it on the side, and melting the wax upon it, and holding the double, rub it along the mark."

Q&L (re: waistband/fall down seam) substitute "half an inch" for "three quarters of an inch" in Taylor.

Q&L (re: buttons) substitute "a quarter of an inch" for "half an inch" in Taylor

Chapter VI.

Of the Theory and Practice of Black Florentine Breeches.

As those materials are of a very delicate nature, I hope the Taylor will be particularly circumspect; as an error committed in things of such value may be very distressing; especially if they should be returned, the loss might be serious to a poor Tradesman; but to proceed.

First, measure from the hip-bone down to below the cap of the Knee, as before observed in former directions; then measure for the width below the knee, very tight. — Your next measure above at the knee slit must be very easy, and also measure easy at the thick part of the thigh; then measure round the small of the body for the waistband.

* N.B. If it should be a tall man you are measuring, you will require two yards and a quarter of Florentine.

Directions at the Cutting Board.

Lay your measure upon your piece, and mark out the place at the top for your pockets, then mark your fall down to the fork, and in marking this bring it straight down within four inches of the top of the leg seam, from which place turn up your line gradually according to plate, and with regularity up to the fork for the stride; afterwards mark your leg seam straight as possible to the knee, then from your side seam make them half a inch wider in the double of the stuff than your measure all the way up the thigh; for there is no stretch or elasticity in Florentine; therefore you have no dependence but an exactitude of the precepts proposed to facilitate your practice of certainty.

Please to observe that you must hollow for the turning in of the seams. All silk must be sewed in this manner to prevent ravelling on the edges. Then turn in the knee under the facing of the glazed linen, the same in the fall down and the tops of the pockets, commonly called the frog-mouth, and face with any thing black. When you are ready for your holes, lay a single bar of silk round them and sew to the Breeches, and gum them on the inside till they are stiff, which will enable you to cut all your holes at one time without the * least fear of ravelling. If you have pieces in your waistband, back stitch them first and afterwards stitch them down to the canvass; and further observe, when you put your waistband in, be sure you pitch them longer before than behind, so that your waistband from the hip to the front may be the greater half. This will cause your fall down to fit clear, for an error in this place will much incommode the fitting of the Breeches as much as bad Cutting. Also take care your men do not follow their usual practice of putting in the waistband what they call half and half. All Silk Breeches must be made very forward in the * waistband three quarters of an inch before the fall down seam, or they will not fit clear when buttoned.

N.B. When you put on the * buttons to the fall down, set them on rather higher by half an inch then the holes would seem to require upon the waistband; the buttons of the pockets the same. With respect to the buttons to the knees, let them all stand below the holes at the bottom, and draw in

Q&L (re: gained by your spring) substitute "two inches" for "three inches in Taylor. But they keep the next measurement of three inches as in Taylor.

Q&L (re: taper gusset) delete "and take the same method of putting in taper gusset pieces" all the way to the end of that paragraph (Ribbed Stocking Breeches) in Taylor.

Re: Chapter VII

Q&L p. 74 which they title:
"On the theory and practice of single and double milled Cassimere Breeches and Pantaloons."

Q&L delete "If you are measuring for a tall man" through the end of that paragraph , in Taylor, and substitute:
"if you are measuring a tall man, remember he will take too [sic] yards of cassimere for breeches, and for pantaloons two yards and a half will be sufficient, and no less. The cassimere must be cut in the following manner,"

Q&L (re: mark your knee straight across) insert:
"and the same at the small below the knee;"

Q&L (re: with this proviso) delete to the end of that paragraph in Taylor, and substitute the following,
"with this proviso, that you make a little allowance, if your customer wants them easy, in single milled cassimere you may cut them to the measure, as it is more elastic than the double milled, they should be cut a quarter of an inch less on the double, if they be wanted to fit tight to the thigh, as this kind of cassimere is adequate to it, if they are wanted tight."

the knee slit, likewise the knee band over the cap of the knee. Pray take care in the pressing you do not right side them, as it will injure the lustre of the Silk; and further observe in pitching of the pockets, that they may lay forward, not straight down the thigh, but right over to the leg seam; put on all your stays, sew your seams, and let them be basted with great exactness; a matter of great consequence to learners; and if they in this state are to the measure, and the other maxims strictly observed, be assured they will fit the Party with much nicety, and give him perfect satisfaction.

There are two sorts of Men who are rather troublesome to fit by young practitioners, either of Silk or Florentine; the one is he that is regularly fat in all parts, the other that is swag-bellyed, very tall and thin thighs; as the Taylor can have no resource for the least error by the stretch or elasticity of the stuff. The latter object with the thin thighs is more intolerable than the former, but in order to fit him take the following Example.

Cut the Breeches out by the previous rule, touching the regularity of the thighs; those answering the properties of your measurements, strike your fall down, then your pockets, and from the places opposite the fork, add a gradual spring up to the hip; and having by your measure held up straight from a regular line of the thigh, up to the top of the hip, you will find how much you have * gained by your spring; and if it is not so much, it must be to the full of three inches; and in cutting your inside, do in like manner up to the hip, and allow the fullness of three inches to be beared on, in setting to the waistband. Make not your seat so round as that for the fat man, for remember it is not so much in the seat (in this case) that the room is wanted, but round the body the place of the waistband [sic]. Let the leg-seam be very straight. If the stuff should be ribbed, let the ribs go straight down the thighs, * and take the same method of putting in taper gusset pieces to the outside and inside of the hips, as is described in the manner of making Ribbed Stocking Breeches.

When you make Breeches of Weymouth Silk, proceed in the same way as is taught in the Florentine.

Chapter VII.

Of the Theory and Practice of Kerseymere Breeches.

The manner of measuring for these sort of breeches differs not from the practice of others before described, by taking the length from the hip to below the knee-cap, and longer, as may be the result of fashion; then measure tight below the knee, and above at the knee-slit, and the thick part of the thigh, and round the waist, as before. — If * you are measuring a tall man, remember he will take a yard and a half of Kerseymere, which must be marked and cut in the following Manner:

First double the cloth with the wrong side towards you, and take care the grain of the wool lies right down the thigh. First mark your pockets and fall down, and having laid your measure at the top, extend it to the top of the knee, and * mark your knee straight across, and let it be rather shorter towards the leg seam, than it is at the bottom of the knee-slit; then mark up the thigh as your measure directs, * with this proviso, that you mark it half an inch less in the double than the measure, as the

Q&L (re: be sure to give stride enough) delete "and make them very high on the hip" through "within four inches of the bottom" in Taylor, and insert:
"and a long spare seam. It is necessary to posses a certain rule for pitching the fork. Take the following: cut your falldown straight, till you come within four inches of the fork or bottom"

Q&L just says "plate" where Taylor says "plate A".

Q&L (re: leg seam) says "six inches shorter" for "five inches" in Taylor.

Q&L (re: shorter than your side seam) after which insert:
"Measure from the hip-bone to the knee-bone, opposite the cap, and to have this the more exact: remember, there is always a little bone like a knob, that you will feel when measuring, and be sure to mark the measure there as below, for the length. This rule is but little known by the trade in general: it is only by chance that they may hit it; perhaps it is often owing to the goodness of pattern, which is too much followed by men at the taylor's business, for want of a methodical system to direct them. Therefore we aver, that this rule is indispensably necessary to our theory and practice; and by following it,"

Q&L (re: and in the making) delete "let your knee-bands be beared on in the sewing, and your tops made very true;" in Taylor, and insert:
"if the breeches be short, let the upper side be beared on the garter; if they are required long, it is necessary that the under side be not hollowed in the ham, but cut straight across, and the garter sewed on full for the rise of the calf of the leg, and on the upper side the garter sewed on plain."

Q&L delete ""seam of the fall down" through "clearly fit the fall down." in Taylor, and substitute:
"the spare seam at the centre of the falldown about half an inch, after they are made up. When that is accomplished, and the button on, button and stretch them so that they will fit the falldown; them mark the fall buttons about a quarter of an inch above the button hole of the fall upon the waistband;"

Re - Chapter VIII & Chapter IX - Q&L p. 78. combines both chapters and entitles them: **"On Cassimere Pantaloons, continued."**

Q&L starts the text with:
"The same measurement that has been submitted for consideration on cassimere breeches, either double or single milled, will answer for the parts above, with this additional measuring; that is, from the small under the cap of the knee to the rise or centre of the calf of the leg, and down the small or ancle, and round the small and calf of the leg, and also the small under the knee, at your lengths run a line across as described in the plate on pantaloons, according to the letters."

Q&L delete the sentence "Observe in those to make the leg seam" and ending with "shew even by inspection.", in Taylor.

stretch of the Kerseymere is adequate to the above less as observed.

If this maxim is not strictly followed, the breeches will be most assuredly too wide, and the customer maybe greatly disappointed, should things of this sort be wanted upon an emergency; besides misfitting causes doubt, and may reflect on the abilities of the Taylor on future occasions. When you have proceeded this far, according to the instructions, lay your measure up the thigh; be sure * to give stride enough, and make them very high on the hip, and a long fall down after the following directions.

Cut it straight down till you come within four inches of the bottom; then turn up gradually, till you make such a shape as is in * plate A, and let your * leg-seam be five inches * shorter than your side seam; this will obtain a certainty of your having given plenty of stride room, and take care your side seam be neat and hollow, and you leg seam be very straight; when this is done, cut your inside round in the seat, and leave no fullness in the waistband; for by cutting your seat round, you will provide fullness sufficient. In order to strike your seat of a proper length, lay the measure from the fork to the hip, and run the measure to the end of the seat; after this is done, cut your fittings, such as waistbands, knee-bands, and top-bits; * and in the making, let your knee-bands be beared on in the sewing, and your tops made very true; and in putting on your waistbands, be sure they are put forward before the * seam of the fall down; and when your tops are finished all but buttoning, stretch them and pull them to their true place, and keep them so much upon the stretch, as will clearly fit the fall down, that neatness and compactness may visibly appear to every observer. Nothing has a worse effect than too loose a fall-down; it carries an indelicacy which decency cannot warrant.

Chapter VIII.

Of Mill'd Kerseymere Breeches.

* The practice of the above Breeches is strictly to adhere to the measure, judiciously taken, in every respect as in the observations already made in regular business, where no advantage or dependence is to be had either from elasticity or deduction; for whatever is repugnant to fair and exact measuring in these sorts of materials, will only tend to bewilder the pupil, and lead him from the rectitude of his bias; and also take notice what sort of stuff the person has on you are measuring, that you err not in the substance by turgidity of one sort, or lightness or frigidity of other, that you may make a little narrower or broader than the measure, as circumstances and occasion vary.

If the stuff you are going to use is different from what the gentleman has on when you measure, for your learner must understand that if we are ever so plain in our instructions, there will always be room enough for him to exercise his own genius; this will ever be the case whilst there is a difference between saying and doing, betwixt description and execution. * Observe in those to make the leg seam straight, and the side seams hollow; as recourse to Plate A will plainly shew even by inspection.

I need not enter into a disquisition of any sort of Cloth Breeches, for you may proceed by the

Q&L at Chapter IX insert at the beginning:
"Imbost cassimere ought to be taken notice of in this place."

Q&L delete from "will answer in every respect for these" through "your side seam also as the stripes," in Taylor, and replace this with:
"neither adding nor diminishing; only in cutting, keep them in your mind, such as milled cassimere, and in cutting and out and inside be careful to let the stripes run down the thigh, that they may not appear crooked, when put on;"

Q&L add at the very end of chapter IX:
"on casimere breeches and pantaloons."

Re: Chapter X
Q&L p. 95 which it titles"
"Of Weymouth Silk Breeches."

Q&L (re: imbost Kerseymere) delete "as is directed in imbost Kerseymere" through"running down the thighs;" in Taylor.

Q&L (re: end of the chapter) delete "of prompt payment without scruple." in Taylor, and add:
"that can be derived from flattery, where praise is not due.

above example of mill'd Kerseymere in every respect; for it is of no use to make puerile or common observations when we have matters of more serious consideration to treat of.

Chapter IX.

Of Imbost Kerseymere Breeches.

* The same mode of proceeding in taking the length and widths as reported on former occasions * will answer in every respect for these — only observe to the same method of particularly providing for the stripes of ribs running straight down the thighs as before mentioned, and may be seen by turning to Plate A of breeches, which will plainly shew the advantage of cutting the stuff, and the proper measures to be pursued, by strictly adhering to the length and widths, neither adding nor diminishing, only in the cutting let them be half an inch less in the double than the measure; leave no fullness in the waistband, but in cutting both the out and inside put in the gusset or splicing bit as before directed; cut your inside round in the seat; let your leg seam be cut straight as possible, and your side seam also as the stripes, and take care your waistband is kept very forward; and as for the practice of making them, there will need no farther comment than wishing you to have recourse to observations made in former chapters. *

Chapter X.

Of Weymouth Sattin Breeches.

The beautiful texture of this very elegant appurtenance, so fashionably appropriated for Breeches, should be handled with a great delicacy, and never be used but upon the most captivating figures, where grace is adorned with symmetry, and manly dignity gives an additional lustre to the brilliancy in the choice of materials. The theory and practice of those sort of Breeches are exactly the same as is observed for the florentine; therefore it may be necessary for the learner to make himself acquainted fully with those instructions, both as to measure, the turning in the seams, and every other maxim thereunto subscribed; and with respect to the stripes or ribs, make use of the same rule as is directed in the * imbost Kerseymere, touching the splicing of the gusset pieces to the hips, to command a straightness in the stripes running down the thighs; — this properly done will confer a smile of approbation from your employer, which will enhance the satisfaction in your own breast more pleasing than the gratification * of prompt payment without scruple.

Re: Chapter XI
Q&L p. 99. which it titles:
"Plain and striped hair Plush, or hair Shag, as it is commonly called."

Breeches and pantaloons were very tight (see the illustration on page 4). Planche says that they were so tight that some extraordinary and absurd means were resorted to to get them on. A gentleman is said to have told his tailor: "If I can get into them, I can't have them."

Q&L (re: plate A) substitute "plate VI" for "plate A" in Taylor.

Q&L (re: beared on the waistband) delete "mind you leave two inches and a half fullness" through "sides of the seat and both leg seams" in Taylor, and substitute:
"Be particular to leave two inches to be beared on the waistbands in the top of the seat, and in making, sew on privately a piece of tape or linen, down to the spare-seam, and up the seat seam. Stay your slits well with linen,"

Q&L uses "pitch" and "drivery" instead of "pinch" and "driving" in Taylor as follows:
"So as to pitch the seam of the two sides closely together, with care, what the trade generally calls drivery."

Q&L delete "Observe that Shag Breeches must always have leather linings" through ""would always want mending." in Taylor, and substitute:
"Remember, that if the party must have linings (we always recommend drawers, as they can be occasionally washed,) it should be advisable to have shamie linings; for the sharp friction of the hair with other materials would soon rub out, and would always want mending."

The above is an interesting observation on sanitary habits of that time!

Chapter XI.

Of plain and striped Shag Breeches.

The many seasonable advantages resulting to the wearer of Shag Breeches, from its excellent qualities touching both neatness, cleanliness, and durability, astonishes us much that the wearing of it is not more in fashion, as it possesses every convenience that could excite a preference to the purchaser or wearer; indeed there may be some objections to it from the barbarous practice in use, for we really think the Trade are more uncouth and farther from proficiency in this appendage of dress than any thing we meet in the streets; this may be a great deal owing to its disuse, not being often enough upon the scale of practice to secure a proper attention; for in the making of Breeches of shag, consistency seems to have entirely bid adieu to the lively imagination and reason of the Trade. Nothing ever was so erroneous as the practice in use.

In order to cut them well, first having taken your measures as in former examples, and the materials before you, take great care how you cut exactly to compass your measure, for remember that the Breeches in every part must be justly cut to it, after they are sewed together, this will convince you of the necessity of cutting them half an inch larger, to procure a natural ease to the wearer. Be sure you do not lose the sight of the drawing in * Plate A, which by inspection will possess you with a clear idea of the mode and shape they should have to prove the effect, which will be conspicuous to every beholder. Make your leg seam straight, and when you cut your inside let it run the same way as the out, and avoid that egregious method of making the inside run up, and the outside down, which from the glow of refection seems as if the shag was of two colours, an error too common and frequently done by people of respectability in the Trade; mind you leave two inches and a half fullness to be * beared upon the waistbands; and in the making baste on privately or sew a piece of canvass two inches broad down the fall down and the leg seam of the outsides; also canvass your slits well, then baste on -- privately sew down the insides, canvass both sides of the seat and both leg seams, and be a little particular in basting them together, that the seams may be true; and keep your left hand thumb and finger straight down, * so as to pinch the seam of the two sides close together with care, what the trade call * driving; these things strictly adhered to, you will find your practice perfect. Observe that * Shag Breeches must always have leather linings, for by the sharp friction of the hair with other materials, would soon rub through, and would always want mending. Take care in lining the waistband that the leather turns over the tops three quarters of an inch (to prevent injury to the shirts by friction).

Note. That striped Shag Breeches must be cut by the same rule of all other striped work, with respect to managing the stripes to run straight down the thigh; and in the same manner as the above directions touching the cutting and making in every respect.

Re: Chapter XII
Q&L p. 102 which it titles:
"The method of cutting Velveteen; with practical observations."

Velveteen was not only popular for gentlemen but was also used for grooms and coachmen.

Q&L delete "The manner of measuring" through "one side of the seams" in Taylor, and substitute:
"The manner of measuring and cutting these is the same as the plush; only in the making up, be sure you seam them in the leg seams, falldown, and seat, with a firm loopstich , and canvass them well in all the parts and tackings."

Re: Chapter XIII
Q&L p. 103 which is the same as Taylor (except that they substitute "plush" for "shag" and which they title:
"Of Corduroy and Thickset."

Re: Chapter XIV
Q&L p. 98 which they title:
"Some practical observations on buff cassimere Breeches and Pantaloons — and on the method of cutting them to fit neatly."

Q&L- this is essentially the same except that you must substitute measurements as follows: "a quarter of an inch" for "half an inch" in Taylor, and "observed on cutting single milled cassimere" for "the other Kerseymere Breeches" in Taylor.

Chapter XII

Of the Method of Cutting and Making of Velveteen Breeches

Velveteen is a most serviceable and valuable commodity, as can be substituted for winter wear; there is a richness in the look of it, added to its great utility, that will always give a distinguishing preference to the choice of those who wish to unite strength, beauty, and convenience together.

* The manner of measuring and cutting these are the same as the Shag, only in the making up, take notice that you have no occasion to canvass more than one side of the seams. If you are working upon Velveteen for a groom or coachman, take care you give them an abundance of stride, and cut them below the knee, even to the springing of the calf of the leg; and instead of hollowing the ham, be sure to make it straight, to prevent a common error too much practiced.

Chapter XIII

Of Corderoy and Thickset Breeches

Both these articles,though of different manufactures, are notwithstanding of the same materials, and to those who make a choice of the wearing, are sure to be satisfied with them in point of duration; for though they are inferior to Hair Shag, yet they are almost equal to Velveteen, being as useful for riding, as they are for common wear in gentlemen's undress, and serviceable in both; and when well cut and made, are likewise very neat, and deserve a very strong recommendation from all Taylors, when their opinions are asked.

Note. The manner of cutting and making Corderoy or Thickset Breeches, are the same as those spoken of above for the Velveteen.

Chapter XIV

How to Make Buff Kerseymere Breeches to fit like Leather

First when you have measured the person after the given directions, cut them * half an inch less than the measure as before observed in the other * Kerseymere Breeches; the kneebands must be proportionably larger, even to the extent of full width taken. With respect to other maxims requisite for the execution of these materials, we shall refer our readers to the rudiments ascertained in the chapter of Kerseymere before mentioned. We cannot pass over this chapter without taking some little notice of the neatness of Kerseymere when appropriated to the above purpose; Breeches of this stuff carry with them a delicate snugness, and in our opinion have a distinguishing preference to leather, both for

Re: Chapter XV

Q&L p. 96 which they title:

"Practical observations on cutting and making Nankeen."

Q&L in the beginning substitute "cassimere" for "Kerseymere" in Taylor.

Q&L at the end of the chapter add:

"By turning your attention to the plate, you can see the different modifications in cutting the pantaloons with feet; showing the turning of the tongue and soles. If strictly attended to, as to the manner of measuring already given in the preceding observations, you will find it will suffice as a direction for all those articles, which at present are in so much demand in this country. We recommend the patent English nankeen, not only on account of the fineness of its texture, but the deepness and durability of the colour, which will stand the process of washing as well as that of India."

Re: Chapter XVI

Q&L p. 104 which they title:

"Some practical observations on Worsted stuff of all kinds."

lightness and ease. It is true that leather is more durable; but then the former holds their rank as to ease and convenience, and will wash like a shirt. This gives them a public notoriety, and much enhances their estimation to every gentleman who prefers their easy elasticity to the buckram confinement of any sort of leather.

Chapter XV

Of Nankeen Breeches

Next to * Kerseymere, we think that Nankeen for the summer wear are most agreeable; and perhaps for riding superior to any thing at such a season. They are cool, easy, and neat; and when they are too much tinged with the soil of the day, they are soon washed and made as neat and clean as when just brought from the hands of the Taylor.

Our practitioners must observe, that these sort of Breeches must be made entirely to the measure; and in making be sure to sew all the seams with thread, for silk turns yellow by the washing. Make the button-holes of twist, and make all the linings loose, only fastened to the waistband. We would also advise the putting of a strip of Irish linen from leg seam to button-hole, to prevent the thinness of the stuff bursting across the knee. Mind that the strip of linen be narrower than the width; this will much strengthen and contract their tendency to laceration or tearing. *

Chapter XVI

Of Worsted Stuffs of all kinds for Breeches

All worsted stuffs must be cut considerably easier than the measure, owing to the necessity there is of turning so much in for the seams. The sizes must exceed the measure by half an inch in the double. As we have said so much in former chapters relative to the laying on the measure, cutting, and other maxims of making, we think it needless to say more, for we are fearful the work will swell beyond our intended limits and expectation when we look forward to the matter we have in contemplation to treat of —With this particular observation that all the waistbands come forward beyond the seam, except where we have said to the contrary.

With respect to striped worsted Breeches the same rule for making the stripe run straight will serve in all cases, by having resource to the first maxim shewn in worsted knit ribbed Breeches.

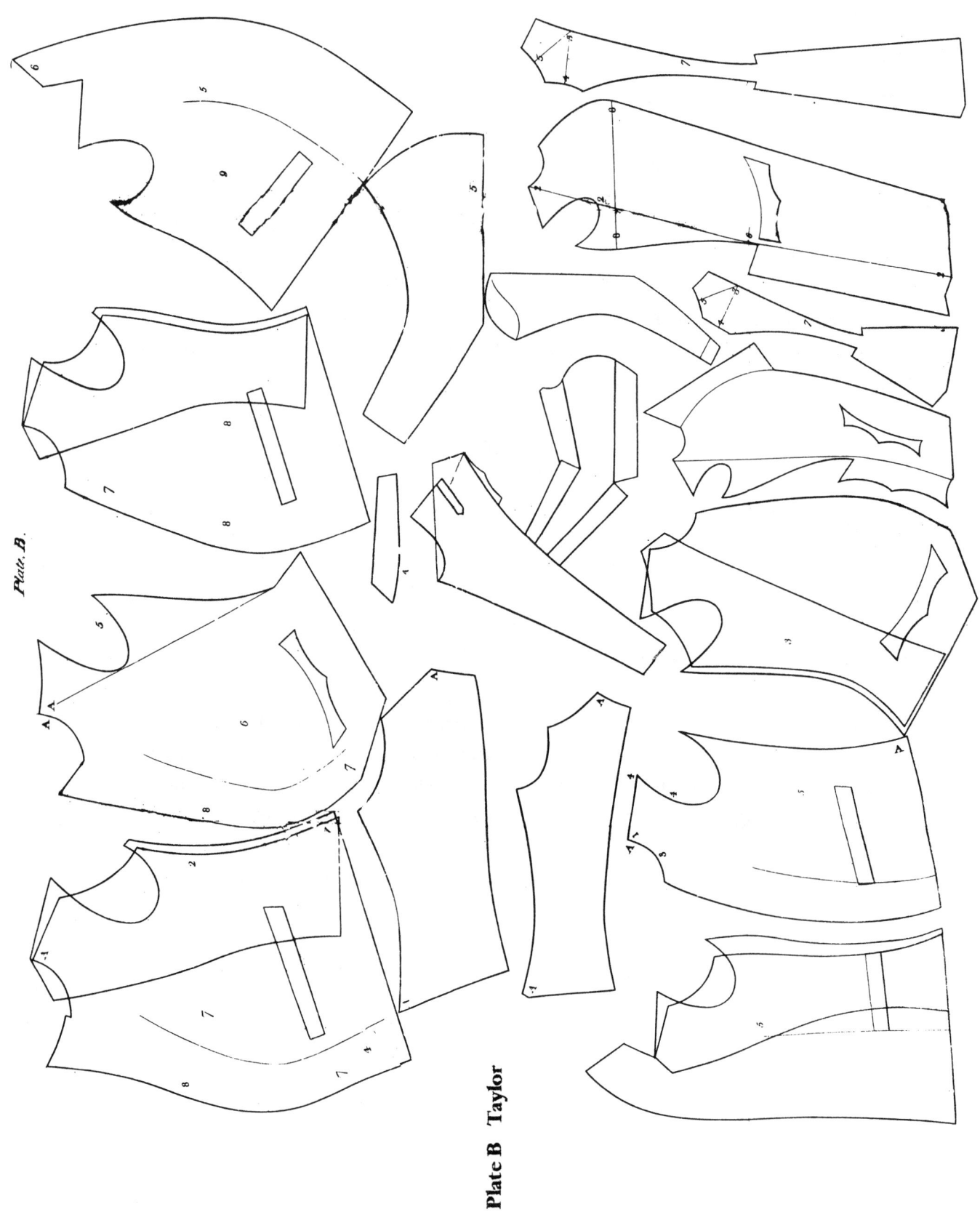

Plate. B.

Plate B Taylor

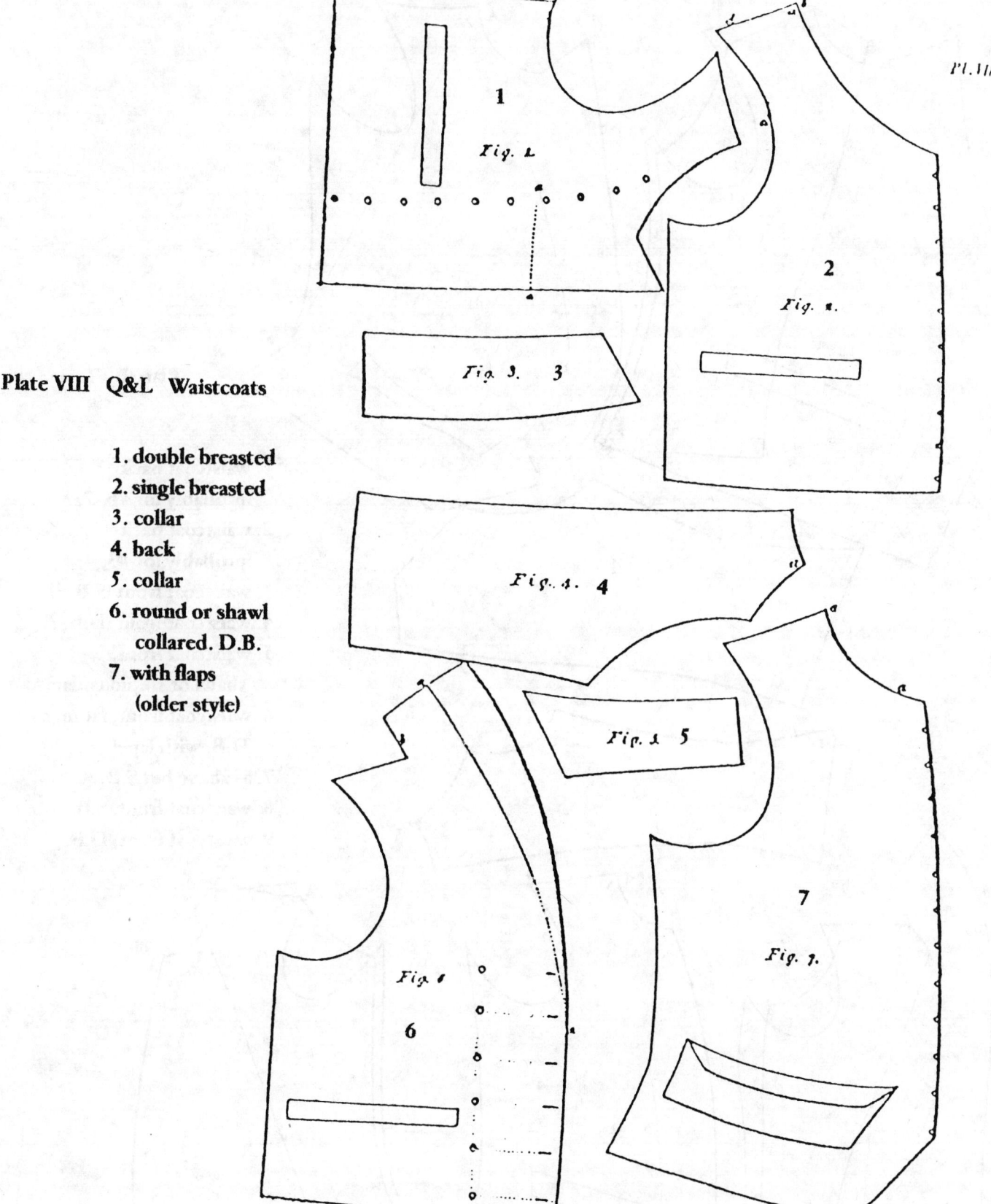

Plate VIII   Q&L   Waistcoats

1. double breasted
2. single breasted
3. collar
4. back
5. collar
6. round or shawl
   collared. D.B.
7. with flaps
   (older style)

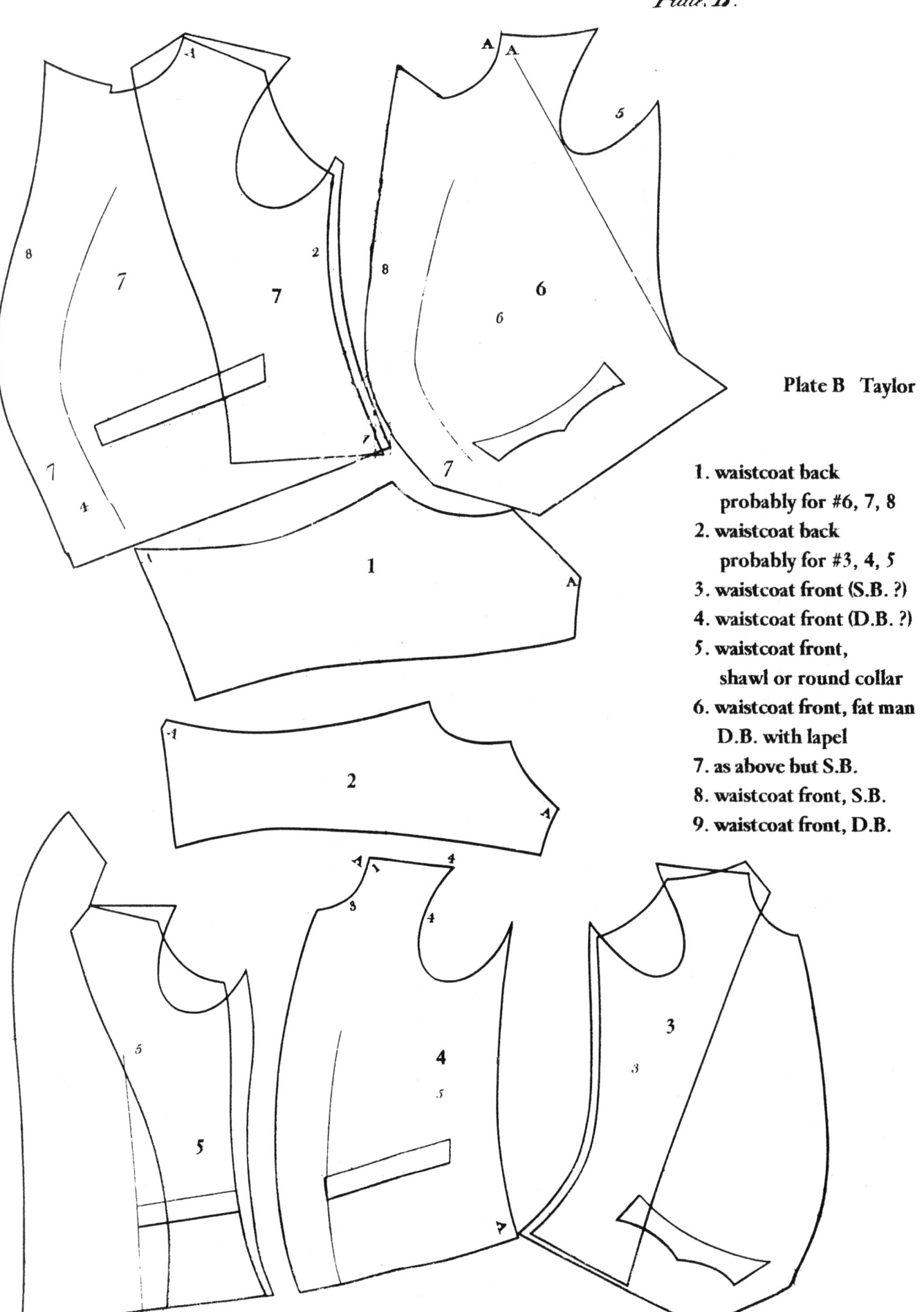

Plate. B.

Plate B Taylor

1. waistcoat back
   probably for #6, 7, 8
2. waistcoat back
   probably for #3, 4, 5
3. waistcoat front (S.B. ?)
4. waistcoat front (D.B. ?)
5. waistcoat front,
   shawl or round collar
6. waistcoat front, fat man
   D.B. with lapel
7. as above but S.B.
8. waistcoat front, S.B.
9. waistcoat front, D.B.

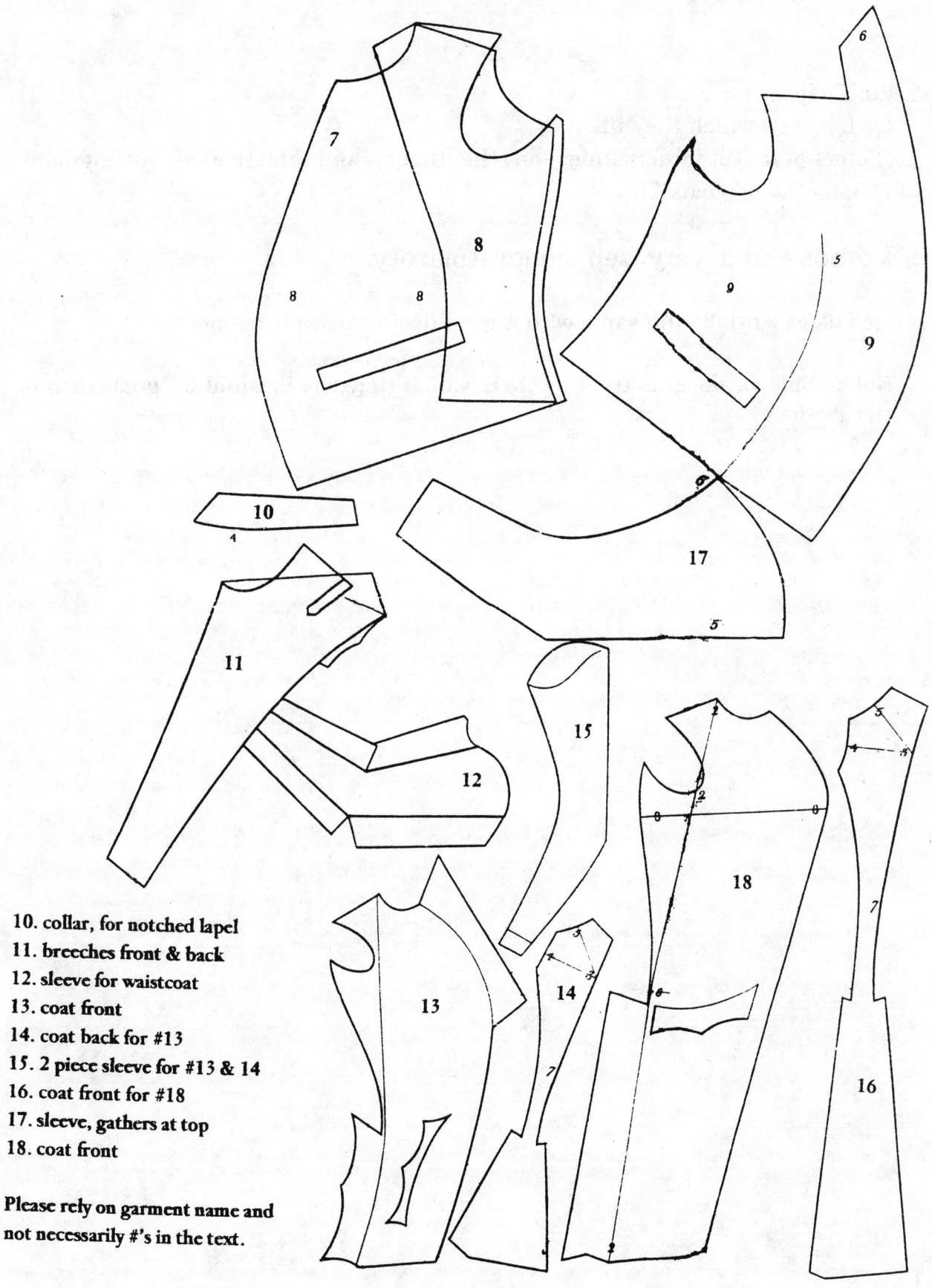

10. collar, for notched lapel
11. breeches front & back
12. sleeve for waistcoat
13. coat front
14. coat back for #13
15. 2 piece sleeve for #13 & 14
16. coat front for #18
17. sleeve, gathers at top
18. coat front

Please rely on garment name and
not necessarily #'s in the text.

53

Re: Chapter I
Q&L p. 110 which they title:
"Some practical observations on the theory and practice of cutting and making Waistcoats."

Verbose and very self congratulatory.

Q&L is essentially the same with a good deal of paraphrasing.

Note: "Billy Beakies" is used by Q&L, which they say is equal to "great men of the Trade."

SECTION II.

Chapter 1

Upon the Theory and Practice of Waistcoats

We shall now draw our Student's attention from the dissertations we have made upon that delicate appurtenance of dress called Breeches, and pursue our further intent of defining the best and most salutary method of measuring, cutting, and making of Waistcoats; to facilitate that part of the business with ease and perspicuity, and thereby avoid all futile undigested maxims too common among the Taylors, and point out a brief criterion in order to accommodate the matter to the most unenlightened person of the Trade, — that no difficulty may hereafter impede the application of all those who may wish to inform themselves of every requisite necessary to compass the theme in question.

We doubt not but many * great men of the trade, who by profusion of business and excessive practice have well lined their coffers, and who may congratulate themselves on the certainty that success carries with it a proof of real abilities above the subordinate rank of any instructions, who may smile at the idea of our dictating or prescribing rules for making of waistcoats, — accounting such flights of fancy as the puerile result of folly and childhood.

Notwithstanding we shall take the liberty of endeavouring to meliorate the pride of such wiseacres, by desiring them to suspend their unwarrantable conclusions till they have had a little recourse to the annexed Plate of Waistcoats. Perhaps a slight inspection there may furnish them with a few seasonable hints, which by comparing with the description and other profound maxims of well experienced practice, may be found worth a few hours reflection, such as may fully compensate their fatigue and labour.

Although they may be pleased to say they well knew the methods before, long before they read the observations hereunto subscribed; this we give them free liberty to say — such ostensiblity will never depreciate the salutary effects that may result from them to the uninformed, whose benefits we chiefly espouse, and whose patrons we declare ourselves to be. As for those very consequential adepts (though not less their friends) we shall only beg leave to remind them of a divine observation — that those that are whole need no Physician.

We write for the general good, and are conscious of meeting success in the minds and sentiments of the truly liberal; and doubt not that thousands now living (who are humble in their pretensions) will rejoice at the opportunity of having such an easy access to the secret purlieus of the business, which neither time nor application could accomplish to their certainly and satisfaction. — The envious asseveration of rancarous [sic - rancorous?] disappointed Men are beneath the notice of true and genuine criticism.

Candour is the source of true genius, and will never disparage the fruitful efforts of any art; whatever is contrary to this is generally directed by spleen and scurrility, and has nothing to support it but envy and malice. Such ill-nature we despise, being too trivial for serious consideration as mean

Re: Chapter II

Q&L continues this on as apart of the previous chapter, this part starting on p. 112.

Q&L (re: when this is done) delete "When this is done" to the end of the paragraph in Taylor, and substitute:

"When this is done, put the measure round the body in two separate places, as, over the breast and the belly. If it be an old man, who wants it long, with skirts, you may take a third measure over the hip; this will be all that is necessary."

Q&L substitute "plate VIII" for "plate B" in Taylor.

Q&L (re: fall away) delete "or it will fall away" to the end of the paragraph in Taylor, and substitute:

"and it will go away gradually to make a rolling collar, which is very neat in the present state of fashion."

Re: Chapter III

Q&L p. 113 again being a continuation of the previous chapter.

Q&L (re: gumming holes) add
"with a little bees' wax"
and substitute "silk florentine breeches" for "silk Breeches" in Taylor.

as calumny itself, the source and offspring of spite and ignorance. Having said so much, we will proceed to the manner of measuring the Waistcoats.

Chapter II

Of the Practice of Measuring and Cutting out Waistcoats

First having the Person before you, lay on at the top of the shoulders and down as low before as the employer may wish to hove [have?] the waistcoat. * When this is done, put your measure round the body, in three separate places, as over the breast, the belly and hip. This will be all that is necessary touching the measurement.

When you have your materials before you intending to cut out, please before you begin to open the book to the * plate B of Waistcoats, and observe well the figures, the modes, maxims, and turnings of the different parts to facilitate the idea and appearance that those separations of things must bear before they are sewed or united together. This will greatly assist your notion when you lay on your measure to mark out for cutting your cloth upon the true scale; and please to mind that it does not appear too round down before in the fore parts, and see that your neck is cut hollow, and at the gorget, spring it forward as the plate directs, upon which depends the chief art of fitting a waistcoat. Keep it very forward to lay close to the neck, * or it will fall away from it; a most egregious error if not guarded against as above pointed out.

There is another matter which requires thought, and that is, in the length of the back to the fore part from mark *a*, in the front, to mark *a*, on the back. Observe that the back must be the same length as the plate directs; and let the back lay on the fore parts straight and easy, and what you call closing the back to the fore part, take care that it answers the same, which will totally prevent the fore parts from driving up on the belly, which is a general complaint, mostly caused by the back being cut too short, and the fore parts too round; both most flagrant errors, and should, to ensure success, be most strenuously guarded against: in order to do this properly, pay strict adherence to the delineations of the plates; these possess all the faculties requisite for compleat fitting, proved and certified by real experience as incontrovertible as demonstration itself. Therefore, the learner cannot pay too great a respect to the shape and manner of those sketches of drawing, to ripen and foster his faint ideas.

Chapter III

Of Silk Waistcoats

When you are about making of Silk Waistcoats, remember the maxim of * gumming the holes as observed in the * silk Breeches, to stick and hold them together, by adhesion you make and work your holes, without danger; and be pleased to make use of glazed linen, instead of buckram for the button-holes.

Re: Chapter IV
Q&L p. 115

Note comments about placing buttons on double breasted waistcoats so that if the front gets dirty the other side can be put forward.

They mention "capes" on waistcoats. Betty Williams says that she has never heard of this and the plates and illustrations from that period do not show it.

Q&L replace "plate B" in Taylor, with "the plate"

Q&L replace "plate B in Taylor, with "plate" also "fig. 5" in Taylor, with "figure 6."

Q&L substitute "slop vests" for "sale waistcoats" in Taylor.

Re: Chapter V
Q&L p. 117 which they title:
"Of the double breasted Waistcoats, in plate VIII. figure 1."

Chapter IV

Of Round Collared Waistcoats

There is nothing very particular in the execution of this Waistcoat more than the common observation of seeing that your back is a right length for the fore part and your cape cut as the plate directs you in * plate B. Should you have a short scale of materials, as the common quantity made use of for other Waistcoats will be too small for broad breast and round collars; therefore in order to assist our learner, we will request him to cut a true shape of the fore part of the lining: first this will enable him to make the best of his outside, and for the length of the back have recourse to * plate B, and draw your inference from that similitude.

Relative to the making of double-breasted Waistcoats, we should recommend the making holes down both sides for the advantage of the wearer, lest any unforeseen accident should happen from dirt, and the wearer's day's pleasure should be spoiled, by not having an opportunity of changing the other side of the breast. Set on the buttons by the mark on * plate B, by the welt of the pocket up to * fig 5; and observe that your pocket welt runs the right way of the stuff, and not as the * sale waistcoats mostly do. Take care in the cutting one of those waistcoats, that you proceed as for one that is lappelled; that you have sufficient room in the breast, nor cut the arm-holes too deep on the breast, but keep them close and small.

'Tis a great error to cut any garment too narrow at the breast. This is the leading incitement to ease, and the place that requires most freedom, an observation that cannot be too strictly adhered to.

In cutting of the cape to be added to the place of the lappell, see that it falls down regular and easy to the shoulder, for the least error committed here, will incommode the fitting of the waistcoat. Please to inspect the plates well we have before been speaking of, and all the rest; as we further treat of them as true similitudes of each theme we mean to define.

Chapter V.

Of Plate B

This plate requires some consideration, for though it is the general size of most in wear, it has difficulties in the formation; therefore our student cannot too closely adhere to the plate. Be particularly careful in making the lappell fit neat, and that the collar fits snug round the neck, and be assured of both the length of front and back parts; observe the neck cut in the plate, it is a particular point, and turn it out as at fig *a* in the Plate. This will assuredly answer the purpose, and fit peculiarly neat and smart. Be careful never to cut a straight collar to any waistcoat, for this method will never answer any purpose; but a chief instrument of frustrating the well designed cutting and fitting of the whole Waistcoat.

Re: Chapter VI
Q&L p. 118 which they title:
"Practical observations continued on single breasted Waistcoats in plate VIII."

Q&L substitute "figure 2" for "figure 5" in Taylor.

Q&L delete "too round before" in Taylor, and substitute:
"too round in the front part of the breast,unless it be for a man who has a large belly, and who may wish it long."

Q&L substitute "of the figure: for "Fig. 1 to Fig. 3" in Taylor.

Q&L (re: gradual sweep Fig. 1) delete "hollow with a gradual sweep to Fig. 1, and turn that part to the neck" in Taylor, and substitute:
"gradual hollow in the gorget, and the point of the back."

Q&L delete "fig. a in ditto" in Taylor.

Q&L delete "Fig. 4, to Fig. 4 in Plate B" in Taylor, and substitute:
"the scye from the point at the shoulder seam,"

Q&L substitute "figure 3, in plate VIII;" for "Fig. 4 in Plate B" in Taylor.

Re: Chapter VII
Q&L p. 120 which they title:
"Some practical observation on Waistcoats with flaps."

Fashion discussion.

Chapter VI

Of the Waistcoats in Plate B

* Figure 5, is a single breasted Waistcoat, and must not be cut too * round before, nor must the shoulder fall too far back, but be cut as straight as possible, only allowing a proper round for the breast and belly. Be careful that the shoulder is kept inclining to the neck, in manner from * Fig. 1 to Fig. 3; and let it be cut hollow with a * gradual sweep to Fig. 1, and turn that point to the neck, and let the back be the same length as the fore part from * fig. *a* in ditto: this will compel the fitting close and straight.

The great difficulty in cutting single-breasted Waistcoats results from an error in not cutting them straight in the shoulder; for if you pitch the shoulder too far backward when you cut it, the effect will be disagreeable, for when it is opened and unbuttoned, it will fall away from the body; when buttoned it will be all in puckers before and of course fall away from the neck behind.

While we are upon this subject, if we might not be thought to digress, we would mention a few hints towards rectifying any faults made in Waistcoats by inexperience, as before mentioned. — First, part the back from the fore part, and when laid on your cutting-board, piece in the neck as usual, of two or three inches at the gorget shoulder seam, and taper it to a point in the middle of the neck, and piece under the arm at the top of the side seam another piece, to prevent the arm-hole being too large; and you must cut off at the shoulder as much as you piece at the neck; we mean down from * Fig. 4, to Fig. 4 [sic] in Plate B. Then take your back and piece it to the length of the fore parts, as the plate will shew, and close it again true to your measure. This done, cut your collar after the manner of * Fig. 4, in Plate B. and when the separated parts are properly adjusted, you will find the Waistcoat fit adequate to your most sanguine expectation.

This is the proper method for rectifying errors in thin men's Waistcoats, when cut too round. For fat men we must pursue other maxims, which will be shewn hereafter.

Chapter VII

Of Fig. D. in Plate B

Though the mode of this cut of a Waistcoat be not much in practice at present, we doubt not but a turn of things from the fluctuating rage will shortly have a change, and that fashion in her mutability may as likely suggest Waistcoats with flaps or any thing else more ridiculous, as they have been worn with much eclat for a long series of years. The taste of fashion is so capricious in all her meanders, that it is hard to say what she will or what she may not espouse. We have nothing to do but humbly watch her motions, and try the effect they may have upon the fascinated million; she is factitious in all her movements, unstable as the wind; and having let our fancies a-gog, she leads us by her power through the whole field of variety; upon which account we think it a duty incumbent upon us for the benefit

Taylor talks about Livery Waistcoats, also "country friends" probably meaning tailors who practice outside of London.

Q&L (re: Livery Waistcoats) delete "and those who have occasion to make Livery Waistcoats"to the end of the paragraph in Taylor, and substitute: "and readers, who mostly retain the former made of wearing flaps, to give a sketch of the forepart, which may be seen in the plate VIII. figure 7."

Q&L substitute "plate VIII" for "Plate B" in Taylor.

Re: Chapter VIII
Q&L p. 122 which they title:
"Some practical observations on Waistcoats with sleeves."

Q&L delete "the elbow" through "and at the hip" in Taylor, and substitute: "Afterwards, measure round the breast and belly, and half across the breast if it be single breasted."

Ostler - stableman.
Postillion - guide that rides near one of the pair of horses on a coach.

Taylor has many typos and this especially is apparent when it comes to identifying the patterns. Also a lot of the original numbers on the patterns have disappeared due to the age of the document.

of our country friends, and those who have occasion to make * Livery Waistcoats, who mostly retain the former mode of wearing flaps to them, to give a sketch of the foreparts in our Plate as at Fig. D in Plate B.

There is nothing to be said of the cutting or making more than we have suggested in the single-breasted Waistcoat of not being cut too round before, nor must the shoulders fall too back, but be cut as straight as possible, only allowing a proper round for the breast or belly. Be very careful that the shoulder is kept inclining to the neck in manner from *a* to *a*, in * Plate B. and let it be cut hollow with a gradual sweep, and turn that point to the neck; and let the back be the same length as the fore part, as the Plate directs. This will compel the fitting close and straight.

Chapter VIII

Of Waistcoats with Sleeves

Though Waistcoats of this sort are not much worn but by ostlers, postillions, grooms and old men, yet they are a particular kind of practice, and requires much care in the formation; for we usually see as much defect in those waistcoats as in any part of the business; therefore that our learner may avoid error in the matter, we hope he will pay great respect to the following method of measuring, cutting, and making, as the only means of accomplishing this arduous task.

'Tis true that the Trade do get through this business with the use of arm-puffs, puckered redundancies, constricted tightness in the shoulder, and other disagreeable defects; but those things are far short of the mastery that is requisite to give a person countenance that he may do his business with pleasure, well knowing that his practice will afford him praise, and give his employer great satisfaction.

To measure for a Waistcoat with sleeves, first, lay your measure from the top of the shoulder before, down as low as the party may choose to have it; for remember that in all things your employer will always have a pre-eminence of choice, though after you have received that, you can always exercise your own judgement by assimilating propriety with their requests.

Secondly, measure from the top of the back down to the bottom behind, then you will acquire a certainly as to your length.

Thirdly, measure from the back seam behind half across the shoulder, and nick your measure for one half of the back; and in measuring for the length of the sleeve, take care the party holds up the elbow level with the shoulder, and at the elbow joint make a nick, and extend the measure as near the hand as your customer may wish for the length of the arm, and mark it; then measure the arm round at the wrist, under * the elbow, and as near the shoulder as you can; afterwards measure the breast half across, and three times round the body; at the breast as high as you can, at the centre of the body, and at the hip; be certain of your marks and measure.

When you cut out your waistcoat, consider well the stuff you are about to make it of, and do not lose sight of the instructions already given touching the nature of the materials, of their elasticity, or other more certain qualities; also if the waistcoat is for a person in any business where great

Q&L delete "and let your back" through "Plate B. Fig. 5" also "Fig. 5 in Plate B" and "Fig. 6", in Taylor

Re: Chapter IX
Q&L p. 125 which they title:
"Continuation of practical observation on Waistcoats for fat men."

Importance of tailoring for heavy men with big bellies.

exercise is required. Consider well the intent, and give a little latitude to the necessity of ease required in such cases; for though we give you exact rules how to proceed, there will always be room enough to exercise your own abilities. If the waistcoat is of fustian, cut it across the shoulder half an inch larger than the measure on both sides of the back, in order that it may be one inch broader across the shoulders, and let your back be cut longer than the measure by two inches; and have a strict eye upon the * Plate B. Fig. 5. Cut your fore parts after the manner of the Plate, and in cutting the fore parts, have recourse to your back, and see it answers as before. Let your fore part run close up under the arm, for that will give great room to the sleeves, and eradicate puffs. Observe well the sleeve, * Fig. 5. in Plate B. for in this there is a difference, whose principal effect chiefly results from the point at * Fig. 6. Give plenty of sleeve top, and spring it out to the fore seam to appear as the plate at the top; for remember the farther you spring your fore seam out at the top, the more room you give for the extension of the arm.

By this maxim you procure freedom and ease to the wearer, without the least restraint or confinement whatsoever. This is the general fault so frequently complained of, and which on no consideration should be omitted to rectify so gross an abuse by every practiser of the art.

Chapter IX

Of a Waistcoat for a Fat Man

The great protuberance of body in fat men requires care in the application, and it would be well for all men of little practice to digest the methods we propose; for the difficulty arising from irregular figures, should excite attention in the workman, that he may be well informed the maxims will answer the intent, and that by such circumstances such means are duly required to produce their natural effect; when he has attained a thorough knowledge of this practice, he will be adequate to the undertaking; for in those, as well as in regular business and well formed figures of men, the practice will be coincident with the Theory.

The most difficulty in fitting a fat man is in a single-breasted Waistcoat. The great prominency of Belly causes so much more width in the round than in the breast, or the hips, that you will find a scrupulous difficulty in the regular falling to the breast, as well as the great nicety of continually hiding the linen between the waistband of the Breeches, and bottom of the waistcoat, owing to the improvident rising of the waistcoat upon the Belly; a very indelicate error, and should be guarded against with all your judgment. — Observe in taking the measure round the Belly that it is put level round, for as you lay your measure upon the cloth straight across, that either rising or falling your hand, will cause an addition to the width, and upon the breast measure the party as high as you can under the arms, then the Belly and at the hip, which must be provided for accordingly.

Nothing can be so egregiously shameful as the rising of the waistcoat upon the Belly for want of properly fitting the Body; this we must own has been a great inducement to our undertaking this treatise, to remedy this as well as other abominable errors, to the scandal of the trade, which shew

Q&L delete "Plate B" to No. 4. in plate B" in Taylor, and substitute "figures on the plate"

Q&L delete "and likewise follow strickly the maxims of the plate in every other particular" in Taylor, and substitute: "and neatly round and fall in at the button;"

Q&L delete "at No. 2 in fig. B. that it" in Taylor.

Q&L delete "attention" in Taylor, and substitute "alteration".

Q&L delete "Cut your neck" to "in that place is" in Taylor, and substitute: "First, cut your forepart shoulder straight, inclining forward, for that of itself is"

Q&L delete "as at No. 5 Fig B." in Taylor, and substitute "at the side seam, and sink or hollow it gradually."

Q&L delete "full in length" to "Fig. 7 in plate B." in Taylor and substitute: "exactly to the side seam,"

Q&L delete "as in the plate at Fig. 4" in Taylor.

Q&L delete "pretty high" in Taylor, and substitute" "as high as the mark on the plate,".

nothing but inattention and poverty of genius.

Observe when you take the length it will be necessary to lay on the measure twice, first from the shoulder to the hollow of the breast; and mark the measure, then down to the bottom of the waist-coat. — Afterwards take a measure all down the buttoning as low as the intended length required; and to the learner it may not be an unreasonable request of us to desire him to measure the length of the back, though this may not be the custom of the trade. We advise it, as fat men are so short behind and so very long before; it will be a means of giving a better idea of the size of the body, and form a proper similitude of the shape of the waistcoat to fit the object.

In order to facilitate this piece of practice to the mind of our students, we would advise them first to have recourse to the * plate B. of the shape of fat men's Waistcoats, and then take great notice of the shape and formation, especially at No. 4 in plate B. that when you cut out you may fall gradually from the protuberance of the belly to the breast; * and likewise follow strictly the maxims of the plate in every other particular; for be assured the rules laid down are not the premises of uncertain speculation, but justified by axioms of well earned experience.

Take care of the side seam * at No. 2 in Fig. B that it be cut short enough for the hind part, in proportion to the extraneous length of the fore part. Some * attention is requisite also to its fitting well about the neck, to prevent its falling away towards the shoulders; a thing very common in fat men. Even so ridiculous are some made, that you may see their linen half way to the shoulder point; nay so great is the abuse, that even the buttoning of the coat will hardly hide the notorious fault; however in order to prevent this excessive blunder in future, stick close to the following Lesson.

* Cut your neck as at No. *a* in Fig. B inclining to No. *a*, for being cut forward in that place is a great inducement to fitting well. It is a most flagrant error to let the shoulder fall too much back. Likewise in cutting the fore part be sure to leave it a great height under the arm, * as at No. 5 Fig. B. Your next remark is upon the back and collar; observe that the back is cut * full in length from No. *a* to No. *a* in Fig. 7 in plate B, answerable to the fore part; for notwithstanding the shortness of a fat man's back, they must be made to assimilate in the length. Cut your collar round at the bottom, * as in the plate at Fig. 4, and straight at the top. With respect to the height at the neck, you must be ruled by the wish of your customer. Place your pockets * pretty high; and in the making of the waistcoat, after being cut with great nicety, draw it in very much over the belly, and likewise draw it in for the breast in the hollow part.

Note. If the waistcoat should be of florentine, or any kind of silk or stuff that will ravel at the edges, when you make your holes wet and rub a piece of gum at the places where you have cut your holes; this will contract and keep your stuff from ravelling when dry, and you may work your holes without difficulty; and be sure for this kind of stuff to use no buckram for the holes or edges, as this will wear the stuff. If you strictly adhere to those rules you will certainly accomplish the business to you own and employer's satisfaction.

Re: Chapter X
Q&L p. 129, which it titles
"Continuation on old men's Waistcoats."

Q&L delete "Plate B and Fig. 3. in ditto;" in Taylor, and substitute "plate VIII. and figure 3,"

Q&L at the end of "measurement you have taken" in Taylor, add: "only diminish on the back in proportion to the prominence of the belly."

Q&L delete "No. 3 in Fig. B." in Taylor.

Q&L delete "Fig. 4" in Taylor, and substitute: "plate VIII. at figure 3."

Q&L delete "No. a to No. a, as in Fig. B." in Taylor.

Q&L delete "as at No. 5 in figure B" to "the buttons requires it."

Q&L delete "Observe in closing on of those kind of Waistcoats, in Taylor, and substitute: "Be careful also in closing on those kinds, if double breasted,"

Chapter X

Of Fig. B. in Plate B. for Fat Men

Our Learners will observe the very particular attention that is requisite in all fat men's Waistcoats, as well as in any other appendage of dress, in order to prevent the too common practice of fitting bodies so irregular and preposterous; for though things may be well conceived, and neatly executed, they will not always have that striking effect as clothes upon more tenuous figures, or men of genteel address. There is a certain ponderosity in heavy men, that when moving disorders the very ceremony and appearance of nice cutting; therefore in order to guard against this as much as possible, take the following directions: To measure first from the shoulder to the hollow of the breast, and mark the measure, and then to the bottom of the Waistcoat; next measure all down the middle from the neck to the intended length before, and measure the length of the back (though not a common practice) for by this you will fully conceive the shortness of the back, and be enabled better to adjust it to the front or fore part.

In measuring round first at the breast as near under the arms as possible, then at the belly, put your measure exactly level round, for either holding up or down your hands will increase the length, which will deceive you when you lay your measure across the cloth.

Lastly measure below the belly at the hips. This will be all that is necessary to measuring, but before you begin to cut, have recourse to * Plate B and Fig. 3. in ditto; and when you have digested well this figure, assimilate the full force of this shape to the scale and * measurement you have taken. Let this be the prototype or living pattern in your mind, bearing it strongly in remembrance to cut the point at * No. 3. in Fig. B. with inclining forwardness; for should it lean off in this part, it will lie off the neck behind and draw it most disagreeably. This is a maxim that cannot be dispensed with; for this, and cutting the collar, and noting the fall of the belly to the breast, are all matters of serious consideration, and should chiefly influence the Taylor's care to provide against them. Nothing gives a gentleman a more disagreeable sense of defection than an untowardly fitting about the neck; and this is a part where most errors are committed. Therefore, we must once more beg our students to be circumspect and also assimilate his collar to the drawing of * Fig. 4; and observe that the back of the Waistcoat must have its proportion of length from * No. a to No. a, as in Fig. B. for however short the back, they must be made to answer in those parts. And please to observe too, that in cutting the fore part, you leave it high enough under the arm * as at No. 5. in figure B. In making up the Waistcoat, draw it in from No. 7 to No. 8, upon the breast and belly; the greater length in this place than at the buttons requires it. If the Waistcoat is striped, let your welt run with the stripe of the stuff; in order to make those Waistcoats fit well, we are obliged to have recourse to the method of drawing in to make it fit close to the lower part of the belly. Should you draw it into a pucker, take a hot iron, and by pressing it a little you will compel it to fit close and snug.

* Observe in closing one of those kind of Waistcoats, lay your measure near half way between the edge of the fore part and the buttons; for should you follow the Trade method of half and half, you

Fashion remarks about round collars.

Q&L delete "sixteen or seventeen years" in Taylor, and substitute:
"twenty seven years"

Q&L delete "Fig. 9 in Plate B." in Taylor, and substitute:
"plate VIII, and figure 2,"

Q&L delete from "When he has taken" to "Fig. 8 in Plate B." in Taylor, and
substitute: "with regard to measuring for those, follow the preceding observation"

Q&L delete "No. 6 in Fig. 9 Plate B." in Taylor, and substitute:
"figure 4, and plate VIII."

Q&L delete "directs from No. a" to "upon the belly and breast" in Taylor.

will too much tighten and narrow it; therefore in this case you must ease it a little in the measure, for irregular figures require irregular means to effect them. With regard to the flap of the pocket, a single view of the Plate will give an idea how to cut it agreeable to the fashion that constitutes it. The taste of the times in this article, as well as the cut of the skirts, will always be a guide to his genius, and prompt him to a modest neatness, which will give a pleasing turn to the whole.

Chapter XI

Of Figure C. in Plate B. for a Fat Man

This Figure describes a round collared Waistcoat, a thing that has been the rage some time, and may continue a few years by some people, but I think cannot be of lasting duration; the idea was borrowed from the great coats that were made in this manner touching the collar about * sixteen or seventeen years ago, but there was an inconvenience attended them, which shortened their duration. The Waistcoats of this fashion in our opinion are full as reprehensible as the great coats, for they are not only inelegant but otherwise uncouth and clumsey; and at all events should be discouraged by fat men, for they help to throw an impediment in the very place it should be most avoided in the neck, where all men of this denomination are particularly short; for in strict justice to elegance and his own appearance, a fat man should wear no collar about his Coat or Waistcoat at all, but what stands up; those seem to help to lengthen the neck, and to figures thus loaded with fleshy shoulders have the best and most pleasing effect, much better than any turn-downs or other substitutes that seem only to be invented to hide the tenuity of long necks; in which case it has its uses, and as they have been long in vogue and have been otherwise sanctioned by custom, we shall let them swim down the stream of time till they sicken and die unnoticed, like many other once brilliant appendages that have had their day, though now no more till time and the whim of some great researcher brings them into life and fashion once again.

However as some gentlemen may choose to hold up its consequence and save it from oblivion; we shall desire our pupil to have recourse to * Fig. 9. in Plate B. which will inspection shew him the very cut and semblance of his proportion. * When he has taken his proper measures of his customer, as from the shoulder to the hollow of the breast, and marked the measure, then to the bottom of the Waistcoat or the proposed length, then measure all down the round of the middle before; afterwards measure the length of the back (though not common so to do) in order to come at an appropriate length to join the back seam to the fore part.

Next measure round the breast as high under the arms as you can, then round the belly very level, and lastly, below the belly at the hips, and every other maxim as laid down in the single-breasted Waistcoat for a fat man in Fig. 8. in Plate B. with this further observation, that for a round collared Waistcoat take care you give a great spring in the cape at * No. 6 in Fig. 9. Plate B. that corner must be sprung as much as the fall of the shoulder may require, only be sure your back and fore parts answer as the Plate * directs from No. *a* to No. *a*. in Fig. 6. Plate B; and in cutting the fore parts be sure to cut

Q&L delete "this place and where the buttons are set" in Taylor, and substitute: "The shoulders and top of the buttons"

Q&L delete "as well as the mode of the flaps in similitude to Fig. 6," in Taylor.

Re: Chapter XII
Q&L p. 136, which it titles:
"Practical Observations."

Q&L delete from "in measuring for Fig. C" to the end of the paragraph in Taylor.

them high enough under the arm, as at No. 5. Fig. 6; and when you make it up, take care and abide by the maxim laid down of drawing it from No. 7, to No. 8. upon the belly and breast, the great difference of length between * this place and where the buttons are set on requires it, in order to make them fit close to the lower part of the belly.

Respecting the cut of the skirts you will always endeavour to favour the fashion that substitutes the manner of cutting them, * as well as the mode of the flaps, in similitude to Fig. 6, with a graceful smartness that may add beauty to the finishing of the Waistcoat.

Chapter XII

Of Plate B. and Fig. 3.

The different figures upon this Plate strongly enforce the necessity of every uninformed mind taking every opportunity of studiously contemplating the points, turns, cuts, scys [sic. scye?], and other appropriate matters in order to symbolize the Plates to the description, and reasons assigned for every cause and effect that is produced by the rules and maxims which they treat of, in order to sanction the judgement where inexperience has not ripened the practice to discriminate the axioms that are so forcibly laid down. There is a kind of doubtful timidity which attends the modesty of genius and youthful experience,which cannot be surmounted but by such a certainty as will justify the proof, which certainty we have endeavoured in every case to possess them of, both by precept and example, and if strictly adhered to will inevitably answer each peculiar purpose ascertained.

* In measuring for Fig. C. follow the same method as in Fig. 3. in Plate B, taking the length from the shoulder to the hollow of the breast, and mark the measure, and then continue the length to the bottom of the Waistcoat as may be required; then measure all down the round of the middle before, afterwards measure the length of the back, for the purpose mentioned in other Plates of fat men, as at Fig. 6. then measure round the breast high under the arms and level round the belly, then below the belly at the hips; and follow the methods prescribed in the other Plates both as to cutting and making, which will fully answer the intent.

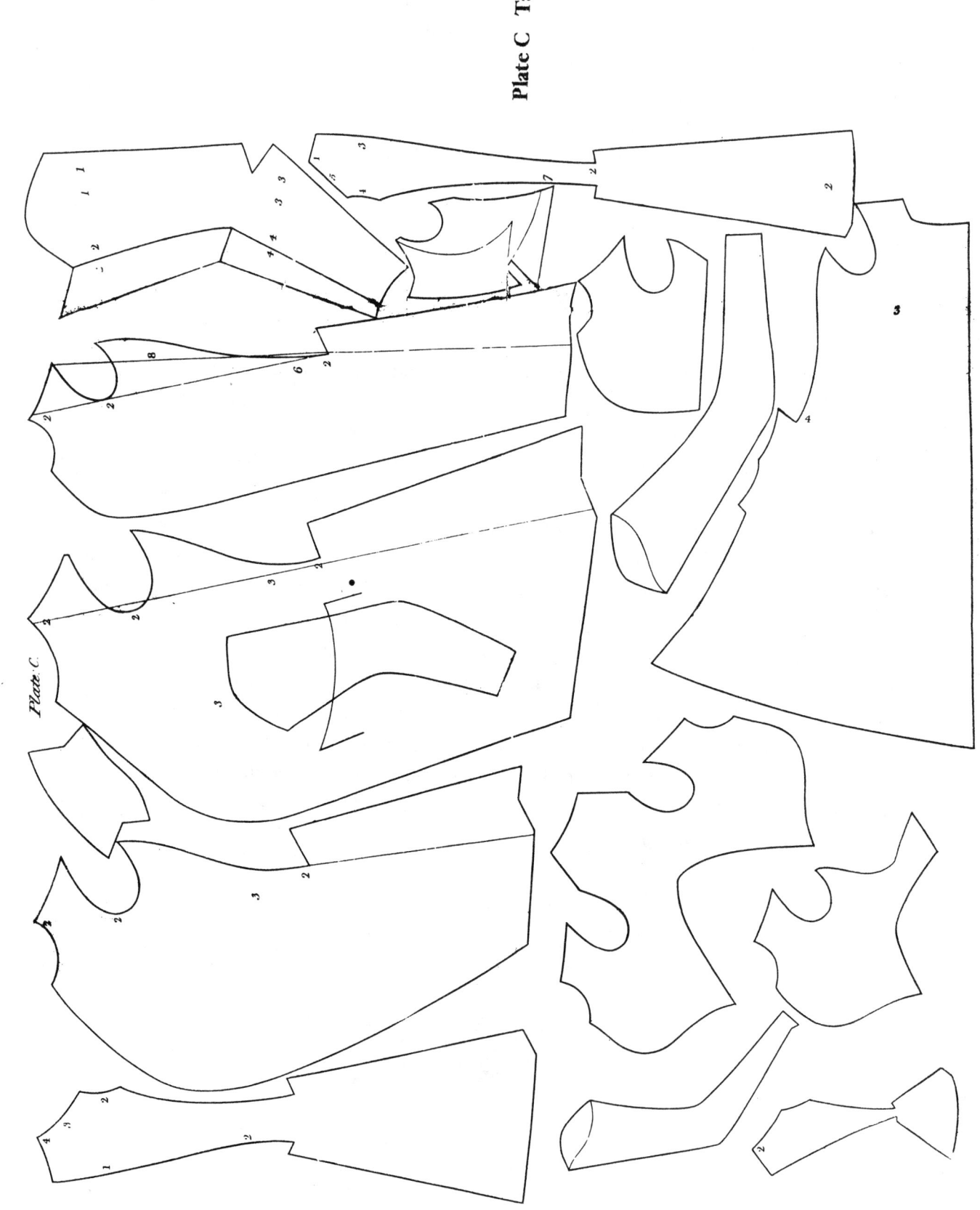

Plate C Taylor

Plate C.

Plate I   Q&L

Single Breasted Coat

1. coat front
2. coat back
3. collar
4. sleeve

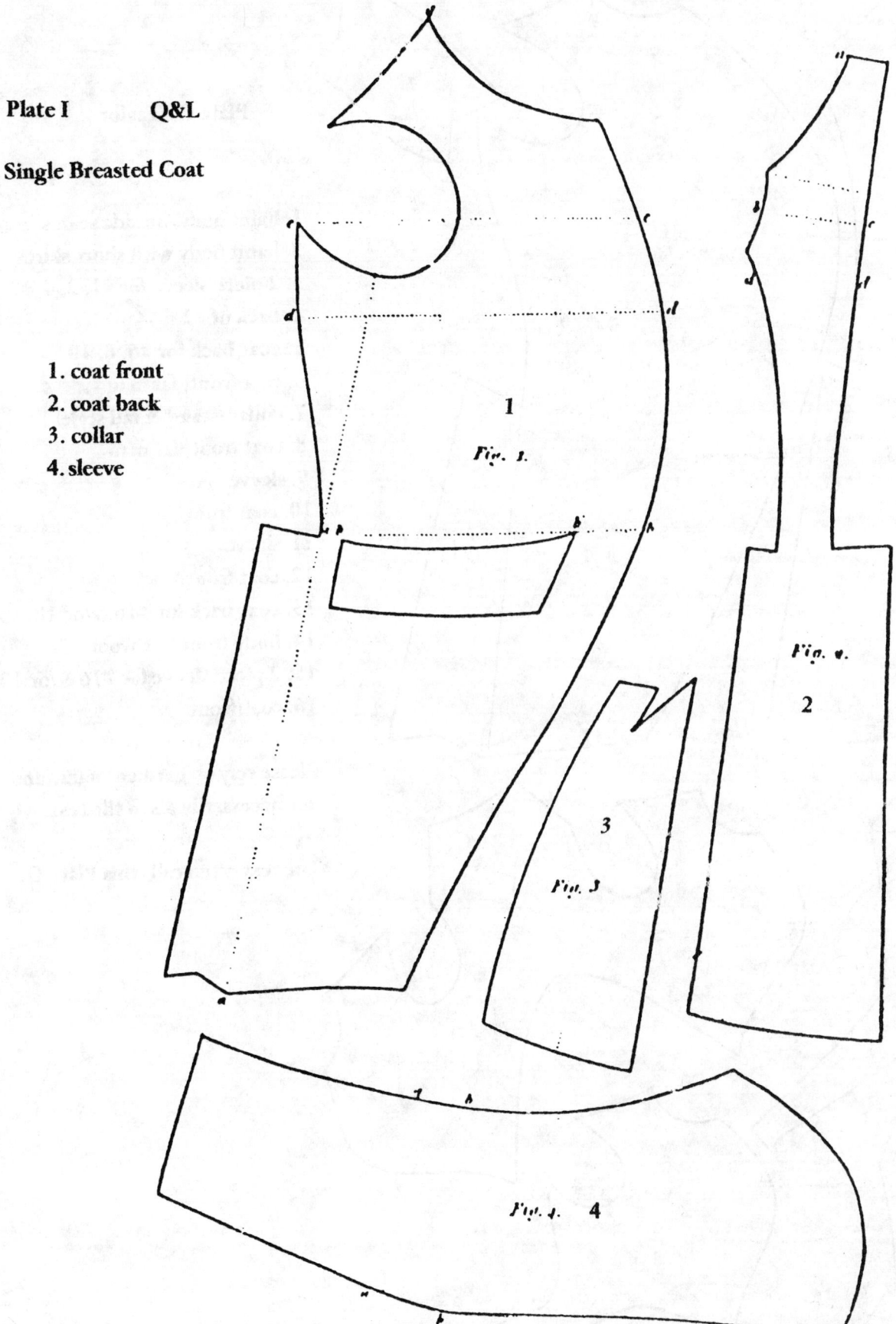

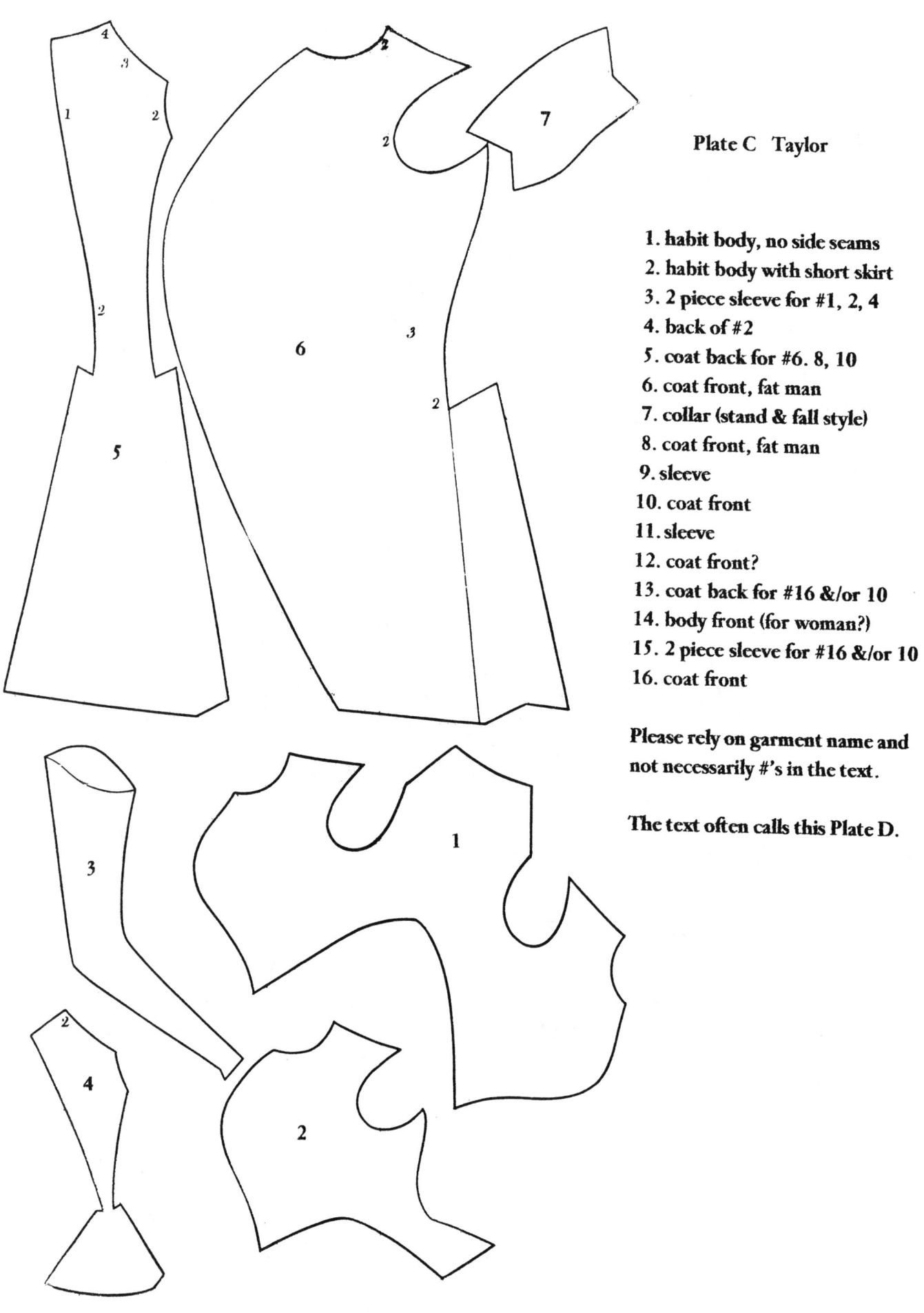

Plate C Taylor

1. habit body, no side seams
2. habit body with short skirt
3. 2 piece sleeve for #1, 2, 4
4. back of #2
5. coat back for #6. 8, 10
6. coat front, fat man
7. collar (stand & fall style)
8. coat front, fat man
9. sleeve
10. coat front
11. sleeve
12. coat front?
13. coat back for #16 &/or 10
14. body front (for woman?)
15. 2 piece sleeve for #16 &/or 10
16. coat front

Please rely on garment name and not necessarily #'s in the text.

The text often calls this Plate D.

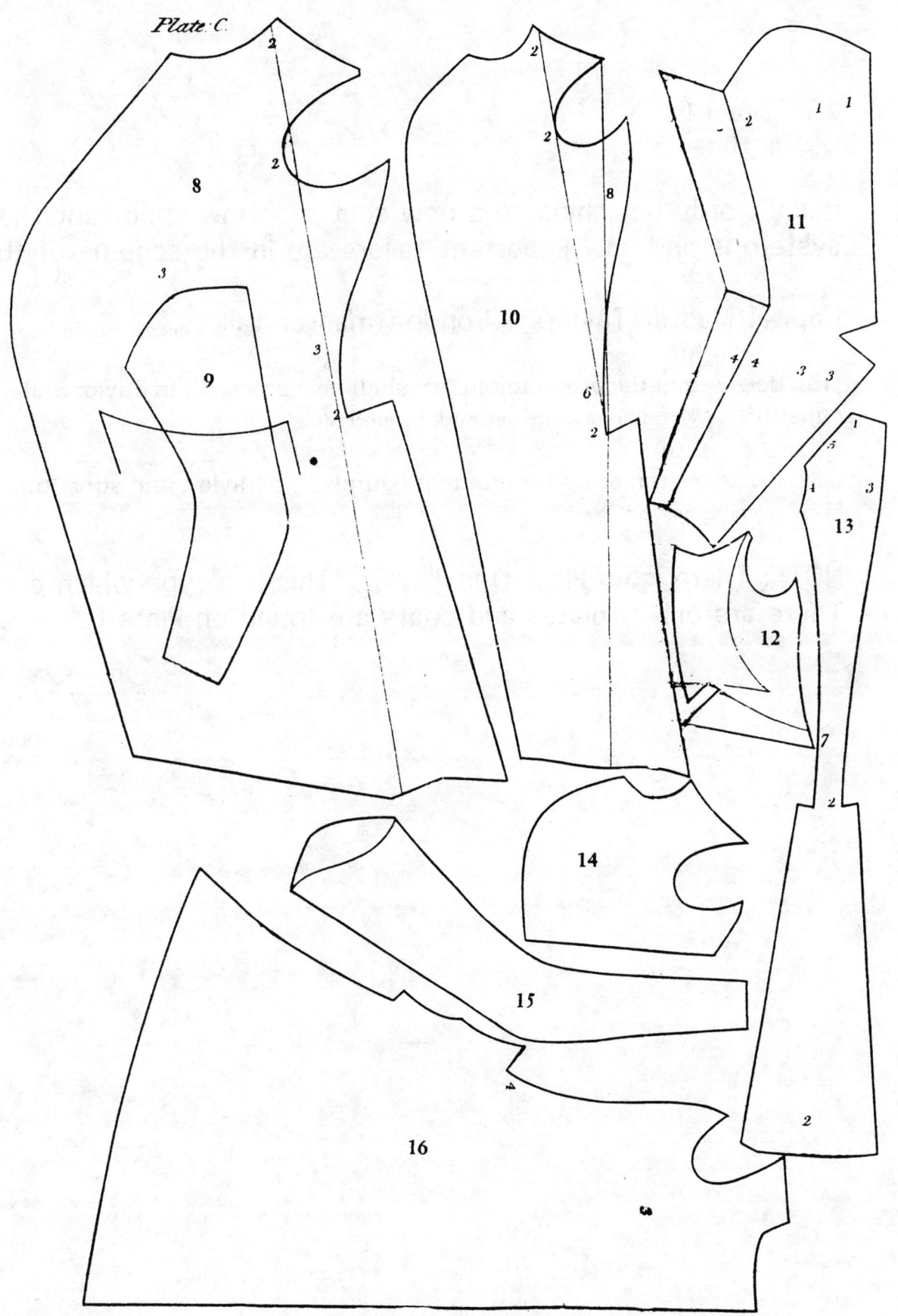

Plate C.

Re: Chapter I
Q&L p. 16

Usual wordy beginning to a new section. How important their
system is and how important tailors are in the scheme of things.

Capital Master Taylors - London master tailors.

Q&L delete from the beginning to "we shall now proceed," in Taylor and
substitute: "We will commence our work by proceeding"

Q&L delete "eleven or twelve hundred pounds; " in Taylor, and substitute:
"a considerable amount"

NOTE: There is no Plate D in Taylor. This is a typo which persists.
There are only 3 plates and coats are found on Plate C.

SECTION III.

Chapter 1

Dissertation on Coats

* Having run through our observations upon Breeches and Waistcoats, we hope to the full satisfaction of our students, we shall now proceed to set forth the modes and most effectual maxims for accomplishing and compleating his practice in the principal part of his business, which is in the measuring, cutting, and making a Coat. In this lays the energy of his pursuit, which when once thoroughly possessed of, he may with satisfaction congratulate himself with the sentiment of being entirely at home.

On the mastery of this great qualification, which has baffled the efforts of all preceding generations, since the revolution of crowns, and new created systems modernized our habits and dresses to the present mode. On the proficiency of this scientific art depends the elements of other arts; for while human nature is dependent upon dress for the grace and embellishment which it bestows upon the well-turned features, the compleat Taylor will always hold a state of pre-eminence in equipping and finishing the exterior of address in a fine gentleman; for nothing can be more convincing, or fully illustrate this hypothesis, than an observation of any of our plays, where the gentleman puts off his real seeming, by assuming the garb of rusticity. This will in a great measure shew the necessity of cutting well, when the effect of elegance depends upon the Taylor's shears.

We mean not by this to infringe upon the distinguishing qualities of either the dancing or fencing-master; we wish only to illustrate our own particular walk, to shew the merit of the art, and what attainments are requisite to compass the matter, for the improvement of our students, and the general good.

By strictly following the dictates of our theory, we hope we shall be able to give such formidable reasons as will prevent in future the necessity of one master Taylor's begging the assistance of another to cut out his clothes; this we know to be a common practice in the trade, by men who have even been in the business and habit of cutting out twenty years. What a depravity of genius, at an aera when every art is striving with a vivid force for mastery.

The Taylor, whose sprightly walk in life is to give grace to drapery, sits down upon the forlorn hope of struggling through without ever inquiring farther than the maxims of his father, or what his master always did before him. Such poverty of genius has always inhabited the minds of Taylors, or they would never have continued so long in such egregious errors, from father to son, or from master to apprentice, without application or enquiry. Like the bell-wether of a flock (if we may be allowed the expression) running over a ditch, and all the rest following after.

It is a notorious truth, however strange it may appear, that we have had capital master Taylors, who at their demise, have left behind them wardrobes of clothes, which have been returned upon their hands by misfitting, to the gross amount of * eleven or twelve hundred pounds; besides what they may have disposed of by alterations and mutilations to less figures, that have made choice

Re: Chapter II

Q&L p. 20, which they title:

"How to measure a thin gentleman for a single breasted Coat: Plate I. Figure 1,2,3,4."

Plate D does not exist.... read Plate C.

Q&L delete "No. 1" in Taylor, replace with "letter a"

Q&L delete "Plate D, Fig. 2" in Taylor, replace with "plate I, Fig. 2"

Q&L delete "No. 3 to No. 4" in Taylor, replace with "letter c to letter b"

Q&L delete "and down to the wrist" in Taylor, replace with "at letter b and down to the hand,"

Q&L delete "as high as you can" in Taylor, replace with "at letter c"

Q&L delete "or as many times round the arm as you please." and replace with "at b, b and around the hand," of the same fashion and colours.

Such circumstances as these must ever happen, while people are content to remain in the field of ignorance. To be uninformed may be the lot of many, whose inexperience have not furnished them with opportunities to compass the matter in question. True genius is not the lot of every one; yet almost every man is sufficiently enabled by application and perseverance in certain rudiments, to accomplish such a knowledge in any common manufacturing business, as will clearly answer the practice of it.

Leave but the road of uncertainly, make one bold effort in the peaceable path of science, and by diligence and modest progressive steps, no doubt but you will artfully reach the port proposed, which is the hearty wish of the authors of these sheets.

Chapter II

How to measure a thin Gentleman for a Single Breasted Coat. Plate D, Fig. P

Previous to our beginning this business, it may not be amiss to warn our student of the great necessity there is of his being judiciously particular in learning from his customer the precise length he chuses to wear his Coat, with how much of the ruling fashion he would wish to imbibe, with other particulars of buttons, pockets, etc. for it is notorious that hundreds of suits of clothes have been returned upon the Taylor's hands by gentlemen leaving it to the Taylor's own taste. The ideas of men are very different, especially in dress; for what is most pleasing to some, is disgusting to others; therefore the safest and most certain mode of giving satisfaction is by a few questions touching the above purposes, and then proceed to measure.

First, take the length from * No. 1, at the top of the shoulder of the back down to the waist, in * Plate D, Fig. 2, and then continue it to the bottom of the skirts for the length; then from the back seam, half across the back from * No. 3, to No. 4; next to the elbow, * and down to the wrist, for the length of the sleeve; afterwards across the arm * as high as you can; then below the elbow, * or as many times round the arm as you please. Observe that the gentleman when you measure, hold his arm level with the shoulder, for too high would make the sleeve too long, and too low too short; then measure round the breast, as high as possible, next below at the belly, and also over at the hips; then measure half over the breast, which will be as much as we conceive necessary, only with this remark; when you measure for the length of the back, mind you nicely hit upon that mode that most pervades your employer's fancy; for by doing this, you will facilitate his wishes, which may give a pleasing sanction to all the rest.

After you have taken and marked all your measures, be sure you keep them distinct, that two alike may not clash at one place, and by a kind of confusion frustrate your ideas. As for your manner of marking, use the only clear method that may seem most familiar to you; and before you leave the gentleman, set down his particular requests in your book of directions that when you have cut, finished, and brought the clothes home, should any dislike arise, you can have recourse to your minutes

Re: Chapter III
Q&L p. 23

Amount of cloth necessary for a coat.

The importance of good fitting.

Q&L delete "Plate D" in Taylor, and substitute: "plate"

Q&L delete "No. 3, to No. 4 on Plate D" and "No. 4 to No. 5" in Taylor and substitute: "a to b in plate II, then move the measure from a to a on the shoulder,"

Q&L delete "No. 7 in plate 2;" in Taylor, and substitute: "in plate I fig. 2" taken from your customer's own mouth, which if you have justly followed, will hold you blameless. A little caution of this kind you will find prevent both anxiety and doubt, and will reflect wisdom on your prudence, and in the end gain both credit and respect.

Chapter III

Of the Points and Maxims of Cutting and compleatly making a Coat

As we write for the inexperienced and uninformed, it may not be amiss for us to define and lay down a certain rule that may be a lasting standard for all such as are unacquainted with the real quantity of cloth necessary to make a coat: take the following method.

Measure by your yard the length of your Coat, as you have taken it from your measure, to which add the length of your sleeve, these two added together will be the precise quantity requisite, and no less will do with any propriety.

When the cloth is laid before you do not omit having recourse to * Plate D, of the analysis of Coats, and pay particular respect to the separated parts, the different modes and turning that they effect, for until these are made (as it were) coincident with your own ideas, the maxims we lay down, we are fearful, will only serve to confuse, without answering the great end we wish to obtain by our labours. — After you have sufficiently digested the plates, and your cloth being before you, mark down the back seam as the plate directs, and strike the shape of the back upon the cloth, bearing the same similitude as the small scale upon the plate, and take care it answers to your measure in every part. Take a large back hollowing, for this will make your back-skirts lap over well, and not part behind; as is too often the case to the abuse of decency.

Be a little curious in the length of the back scye; should you make it long, see that the shoulder seam lies very high, and in order to prove that, when you lay your measure across the back from * No. 3, to No. 4 on Plate D; then move the measure from * No. 4 to No. 5, on the shoulder, and mark down the shoulder at the end of the measure for the shoulder seam, afterwards strike the mark of the back scye at the end of the measure according to the plate, as low as you perceive it necessary; but be a little nice in this top of your back, and cut your back narrower at the shoulder across, than it is at the bottom of the back scye.

This maxim will make your sleeve, when all is united and put together, come up well on the shoulder, from which effect you will learn, that if your back is broad, your fore part must be broad also; in which case the sleeves cannot come up to the place they should be at, both the back and the fore part prevent it, but by cutting the back and fore part a little away and adding so much to the sleeve, you may command the sleeve seam at the shoulder top as much over the rounding of the bone as you please; but more of this hereafter.

In order to finish the back down from the back scye to the hip, strike the back side seam as smart and neat as you can, by inspection of the plate, and in the back seam be sure you do not begin to hollow till you come to the appropriate place * of No. 7 in plate 2; for should you do this, you will

Q&L insert before ""If the Fashion" in Taylor: "Another, and more certain rule is, to make your waist of the same length as your measure from the middle of the back to the elbow."

Q&L delete "and next of the fore part as at Fig. 6, in plate 2. for on this depends the very continuity of the whole coat." in Taylor.

Q&L delete "No. 8 to No. 8" in Taylor, and substitute: "letter d to letter d"

Q&L insert "button" before "holes" in Taylor.

Q&L delete "Fig. 2 in Plate D as at No. 7" in Taylor, and substitute: "a and at letter a" disorder the economy and fitting of the whole coat; for by too much hollowing the back under the shoulder, you will force it to kick up and hang loose at the hip, which is a very great error. To find the true length of the waist, it must be cut from the top of the back-slit (or what is called tack over) longer by three inches than the skirts. *

If the fashion should create a broader mode of making of the backs at the hip than at present, and our student should not have considered this, till practice has availed him of the methods more prompt to his purpose, let him mark out his narrow back that he has been used to with all its leading features, and add to the side seam as much as is required; — but remember that whatever is added to the back must be taken from the fore part, and this will answer his purpose, * and next of the fore part as at Fig. 6, in plate 2. for on this depends the very continuity of the whole coat. Observe well the cut and contour of the plate, mind the prominency and round of the breast, for on this will depend the graceful seeming and elegance of the cut, which is so requisite to display the beauty and perfection of human nature.

To make the fore part answer to the back, lay the back upon the fore part, and from the same shape according to the plate down before. Extend you measure across from * No. 8 to No. 8, and lying one half of your back to the extent of your measure, mark the width of the fore part at the side seam, with a proper allowance for laying in, and also room before for paring and making up the edge, with allowance for the projection at the end of the * holes; then across for the Belly and make it somewhat less in proportion to the Measure, as smartness and neatness may require, and the same at the hip, and mark your skirt agreeable to the plate, and the same length as the back skirt, then make the fore part skirt.

Notwithstanding we have said so much about the cutting, measuring, and making of a coat, yet we have a few most essential points further to propound to our pupil, which he will find of serious consideration, and tantamount to his purpose, as they are the very leading features which symmetry has prescribed to facilitate and harmonize the whole.

In the first place we must inform him that however essential every component part is to the unity of the thing intended, yet there are a few prevailing causes which give energy to the theme, and which cannot be dispensed with if the coat is designed to fit neat, clean and clever in every part. — Observe the following rule, that it is a maxim in our Theory that the top of the Coat commands the bottom; for instance should you want to find where the square must be marked, this must be done by laying your measure or yard, or any thing you have that is long enough, first at the shoulder point in * Fig. 2 in Plate D as at No. 7, and continue it straight down to the hip where it closes to, and carry it down the skirt to the bottom; and where it falls at the extreme end of the skirt, there you must mark your place for your square.

When you plait up the coat you must mind that the fore plaits are exactly in the line from the top of the shoulder to the hip, and down to the bottom of the skirts, for your square will be always in a right line from the shoulder and hip. Thus far we do infer the shoulder point always rules your square, and always will, let the rage of Fashion be ever so preposterous. Notwithstanding any alteration of long or short waists, narrow or broad backs, this rule is plenarily just and cannot be dispensed with for any elegant coat whatsoever.

Q&L delete "Plate B. in Fig. 2" in Taylor, and substitute: "plate I. fig. 1,"

Q&L delete "No. 2. in the plate at the shoulder, and at No. 2, at the scye arm-hole, and at the hip" in Taylor, and substitute: "at a and at a at the hip"

Q&L after "shoulder point" in Taylor insert "the gorget"

Q&L replace "trim" in Taylor, with "train"

Q&L delete "for it would be awkward" to the end of the paragraph in Taylor.

Q&L delete "the Fig. of the sleeve in Plate D," in Taylor and substitute: "fig. 4, plate I"

Q&L delete "and those must be straight, not in the least hollowed, as reason must suggest to every searcher of the art" in Taylor, and substitute: "For further instructions on this subject, see plate II, fig. 4."

The next great point to compleat the cutting lays in the symmetry of the fore-part, which is perfectly described upon the * Plate B, in Fig. 2, which bears a just proportion, and must be the same in likelihood and similitude when marked and cut upon your cloth; and be sure you note the following maxim, that is, to lay a line from the hip to the shoulder point at the gorget, I mean the point at No. 2, in the plate at the shoulder, and at * No. 2, at the scye arm-hole, and at the hip; and be assured of this, that if those three leading points are not all in a direct line, that it will baffle the very hope of possibility ever to make the coat fit. This maxim we do affirm to be an indispensable certainly, and though but little understood by the trade, we give it as its choicest criterion, and of much more value to our pupil, than any rule in the whole branch of business.

After your fore part is fashioned after the manner we speak of, and those other rules strictly adhered to, you must be careful that your back and fore part are both of a length; and in order to ascertain this matter truly, lay your back and fore part together at the hip, and hold them fast, and also lay hold of the corner of the back at the top of the neck at the shoulder seam, and try how high you can make it reach without straining, and then strike your shoulder across for your fore part shoulder seam; and that point of the back that is the shoulder point, * must fall just in the middle of the shoulder seam. This will ever be a judicious guide for all thin people. When the fore parts and backs are in this * trim, be assured that the very power of distortion is destroyed, your practice being commensurate with symmetry, and error is totally divested of its power.

Now we have taken so much pains to shew how effect is to be given to drapery, and the body graced by the influence of the cut of the fore part, we are not to establish this as an invariable rule to suit the fancy of all opinions; the gravity of some customers would rather think this mode of cutting an imperfection, than a pleasing maxim to be guided by; therefore all allowance must be made touching circumstances, the age and avocations of different people: * for it would be as awkward and truly laughable to see a hackney coachman in a Coat of this graceful cut and seeming, as Tom Errand in Beau Clincher's clothes, in the Trip to the Jubilee.

Clothes that would grace the first officer of a regiment, would be unsuitable for the back of a porter. Observe the requisites of fitting the body, and you may follow the wit and sport of fashion to every extreme. The ornament of lappells or other modes of making, will never impede the system we treat of, if you do but follow the dictates of our theory; for be assured, that good fitting is the ornament of fashion, and gives a most graceful lustre to every thing attending it.

With respect to the sleeve, we must still urge the necessity of strictly adhering to the cut and matter of the Plate. Take care you do not hollow your fore seam otherwise than we direct. Cut the sleeve all down the fore seam, in the matter of the * Fig. of the sleeve in Plate D, a little hollow from the top to the bend of the arm, very full and nearly straight; and then from the hollow down to the hand, according to the success of the figure in the Plate, full, and to fall off agreeably; this will prevent the cocking up, so much complained of. Though this mode of practice may differ from your own, and create a surprise at the novelty of the method, you may rest assured it is a paradox not more strange than true.

In order more fully to demonstrate this matter to our learner, we would have him turn his thoughts upon the cut of the patent sleeves, which are made without seams, either before or behind;

Q&L delete "left by bad practice they should prevent its fitting at the arm-holes." in Taylor, and substitute:

"which must be held on from c to a, in order to form an elbow," and which are known to fit neater and much better than those that are made with seams; * and those must be straight, not in the least hollowed, as reason must suggest to every searcher of the art. Have an eye upon the men's sewing of the sleeve, * lest by bad practice they should prevent its fitting at the arm-holes.

Observe they lock in the inside at the top four inches down, and take it in less than the outside full an inch; this maxim will compel it to fit the scyes, and not appear too full under the arms, as is too frequently the case by the generality of the Trade. This has long been a most egregious error, and has escaped the observation of many, whose studious application has given them great credit in this particular, as well as other brilliant efforts in many other parts of the business, to the attainment of the matter we are treating of, which has ever distinguished them by the neatness of their work.

The Taylor text refers to Plate D for patterns for this section. There is no Plate D of course and so they mean Plate C...which is found on pages 76 and 77.

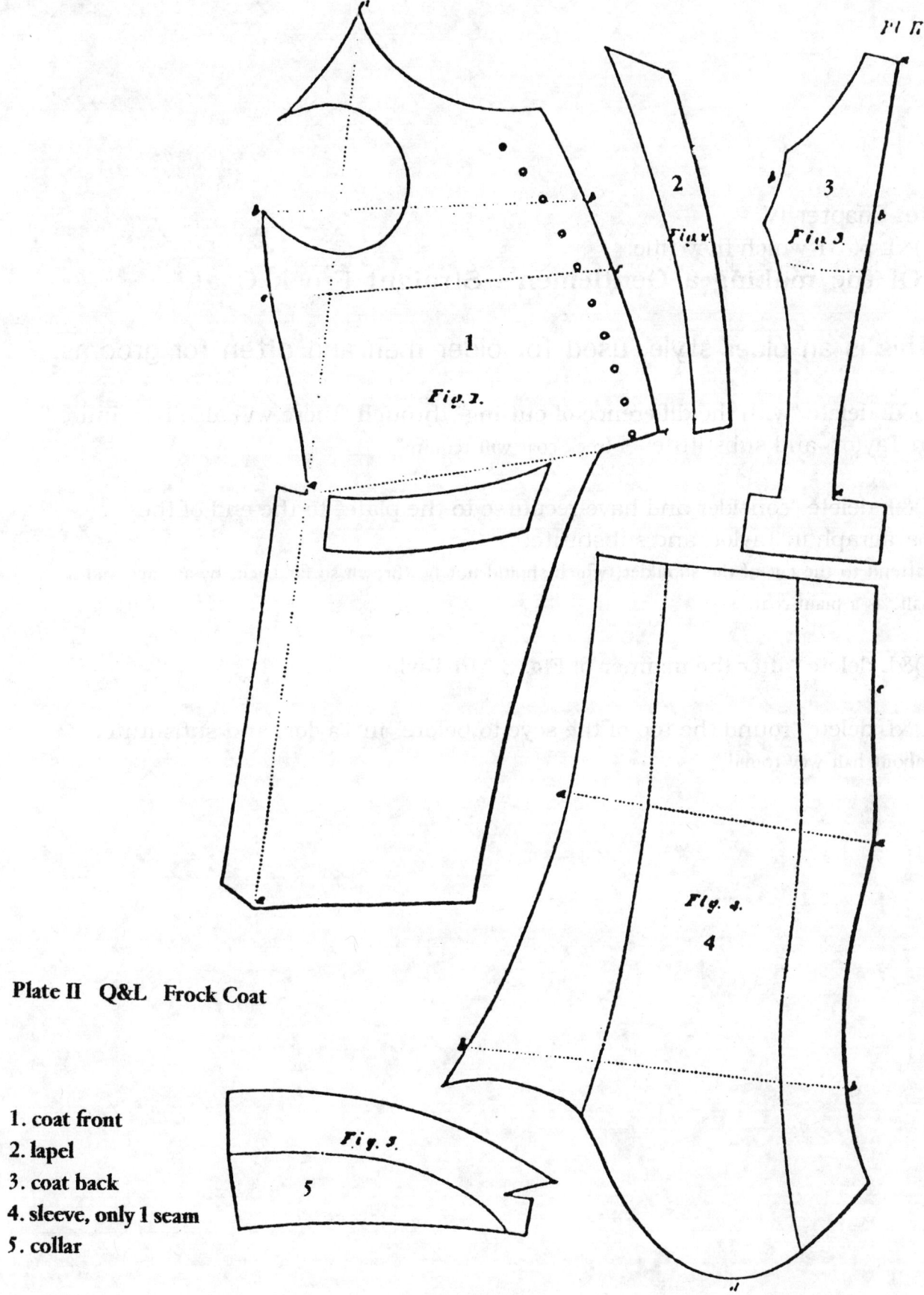

Plate II   Q&L   Frock Coat

1. coat front
2. lapel
3. coat back
4. sleeve, only 1 seam
5. collar

91

Re: Chapter IV
Q&L p. 31 which they title:
"Of the making a Gentlemen's Straight Frock Coat."

This is an older style, used for older men and often for grooms.

Q&L delete "with the difference of cutting" through "there will also be required" in Taylor, and substitute: "a frock coat will require"

Q&L delete "consider and have recourse to the plate" to the end of the paragraph in Taylor, and substitute:
"attend to the cut of the shoulder, which should not be thrown so far back, by an inch and a half, as a plain coat."

Q&L delete "after the manner of Fig. 3." in Taylor.

Q&L delete "round the top of the scye to before" in Taylor, and substitute:
"about half way round,"

Chapter IV

Of the Making a Straight Frock, for either Gentleman or Groom

Our previous observations in the Coat for a thin man will answer every purpose of measuring for the subject in question, * with the difference of cutting in the fore part, which is properly described in Plate D, Fig. 3; here you will discover the effect by the similitude, and by inspection perceive how much in addition is necessary to the fore part to accomplish this piece of business: there will also be required an additional width to the back in that place upon the hips, between the buttons, and likewise a little wider skirt for the back.

In cases where persons are a little long in the neck, to remedy which, add to the fore part, before a full inch more than another kind of coat, that it may button over the top button with much ease, that no restraint or constriction may in any wise impede the free extension of the arm. Touching the difficulty resulting from the flying off of the frock, we cannot be too pressing in our requesting most seriously to * consider and have recourse to the Plate, for that will infallibly shew him the manner of cutting, and how the shoulder must lie.

The fore part must be cut as straight as possible, and square across the bottom, * after the manner of Fig. 3. With regard to the sleeves, collar, etc. proceed according to our directions of a Coat for a thin man. Take notice in cutting the fore part before that you do not cut it shorter than behind; this is a terrible fault, and but too often exposed to our sight.

In order to make a frock hang straight, you must take from the skirt at the bottom behind three inches to make it shorter behind than before; this done, it will hang straight and level all round, to the satisfaction of the wearer.

When you clear the scye, you will remember that clearing it from the closing of the side seam, and round before, according to custom, is erroneous. This we have thoroughly proved from various examples, in altering the mistakes of inexperienced Taylors. In our theory clearing the scye will be unnecessary if you adhere to the plates, and the maxims here treated of. If you cut by the rules laid down, and find an occasion, begin at the back scye very near the shoulder, and clear it * round the top of the scye to before, and not under the arm, as is the common practice.

Be careful in this point, for any irregular cutting away before, will totally dispossess the coat of its other genuine merits; for by cutting the scye too forward, you will force it into wrinkles under the arm. The more you wound the fore part, the larger the scye will be, and of course the fore part will fly to the flesh; the sleeve will force the fore part, and with the additional weight of the Coat, it is dragged to fit close at the arm-hole, to the prejudice of ease, and every convenience, and sometimes chafe off the skin under the arm.

In order to facilitate this nice piece of business, and rectify any errors of this sort, first take in the sleeve behind, the inside only, leave the outside as large as it was before, only lock in the inside to fit the scye. By this maxim, your Coat will receive a peculiar advantage, and give ease and freedom to the wearer; and in such a case, when a coat cannot be worn, through thightness [tightness] or

Q&L delete "pinned up under the arm" in Taylor, and substitute:
"being basted at the side arm"

Re: Chapter V
Q&L p. 35

constriction in the scye, let out the shoulder (for we hope you will always lay in there as well as at the side seam), as this is the place from whence relief must be had. You must not let out the side seam at the top, as is usually done; this will only make it wider in the breast; nor will letting out the sleeve and side seam answer any purpose towards easing the coat, without letting out the shoulder also; for all cramped scyes must have ease from the shoulder and sleeve; for often the shoulder is peculiarly fleshy and round, which demands extraordinary room.

In those cases, some say the scye is too little under the arm; but this is wrong, for the cause is before the arm at the fore seam of the sleeve, and round the top of the shoulder; in consequence of which it would be well to help the hand of inexperience by urging the necessity of laying in the shoulder fore part where the grievance lies; for in any constriction, letting out the sleeve of the fore-arm, and giving room on the shoulder, will effect a radical cure.

The reason of our hint for laying in the side seam is to provide you with the means on any occasion of making the Coat wider upon the breast, either from the fault of your own practice, or by rectifying the errors of others.

If you would wish to prove the prescribed maxims by experience, make an effort upon your own Coat. Take and pin your own Coat in at the shoulder, about one inch double on both sides, then slip it on your back, and you will soon find the effect it has upon you, and how different from the same quantity being * pinned up under the arm

There requires much judgement to alter clothes well, that have been spoiled in the cutting, and it is with regret that we speak it, that too many of this description have come within the scope of our practice.

Chapter V

Of Great Coats

Having treated upon the various kinds of dress, we should hope by this time our student begins to possess the power of discrimination, and a few hints now will serve to lead him, we hope, to the seat of proficiency, where he may have leisure to contemplate on the perplexity of his pursuits, and with a grateful sense of his own application, rejoice that perseverance has at length brought him to the summit of all his wishes.

A great coat is the very exterior of all dress, and though it is only used against the inclemency of the weather, has notwithstanding its merits as well as conveniencies; for whatever merit your inner dress may possess, if there is the least defect in the surtout, your whole body will be deformed; therefore we propound the few following observations as a guide to the pupil's genius, and beg he may not slight the advice, as they are of more value than he may imagine, for we know that many of the Trade too wantonly sport with the maxims of making a top coat.

In the first place we would advise them to cut it full and large to answer the intended purpose, the fore part must be cut somewhat longer in the shoulder than a strait coat, to facilitate its

Q&L delete "and wider in the arm-hole" in Taylor.

putting on; the sleeve to be cut three quarters of an inch wider in the double than a small coat, and also longer by an inch * and wider in the arm-hole, and easier in every part by three quarters of an inch, both in the back, across the shoulders, and in the width of the body. There is often a great error in not being cut long enough before, this is chiefly owing to the cloth going straight along the bottom, and not taking three inches off at the wealpiece [wheelpiece]; and begin cutting from that point to the front to nothing. This method will make the coat hang neat and straight round the bottom. Cut the shoulder as straight as you can, for fear the coat should fly back; for all great coats buttoned or unbuttoned should hang neat and straight down before, and with width to lap over, which is the intended purpose, and the end is answered.

The Taylor text refers to Plate D for patterns for this section. There is no Plate D, of course, and so they mean Plate C. This can be found on pages 76 and 77.

There is also a difference between the Riding Habits that they are talking about here and the Patent Riding Habits (or habits without seams) they are discussing in Chapter XI on page 127.

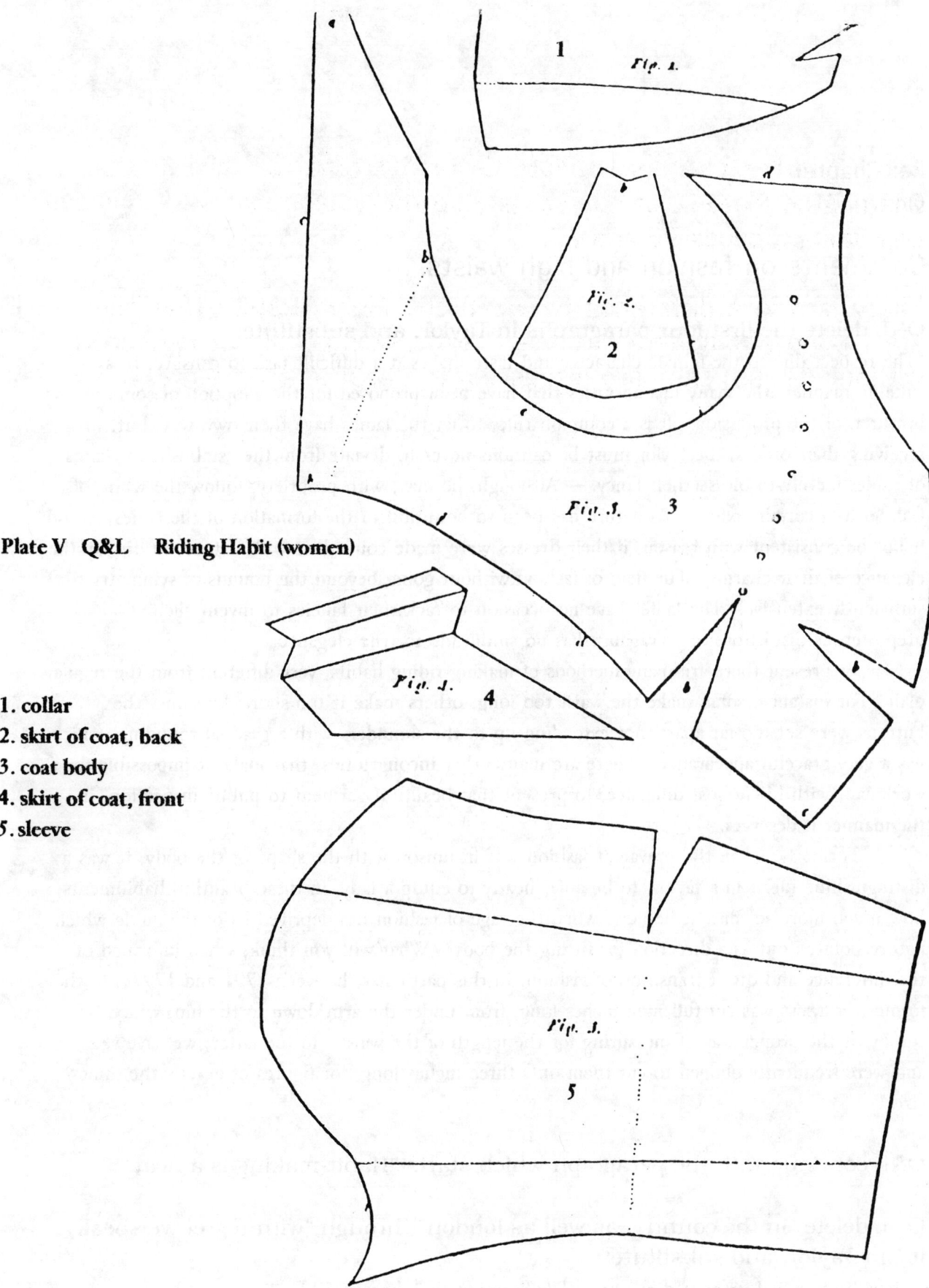

Plate V Q&L   Riding Habit (women)

1. collar
2. skirt of coat, back
3. coat body
4. skirt of coat, front
5. sleeve

1

Fig. 1.

2

Fig. 2.

Fig. 3. 3

Fig. 4. 4

Fig. 5.

5

Re: Chapter I
Q&L p. 51

Comments on fashion and high waists.

Q&L delete the first four paragraphs in Taylor, and substitute:
"The respect due to the female character and taste makes it a difficult task to censure, in a suitable manner, the many incongruities that have been proposed for the adoption of some of our brethren of the profession. It is a common rule, to let the ladies have their own way; but, in receiving their orders, the taylor must be cautious never to deviate from the established maxims of trade, merely to please their fancy. — Although, he may, with propriety, follow the whim of fashion to a certain extent. As nature has been so bountiful in the formation of the ladies, would it not be consistent with reason, if their dresses were made coincident with nature, to display the elegance of their charms. The field of fashion,without going beyond the bounds of symmetry, is sufficiently extensive. The ladies have no occasion to rack their fancies to invent such preposterous distortions; extravagance has no similitude to true elegance.

At present there are many methods of making riding habits, very different from the regular plan. For instance: some make the waist too long, others make it too short; by some, the buttons were set too far apart, not extending up to the shoulders with a gradual rounding, which has a very graceful appearance. There are many other incongruities, that make it impossible for a workman, with his utmost diligence, to present that beautiful garment to public inspection, in the manner it deserves.

Formerly, when the prevalent fashion was in unison with the shape of the body, it was a distinguishing merit in a taylor, to be able, neatly to equip a lady, in these beautiful habiliments; how much more so must it be now, when the rage of fashion has deprived us of the guide which nature pointed out as a direction for fitting the body? What will you think, when informed of the difference and quick transition of fashion, in this particular, between 1791 and 1797? In the former,the waist was cut full nine inches long, from under the arm down to the hip, which by the by, is the proper way of measuring for the length of the waist. In the latter, we have seen, and were frequently obliged to cut them only three inches long, for figures of exactly the same size."

Q&L continue with the paragraph which starts "Habit-making is a neat..."

Q&L delete "in the country, as well as london" through "with regret we speak it." in Taylor, and substitute:
"might be supplied without difficulty. —We mention this, because"

SECTION IV.

Chapter I

Of Ladies Habits

* The great veneration we have for the Ladies makes us a little cautious how we arraign the inconsistency of the prevailing rage and fashion of making Habits; yet surely it cannot be wrong to say that no furor, however outrageous, could be so truly ridiculous as the mode they now have adopted for adorning the most finished part of the creation, and should be stiled [styled] the Sport of Lady Fashion in the year 1796.

As nature has been so delicately graceful in the formation of the Ladies, would it not be more consistent with reason and elegance, if dresses were made consistent with nature, to display the beautiful appearance of their charming features? Fashion hath as many changes as variety, and all within the pale of symmetry and gentility; the Ladies have no occasion to rack their fancies with preposterous distortions; the whole arcanum of extravagance is totally dissimilar and foreign to graceful elegance and ease.

The present mode of making Riding Habits is much out of the regular method, for such short waists and broad lappells; buttons set so wide, and other incongruous maxims, that the maker with all his application is totally incapable of setting the beautiful finishing of nature in any point of view fit for public inspection.

A few years ago it was a distinguishing merit in the habit maker to equip a Lady neatly in these habiliments of Diana, even when taste was in unison with the shape of the body; what must it be now when the rage of extravagance has stripped us of every guide that nature pointed out as a direction for fitting the body? What will future workmen say when we declare the difference and quick transition of * fashion in these particulars between 1793, when we were wont to cut waists full nine inches long from under the arm down to the hip (which by the bye is the choice way of measuring for the length of the waist), and in the year 1796 we have been obliged to cut them but three inches in the same place for the length, to figures of the same height and stature?

* Habit-making is a neat and delicate piece of practice, and understood but by a few; seldom practiced, and unknown to thousands of Taylors; and though by many may be thought a part of the Taylor's branch, is quite dissimilar and as different as joinery and cabinet-making. Yet 'tis a pity that it were not a little more united to the Taylor's Trade, and become a matter of instruction to apprentices by which means it might be diffused generally amongst the Trade in the country, as well as in town; then Ladies might be served upon any emergency * in the country, as well as in London; for it is with regret we speak it, we have known Taylors both in town and country, who have done the Tayloring business as well as their neighbours, who rather than modestly own their inability to habit-making have undertaken this business in families to the spoil of materials, and loss of their whole work, when they in other matters had for a time given decent satisfaction. A man should not be blamed for what

101

Q&L delete "thirty years" in Taylor, and substitute: "twenty years"

Q&L delete "Franklin's wife" in Taylor, and add "mechanic's daughter"

Franklin - an English free-holder or substantial land owner.

Q&L for "habit" in Taylor, substitute" "habit and skirt"

Q&L delete from "straight down to the hollow " through "round the arm at the top" in Taylor, and substitute:
"at letter e, on plate V. at the scye, down about five inches; this you must calculate yourself according to the size of the lady you are measuring, to letter f, as the plate directs; there mark the measure, which will be the length of the body. Next down the back, from the top at letter b, at the bottom, then across for the breadth of the back,from the crest or back seam at letter e, then down to the elbow and hand. Remember to mark the measure; you next measure round the body, as high as possible under the arms, and round the wrist; you next measure round the arm at the sleeve top, as far in upon the body as you can for the scye"

Q&L delete "from the hip down to the ground" through "the leading feature." in Taylor,and substitute:
"or skirt, measure from where you left off at the side, at letter f, down to the ground, and any other part you may think proper; you will do well to measure from the top of the back, to the lower point of the back scye, at letter b, as these are the leading features in measuring."

Q&L after "half breadth in the skirt" in Taylor, add:
"which is very seldom the case now,"

Q&L for "petticoat" in Taylor, read "skirt"

Q&L for "placket" in Taylor, read "pocket"

Q&L delete "three inches" in Taylor, and substitute:
"five inches plain before, for the apron"

he does not know. — 'Tis a pity country Taylors have not paid more respect to the nature of Habit-making; they have certainly neglected the most pleasing appendage to the Business; for what in any situation can so strongly recommend them to custom and establishment, as the good opinion and favour of the Ladies? Besides considering the improvement of dress and manners, the popularity, riches and industry, of this country within the last * thirty years.

It becomes not only a matter of merit but a cause of necessity for every man to make himself acquainted with every part of his business for his own benefit; the luxury and profusion of the times require it. At the aera we have mentioned, where there was one habit then made, there are fifty now — for you hardly see a * Franklin's wife, or a farmer's daughter at a market, fair, or country wake without a Riding-Habit on. This makes the knowledge and practice the more essential; therefore to all our brethren of the Trade who may not be so well versed in this point of neat practice, we shall use our best endeavours to ground them thoroughly in every particular that will tend to their improvement and accomplishment, and what they have lost by lack of practice, they will make up by doubling their diligence, and strictly adhering to the maxims that we shall point out and illustrate in the plates and figures annexed; we hope every searcher of the matter in question will be able to avail himself of it uses and advantages.

With respect to the measuring for a * habit, take the following method:
First, measure under the arm * straight down to the hollow by the hip, there mark your measure, which will be the length of your body; next down the back seam to the hip, then across the half of the back; mark the measure, and then proceed to the elbow, and down to the hand; next measure round the arm at the top, and afterwards in as many places as you think proper; but be very correct in measuring around the wrist, as that is a principal consideration, and must fit close and neat; then round the body as for a coat. With respect to the breast, be delicate and judicious, and take half across, with a proper consideration of ease for the rising prominency; measure likewise * from the top of the shoulder to the bottom of the stays before, or to what length the Lady may wish, or as the ruling fashion may suggest; then for the length of the petticoat * from the hip down to the ground, and any other part you think proper, but this is the leading feature. These measurements being taken, if it is required of you how much cloth will be necessary, you will be able nearly to ascertain by the following rule:

If the Lady requires a half breadth in the skirt, * you must have full three times the length of the skirt. If you should be at a loss how to put in the half breadth, observe our remarks in cutting out the habit.

Take your cloth and measure and cut off the * petticoat first, then lay your cloth straight, and cut the edges where the seams are to be exact by a line, then open the petticoat piece to the full width, and cut your * placket holes six inches from the seam in the breadth, that is for the front, then lay a line from the top of the * placket holes to the half of the breadth before; let it fall from the top two inches, to make a hollowing, and cut it off that it may not be too think and clumsy in the binding. — After your seams are sewed, you will find more width in the breadth behind than before by twelve inches, which habit skirts require. In plaiting up the coat to the width of the waist, mind you lay all your plaits towards the hip in the front; in the front breadth leave to the front about * three inches plain, and in the breadth behind lay the plaits from the hip to hang in such a way that the inside of the plaits

Q&L delete "three inches wide" to the end of the paragraph in Taylor, and substitute:

"two or three inches wide, at the top of the skirts before, if it be not fastened to the inside of the waistcoat."

Q&L delete "its double breast, large lappets" through "back as possible, holding" in Taylor, and substitute:

"in the breast, and the pieces that are to be cut out, in the front of the breast, and at the bottom, which are to be fine drawn up again, this answers for ease in the breast.

The back rows of buttons may be sewed on, beginning at the fine draw below, but keeping"

Q&L delete "at figure 2 the top of the back (in plate D,) just in the point" in Taylor.

Q&L delete "pigeon breast" through "adequate to your measure" ion Taylor, and substitute:

"round the breast, a single breasted is entirely the fashion."

Q&L delete "that when you baste it" through "answer to the back skirt, and" in Taylor, and substitute:

"for the fore parts are to be fastened at letter b, and f, across; and when you have it on, you will find it corresponds to the back skirt, which you may cut to tack over like the back of a coat, or in one piece like the back of childrens' jackets; you will find that adhering to the form of your forepart skirts," behind may seem like the outside of the plaits before, and mind you lay all your plaits full at the hips; this will give a swelling appearance to the coat, and add much to the effect. Should you want half a breadth more in, take the remaining part of the cloth and split it in two, and put the pieces on each side, then the petticoat will hang properly, and the seams not out of their places; still remembering to make your pocket-holes twelve inches within the half breadth, that is six inches on each side as before; and after it is plaited, but a band of cloth * three inches wide at the top of the coat, both before and behind, and in the front fobs for the watches.

In cutting the Jacket part of the Habit, pray be a little circumspect, as some taste and genius is required.

First mark your back according to the Plate, and take full as large a back hollowing as the Plate defines; for in this part we see errors in many of the principal habit-makers. For want of a sufficient hollowing in the back the Jacket shirts part behind; but if you follow the dictates of the Plate, you will find the back will lap over behind when the seam is sewed up.

Yet this hollowing of the back must be done with discretion, for should you do it to excess, you will spoil the economy and filling of the whole Habit, and make it wrinkle both across the back and under the arm (a common error you too frequently see). — Observe also you cut the top of the back wide in the shoulders, for women are in that part proportionably bigger than men up to the back of the neck; this may be owing to their having less restraint upon this part than men.

Take notice in cutting your fore part you mark the turn of the plate, * its double breast, large lappels, and the mode of putting the buttons on as far back as possible; holding this maxim in view, that the change or mutability of Fashion will make no alteration in the rule for fitting the Body.

Of cutting the back and fore part to answer each other so as to fit with ease and elegance, in order to make the back and fore part both in unity, lay the hip of the back to the hip of the fore part, and stretch the back up as high as you can, * at figure 2 the top of the back (in plate D,) just in the point, there mark your fore part shoulder across, and cut it to the likeness of the Plate, with an agreeable * pigeon breast, and beautiful small waist adequate to your measure. If it is required that your jacket part should be a single breast, consider that a round prominent breast is the chief ornament, and give your side seams the same shape as the Plate; likewise your skirts according to the direction laid down, * that when you baste it on, you will find it agreeably answer to the back skirt, and they will all fall easy together.

These considerations you will find worthy your closest application. — Many of the maxims are but slightly understood. In joining the back and fore parts pray avoid the old trite custom of bearing on either the fore part of the back; 'tis pity that many decent practitioners of the Trade will still follow this method of bearing on the front in one place, and the back part in another, without considering that bearing on the fore part drags the back, and bearing on the back drags the fore part; though this perhaps may not be seen in the first instance, as pressing will sink the parts of a time, but in a few days wear the disagreeable effects will appear, and the lady instead of receiving an addition to her shape, will appear crooked and deformed.

By all means sew the seams straight, this is the genuine way, and a truism so trite in nature, that every practitioner must be convinced of it; if he considers the habit bodies without any seam at

Q&L at "Be careful how you cut" in Taylor. add the following before it:

"Observe the figure before you, of the habit without seams, will answer every purpose; only look to the line where the side seam ought to be, and it will teach you how the back ought to be cut; and you must remember a back, if it has seams, hollows it."

Q&L (re: at the bend of the arm) delete "a little" in Taylor, and substitute:

"at fig. 5, cutting the piece out,"

Q&L delete "the sleeve at the top" through "clear that too frequent" in Taylor, and substitute:

"the sleeves, remember to let a piece of outlet be in the under seam, hollowing it according to the plate, below the sleeve top, — Be sure you hollow it according to the plate at the top; which, when put on, will clear that"

Q&L delete "which bear on the back scye" to the end of the paragraph in Taylor, and substitute:

"you may hold the body easy on the sleeve, from the side seam, nearly to the fore-arm seam; and from it, you may keep the sleeve top full on the body, to within three inches of the shoulder seam. Your scye ought to be lined all round the body, as by friction against the body, if the lady wear whalebone vests, in the inside, under her habit waistcoat, it will soon wear out under the arms."

Q&L delete "and make a large slit" through "same tacking as a coat" in Taylor, and substitute:

"on the bottom edge; make a straight sleeve, without fore arm or back-arm seam, as they look much neater."

Q&L for "size" in Taylor, read: "scye"

Re. Chapter II (see next page)

all, there the cloth is straight without bearing on, and so must all Habits with seams, or they will never fit the body.

* Be careful how you cut the shoulder of the fore part, for should you make it too short though but one quarter of an inch, your Habit will wrinkle under the arm and across the back. Some Ladies, through a protuberance in front, require a long fore part, which will baffle anything but great experience, and must be provided against. Touching the sleeve, you must have recourse to the Plate for the form and manner; draw it in at the bend of the arm * a little, for the Ladies through custom have a manner of holding their arms more upon the bend than men, which requires the sleeves to be cut more crooked and bent; also in making * the sleeve at the top, be sure in the sewing to lock in the inside full one inch, this will make the inside less than the out, which when put on will clear that too frequent superfluous part under the arms, which is an egregious fault too often exposed to our view.

Clear your arm hole before you put in the sleeve, * which bear on the back scye to the sleeve up as high as the shoulder seam; then bear on the sleeve on the shoulder to the front and make the body with large scye pieces, as the friction of the arm against the stays very soon wears them out.

Cut the collar as is shewn in the Plate, on the bottom edge, * and make a large slit at the hand that the sleeve may come off easy. A Denmark sleeve with four buttons is most suitable to draw off, and may be made to button close and neat to the wrist; the plaits take the same tacking as a coat, and we would recommend the skirts to be rantered on, as the body will by this means look much neater in the wearing.

Also note, if you cut your back too wide across the shoulders, it disconcerts the fitting upon the top or neck of the shoulders, and will keep the sleeve from coming up and make a disagreeable appearance of the sleeve seam lining down on the arm, which is too frequently complained of.

The way to prevent any faults in this place is to cut the back narrow across the shoulder, and give more sleeve to answer this; for whenever you take from one place, you must add to the other to make out the * size. We have in the course of our practice met with Habits that the seam of the sleeve has turned upon the top of the arm, and the same Habit returned from alteration several times with the common fault till we saw it, and found the defect arose from not having pitched the sleeve right.

The proper way of doing this is, take the habit body, lay it with one hand two inches from the hip, and the other hand in the arm hole, and where it folds, which may be about two inches from the shoulder seam, from which place double it under the arm, then double it from the back scye to before, and where the mark falls there let the seams of your sleeves be put, as that is the right way of dividing the arm-hole in four parts, which will cause the sleeves to hang true without twisting.

Chapter II

Habits Continued

Before we leave the subject of Habits, we wish to impress our students with a few material hints relative to alterations of such as may fall into their hands for amendment, being injudiciously made by

Re. Chapter II

Complaining about other tailors and how good the authors are. Very pompous, especially at the end.

Q&L p. 63 - this is very different, as follows:

"Before we leave the subject of habits, it is necessary to inform our readers, that, according to the newer mode of cutting the skirts, the general pattern for a middle sized lady is three yards, and those of a larger size from three and a quarter to three and a half: but this you can calculate according to the size. From the middle size, and any under this standard you can calculate; — say, from two and a half, to two and seven eights. It must be cloth of the superfine breadth, as in the skirts we have just mentioned; but there is not near as much cloth put in. Remember also, that the length of your skirt must be cut about a quarter of a yard in, on the double of the cloth at the top, and run on a straight line down to nothing at the bottom, on the selvage edge of the cloth. Your front piece, or apron, may be cut at the top of the waist, and down at the bottom; you need not exceed a quarter of a yard in the breadth of your piece; this will be very little more than the half breadth of your cloth on the double, and not half that above; — this will make it full enough; and is a great saving of the cloth, which some years ago was only uselessly plaited up. Your front piece need not have more than two small plaits on each hip, and your back piece plaited to the measure.

other people, who by incapacity had brought themselves into such a dilemma that neither genius or experience could acquit them to their employers, or justify the practice to their own feelings.

A thing of this kind lately came under our inspection, by an insignificant person of the Trade, who with a woeful complaint of the great danger he stood in of losing the countenance of a lady of the first fashion, whose recommendation had brought him into repute; we commiserated his case, and learnt that the great grievance was a pinching under the arms, and a very disagreeable wrinkling from the lower part of the arm-pits quite across the back.

We instantly informed him the fore part was too short for the back, and ordered him to unrip it and take out the sleeves, then told him to lay the back upon the fore part joining at the hip, afterwards to holdup the back to the top corner next the shoulder point at the neck, and extend as high as the back shoulder; he then found it reached over the fore part two inches, in consequence of which he naturally pieced two inches to the forepart shoulder, and another piece half down the neck, and cut off the remainder at the scye, that the fore part might not exceed the length of the back, and then joined it together again; but alas! when this was done, there still remained another fault: the scye was too big for the sleeve; on second application we told him he should have put the back two inches lower at the hip, and sink the fore part under the arm as low as the back scye required, and cut off the back skirt as much as the back was too long, which was lengthening the fore part without piecing, and fashioning the body so as the back and fore part answered each other, and the arm-hole made no longer than it was before.

Having thus proceeded, he had it closed together again, when the Jacket fitted the body with the greatest nicety. This being done, he had another complaint in the petticoat, which seldom happens with people of almost any practice; this fault was, the coat would not hang down straight before, but rose up on the belly, which totally disfigured the Lady, and shewed her in front in a situation which circumstances had not in the least entitled her to; this was an egregious fault, which we told him was owing to the coat being too much hollowed before, which dragged it up and made it stand out so in the middle, as the hollowings were not cut off; this matter was easily remedied. We told him to let it down two inches before, and that would settle the business.

Had the hollowing been cut off, the whole dress would have been spoiled; after this matter was adjusted, he carried and fitted on both Jacket and Coat, which sat extremely neat upon the Lady, and gave great satisfaction. The grateful acknowledgements of our brother Tradesman, after he had accomplished his point, was adequate to the favor we conferred upon him.

Bad cutting is a fore evil, and very fatal to many of our Brothers of the Trade; numbers to our knowledge, men of great sobriety and diligence, have ruined themselves by the cut of their own shears.

Before we began this undertaking, we had premised a scheme of keeping a public office, where one of the society would have daily attended to have given instructions in every case and matter of the business that might require assistance; but this was over-ruled by a supposition, that the task would be too arduous for one person, owing to the great lack of genius that appeared so palpable in the Trade; therefore struck upon the method of Publishing our maxims, as having a general tendency and likely to diffuse precept, which properly attended to would be for the universal benefit of mankind.

Re: Chapter III

Q&L does not have this chapter.

Chapter III

Of Making a Coat for a Fat Man

This is a difficult piece of business to the learner, and wants a great practice, but we hope with a little application and strictly adhering to the turn and manner of the Plate, he will be able to compass it with great nicety.

The mode of Measuring a fat man differs not from the rules already laid down, for men of reasonable size. When you begin to mark for cutting out, be sure to make a long back scye, and give plenty of room on the top of the back shoulder; this will assist the ease of the arm-hole. In cutting the back, do not begin to hollow till you come to Fig. 2, and keep gradually down to the back slit, your side seam make with an agreeable hollow as is shaped in the Plate, and take care you are not too wide over the shoulder, for this would be a conspicuous error, and disorder the sleeves much more than in a thin man; without these things are noticed, it will be difficult for a fat Man to sustain his coat upon his shoulder, owing to the fleshiness of them, and the short neck.

When you lay the back upon the cloth for the fore part, give it the same sweep as is shewn in Fig. 3, Plate D, and make your side seams straight; for by throwing the fore part shoulder so back, it requires the side seam to be partly straight, the same as the fashion of the Plate, for what is wanting in size give it before. When you want the length of the fore part united take the same method as is defin'd for a regular size, with this proviso, instead of making the back at Fig. 4 come in the middle, make it come at the point next the shoulder, for this will augment the length of the fore part shoulder, which addition is required in a fat man much longer than in those of a regular size. We should wish the student always to lay in a little at the shoulder of a fat man, for the shortness of his neck will contract the shoulders, and make the Coat wrinkle under the arm; by laying a little in, if he finds the shoulders too short, he can easily let it down.

To make the square, from the point of the shoulder down to the hip, and wherever the mark falls at the bottom of the skirt, there must be the square, and the same rule from the hip to the scye, and then to the point of the shoulder next the neck, from Fig. 2, to Fig. 2; and be a little particular in cutting your scye or arm-hole, by keeping strictly to the manner of the Plate.

Observe well the round of a single-breasted Coat, as is described in the Plate; and if you should want to make a fat man's Coat lapelled, you may make this addition, or any other that fashion may constitute, when you thoroughly understand the previous maxim of cutting a single-breasted Coat. Observe the neck of the Coat must be short; for should you make a long gorget to the fore part of the neck, the collar will be on the breast; as you have the shears in your own hand, you can use them as discretion may suggest.

Re Chapter IV

Q&L does not have this chapter.

Re Chapter V

Q&L does not have this chapter

Chapter IV

Of Altering Clothes badly made

It is not to be wondered at that so many mistakes happen among Taylors who have no rule or criterion to go by, but leave every thing to blind chance, or what is almost as bad, following the maxims of ill-informed masters, without ever consulting either reason or nature whether such practice was within the pale of likelihood to succeed.

A suit of clothes lately came to us for alteration, subject to the following faults; first of the breeches, which were full three inches too short; this we did perceive had been a fault in the measuring, for had the Taylor took his measure from the hip bone down to below the knee-cap, he would have prevented this disagreeable disaster.

The Taylors have a method of measuring by the old Breeches, without considering how much their weight and wear has sunk them into wrinkles. This often deceives them, when if they would measure as before observed, they would prevent such errors in future.

Chapter V

Next of the Waistcoat

This was cut so short in the back,that whenever the wearer rose from his seat, the waistcoat rose up to his stomach. As we have written so copiously of the maxims of making Waistcoats to fit, we beg to refer our reader to that chapter, which will inform him of the true method; and by having recourse to the Plate, when he takes any Waistcoat that misfits asunder, by trying it by these rules, he will instantly find the cause of error, and be able to apply a proper remedy.

After this, we observed the Coat, which pinched under the arms, which is the first general complaint; it was too strait over the shoulders, that he could not bring his arms forward: it was too wide over the breast, so we took out the sleeves and unripped the coat, found the fore part too short for the back.

We instantly sunk the fore part hip two inches, and put the hip of the back to the same place: then found the back and the fore part to answer as the Plate directs you. We pieced a usual [sic] to the fore part neck, and then took a piece off from the fore part of the shoulder, and in cutting it away, we continued it round to the scye before, and then cutout a full inch and half, as the breast would admit of it: this gave room to the part behind, and eased the confinement of the shoulders.

We found by giving the body of the Coat this liberty, we wanted our sleeve two inches longer, and the sleeve to be wider in the top: this happened rather lucky, as the sleeve was laid in on the inside of the fore seam, which we let out, and sunk the elbow the two inches we gave in the shoulders, and made the sleeves three inches longer at the wrist: after this we cut from the bottom of the back as

much as we had sunk it down, made up the Coat again, put on a new collar three inches longer than that which had been put on before; and when the gentleman put on his Coat again, he was happily freed from the inconveniencies, as they fitted him with great satisfaction to himself, and credit to us.

Our learner will understand that this coat was made to the measure of the man's body, but not containing the scientific points requisite to ease and elegance, the errors became both problematical and paradoxical.

Youth's Dress: A jacket and trowsers a la militaire, of Windsor grey cloth. White Marseilles dimity waistcoat, ornamented to correspond: collar and frill in the antique style: hair a waved crop. The pomposo, or Moorish half-boot, of yellow or black Morocco.

Lady's Opera Dress: A round robe of imperial violet net-crape, or leno, with a long sleeve of the same, worn over a white satin under-dress. A cottage vest, or bodice, of Chinese crape, tabinet, or satin, laced and tagged with correspondent cord and tassels.

Ackerman's July 1811

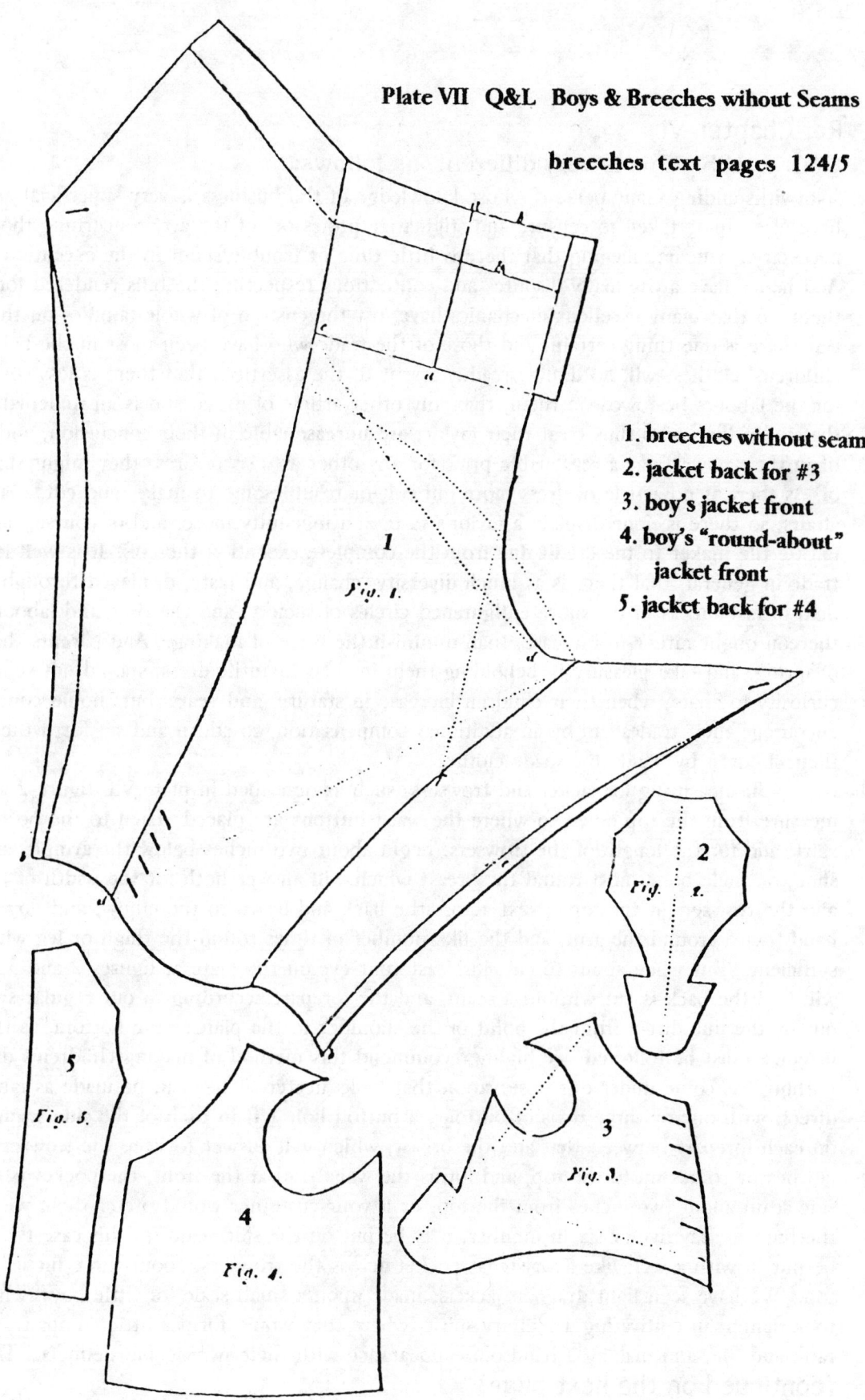

Plate VII Q&L Boys & Breeches wihout Seams

breeches text pages 124/5

1. breeches without seam
2. jacket back for #3
3. boy's jacket front
4. boy's "round-about"
   jacket front
5. jacket back for #4

117

Re: Chapter VI

Q&L p. 135 - this is very different, as follows:

"Notwithstanding many persons whose knowledge of the business is very superficial and limited, have often undertaken to censure and stigmatize professors of the art, concerning those small, but necessary garments; alleging that there is little time or trouble spent in the execution of them. — And hence have arose many disputes and contentions respecting the bills rendered for making of them, so that many excellent mechanics have lost the custom of whole families on this account. But there is one thing certain, and those of the trade who have been most in the habit of making childrens' clothes, will no doubt, readily assent to the assertion, that there is less compensation for the labours bestowed on them, than any other article of dress; and is an undeniable proof, that individuals who thus treat their taylor, are unreasonable in their conclusion, and would not (if in their power) pay a reasonable price for any other articles of dress they might stand in need of. As there is no article of dress more difficult or troublesome to make, and cut, than those little affairs; so there is none displays a taylor's taste and ingenuity more, and of course, ought to entitle the maker to the credit due from the complete execution thereof. It is well known by the trade in general, that there is as much diversity, change, and taste, displayed throughout this little field of fashion, as in the more enlightened circles of society, and the time and labour bestowed thereon ought rather to increase, than diminish the price of making. And parents that love their offspring, and take pleasure in beholding them in their infantile dress, should not suffer their curiosity to abate, when their children increase in stature, and years, but should continue to encourage their tradesman, by an additional compensation, to adorn and set forth the beauties of their children by handsome made clothes.

In measuring for jacket and trowsers, such as described in plate VII. figure 2 and 3, lay the measure from the top down to where the waist buttons are placed. Then to the bottom of the skirt, and for the length of the trowsers, begin about two inches below the armpit, and to the shoe, or ancle bone; next round the breast which will answer both for the width of the jacket, and the trowsers at the top. Next across the back and down to the elbow, and down to the hand, twice around the arm, and the like number of times round the thigh or leg will be sufficient. But when about to cut, just cast your eye on the plate at figures 2 and 3, where you will find the back is cut without a seam, and the forepart according to our regular system marked out by the line direct from the point of the shoulder to the plait at the bottom, as this in every instance must be followed; we highly recommend this method of making children's dress, as nothing has come under our observation that looks neater. They can be made as fancy may direct, with one or three rows of buttons, a button hole left in each of the side seams, and two on each forepart between that and the breast, which will answer to keep the trowsers up. The fall bearer comes up to the top, and forms the waistband at the front, the pocket is put in the side seam about two inches from the top, or if your customer would prefer them without a fall, the buttons, say five or six in number, may be put on the side seam, in this case the pockets may be put in with a welt like a waistcoat pocket across the trowsers, about three inches from the top. We have seen light dragoon jackets, made upon a small scale for little boys, whose parents took delight in cultivating a military spirit, where they would form a little company, marching rank and file, and making a handsome appearance with their swords and helmets. This occurs

(continued on the next page)

Chapter VI

To make a Jacket and Trowsers for a Boy

This little appendage is usually the first change the parents give their children, when they are tired of seeing them in frocks, and we think as easy and simple (well made) as any thing that can be substituted. The way to measure those infants, as you can have no guide by other clothes made, or from their frocks, is from the hip-bone down to the joint of the ankle for trowsers, and measure every other part you please, by the joints, and allow them of such size as they may fit with ease, that nature may have room to extend her improvements.

When you have easily measured, leave room for your seams, and have recourse to the Plate for the figure of the dress, and be sure to cut the leg seam of the trowsers exactly straight, and do not make them too wide as many do; let moderation be your guide, for nothing is more disagreeable than to see children overloaded with cloth in the first instance.

Cut the seat small, and high enough upon the hip, and put on a band with pockets for the child's convenience; and at the bottom of the trowsers, put on three or four buttons, not too tight, and strings, which will give a smartness to their little legs, and let the jacket button under the trowsers; and if the seat is not cut too large, and the jacket cut after the manner of the Plate, you will be sure to complete the matter with neatness.

There are various other kinds of dresses in use for children, but for the first we think the above as good as any; the most ridiculous are those that are made after the manner of grown up people, with Coat, Waistcoat and Breeches, making them appear like dwarfs, or little old men.

We believe it is a kind of custom which ignorance and inexperience have invented to recommend to their employers such modes of making things as is most familiar to their own ideas; for it is very natural for mothers to make choice of those fashions that the Taylor says the child will look the best in.

A circumstance of this sort lately happened on a journey we had into the country, where calling at a very respectable public-house, by the road side, we saw a pretty boy newly habilimented, but in such a way, as would have provoked risibility in a stoick [stoic].

The dress was a Jacket and Trowsers; but surely nothing ever looked so truly ridiculous; the child looked like Scaramouch in a Harlequin entertainment; and to heighten the scene, a few neighbours were drinking down the landlady's spleen with their own comments in a glass of good ale.

The Trowsers were wide enough and almost long enough for his father, and what was worse, the child was obliged to hold them up with both hands, and when he had pulled them up to the height, they were still long enough to sweep the ground; the Waistcoat was too short by five inches, so the little shirt was obliged to make up the defalcation between them; and in order to garnish out the force of risibility, the Taylor had ornamented the Jacket with what is called flash-flaps, turned the wrong side before; for he had put the seam of the flap towards the back, and the points of the flaps to the fore part, with three buttons to each flap, one at each corner.

but seldom, as the expense and trouble incurred thereby is so great, few parents choose to gratify their children in this respect, and in [sic] indeed taylors need not covet this kind of work unless they are well paid for it, as scarcely any journeyman is willing to have any thing to do with them.

The next form on plate VII. fig. 4 and 5, is a round-about jacket, the trowsers button over the jacket and the holes are put on the waistband or upper part. But we recommend them to be cut without waistbands entirely, as it looks much neater to have them all in one piece, about six button holes may be made, marked round. In cutting leave the upper and under side of the same height at the top. The seat is to be made rather full in the seat seam, down to within three inches of the fork. To be more explicit, do not hollow them in the seat as you do the spare seam, but in a straight line from within three inches of the fork, up to the top, equal with the upper side. By this means, sufficient room will be left for the seat. The same measure may be taken as for those last mentioned with this exception, you must measure down the back, as the foregoing have small skirts, these have none, but are quite round. We have often cut this kind without back or side seams, which fitted equally well. We have given but two forms of this kind of children's jackets, on the plate. We had to crowd the different parts of figures, of much more importance on the plate, and we think these may suffice, for the second and third size of children; we recommend skirted coatees and trowsers; this is more becoming for boys of nine years old and upwards. As we have descanted so largely on measuring in the different sections of this work, we think it unnecessary here to say any thing farther on this subject, only follow the directions given, and examine the joints and symmetry of the boy, or child you are measuring, and you may follow the formation of nature in them in the same manner as larger sizes, and you will find this little nursery of fashion worth of your greatest care and attention, and experience in cutting and making those and becoming a masterpiece at them. It will be a kind of prelude to ripen and facilitate your growing ideas in the performance of still brighter displays of skill in your profession; so that the trade you have devoted a portion of your time to acquire, may not only bring you through life comfortably, but in like manner give celebrity to your names, in your own day; and hand down to posterity unequivocal proof of your abilities and usefulness in society."

Re: Chapter VII
Q&L p. 71 which they title"
"Some practical observation on Ladies' Coats for riding on various occasions, either in a post-chaise or phaeton."

Fashion comments.

Q&L delete "and have only their admirers" to the end of the paragraph in Taylor, and substitute"
"and the substitute for some time back, has been police [pelisse] coats, made of cloth for that purpose; or velvet which looks very rich, more so when it is not tabby but silk. Of those there is various shapes and diversities. — But they are principally executed by mantua makers: and so much the better for the trade, as we need not covet any thing in their garments, but in the woolen line."

The landlord hearing the different remarks of his customers, said he did not so much mind the spoiling of things, as the fun that every body made that looked at the child; as the boy was pretty and remarkably straight, the Taylor had all the blame.

A farrier, as he emptied his mug said, if it had been a child of his that had been so disfigured, he would have pared the Taylor's hoof, but he would have made him fit the boy better; an exciseman replied, for his part as there seemed to be cloth enough and to spare in the Trowsers to make all good, he would have the child fresh gauged, and the things altered and made to fit him.

"You say right, Mr. Figures," cried the landlady, "that's what I say to my husband; for to have the child laughed at in this manner, all through a cabbage-headed son of a cucumber; why," says she, "it was only yesterday, as Mrs. Caudle, the nurse, had hold of the arms of poor Mrs. Feeble, that Doctor Forceps lay a few weeks ago of the two boys, was going to be churched, (for by the bye the church-yard joined the public house) she fell into such a titter of laughing at the boy, that she had like to have fallen with her nose against the church wall. I say, if I was my husband, I would send for Mr. Bodkin, who is something like a Taylor, makes for the quality, and let him alter them as they should be, and Tom Thimble shall never press a button-hole for me again, as long as he lives."

At these words in came the Taylor, for it was about the time of his allowance. — "O Mr. Thimble, are you there? — Did you ever see the like, gentlemen — I will assure you, sir, my child shan't be the laughing stock any longer in those things." — "Why ma'am, what's the matter?" — "Matter," quoth she; "look at this sweet boy, was he made to be the butt of your blunders?" — "Why, to be sure ma'am, the sleeves are a little too short, and rather too wide, and so are the Trowsers, they may be said to be too long and wide, but those are good faults, and the Waistcoat is a few inches too short also."

After this Mr. Thimble acknowledged, he made them after the manner of some which came from London, and he thought they were fit for any body to look upon; he said he knew his business, or else it was a pity, for he had been above twenty years at it.

Such vain stupidity as this, is unbearably pitiable, and almost too ridiculous to laugh at. However, we hope in future, such vanity and folly will be done away, for if men will but read, and apply themselves to the preceding sheets, they will be able to do all their business with ease and satisfaction.

Chapter VII

Of a Lady's Levett, or Great Coat

Those dresses are worn by some instead of habits, but they are mostly out of fashion by people of rank, * and have only their admirers in the country amongst the farmers' wives and daughters.

There is much neatness attached to them when they are well made, and require as much delicacy in cutting and making as a habit; the principal difference is, that the skirt of the Levett is fastened to the body, and the Jacket and Petticoat of the Riding Habit are two abstract matters. If you please to

Re: Chapter VIII
Q&L this is a continuation of the previous chapter, starting on page 72.

Q&L for "five inches" in Taylor, substitute: "three inches"

Re: Chapter IX
Q&L p. 64 where it starts with the second paragraph.

have recourse to the Plate, you will find the turns of the same nature as the Habit.

Bind the front breadth from the pocket-hole with a band to button on the body before, and plait it in the band the same as in the Habit Petticoat, with any other addition of ornament, which fancy or fashion may dictate.

Chapter VIII

Of a Lady's Phaeton Coat

This is made after the manner of a coachman's Box Coat, with as many capes, etc. and the only difficulty attending this business is in fitting the capes, which is done in the following manner: — When your shoulders are closed, and the side seam, open the Coat, and mark if the back and fore part shoulders lie flat upon the board; if so, then cut the capes exactly as the shape of the neck is, and when they are on will fit snug and easy; this is as easy and general a way as we can devise for the uninformed; adepts may take other methods.

Observe that the back and fore part must be both of a length at the top, the back must not drop in the middle of the shoulder, but like the neck of a Waistcoat, come close up before; but at the bottom before it must be * five inches longer than the back behind, or it will not hang well; when on, it will be shorter before than behind. — The very like must be a coachman's Box Coat in every part. Stand-up collars are sometimes made to ladies' coats, but Box Coats have fall-downs, but both must be cut long in the neck, to be plaited on under the collar to give ease upon the shoulders.

An inexperienced man in these matters would hardly suppose the quantity of cloth made use of in these capes. We have known four yards and a half used (of narrow cloth) in one of them.

Having led our pupil thus far, we hope he will be able now to find his way without assistance. If his application is but adequate to the desire we have had to serve him, he will, we make no doubt, cut a very brilliant figure in the Trade, after he has had a little practice to justify our maxims.

Chapter IX

Of Patent Elastic Habits, and other Clothes, made without the Accustomed Seams

This very delicate piece of practice is not an invention of our school, though we are taking upon us the authority of defining it to the world. We must own we are possessed of the liberal sentiments of the author, and wish to pay him every praise adequate to his great abilities in the Trade, as well as his condescension and generosity in permitting us to publish it in our work.

The inventor is Mr. James Key, late of Bond-street, born we are told at Atherstone in Warwickshire, a man of attention and great application in business, and who for this very distinguishing

Re: Chapter X
Q&L p. 105

Q&L delete "Plate A" in Taylor, and substitute: "plate VII. and figure I."

N.B. Plate VII is on page 117

Q&L insert, after "striped stuff" in Taylor, "either stocking or silk web"

Q&L delete "kerseymere, stocking" in Taylor, and substitute: "cassimere"

Q&L after "Figure" in Taylor, insert "I"

Q&L substitute for "stocking, kerseymere, etc" in Taylor "stocking web or cassimere"

Q&L delete "stocking or corderoy" in Taylor, and substitute: "stocking web or cassimere"

Q&L delete "four inches" in Taylor, and substitute: "six inches" maxim and delicate piece of practice in the execution of making clothes and habits without the accustomed seams, (in the sleeves, etc.) received his Majesty's Royal Letters Patent.

It is not for this invention only that our tribute of praise is so pointedly levelled, but in every other branch of the Trade; for we have made it our business to come at ladies' habits, and clothes of every sort of his making, which we have unripped, to possess ourselves of his methods, which we must own has given us great satisfaction, for we think him a compleat master of the shears, and one of the Trade's greatest ornaments.

Chapter X

Of Breeches without the Accustomed Seams

Before we proceed in detail, we shall beg our readers to turn to * Plate A, where he will find a sketch of a pair of Breeches without leg-seam, side-seam, waistband, or knee-band seams, they being all left in the stuff, and which are made to answer as well as those with seams, which we think much neater, especially for ribbed or striped stuff, * broad or narrow cloth, * kerseymere, stocking, or any stuff that has the least elasticity in it. They fit so neat to the thigh, and are in no danger of injury by the workmen's bad practice in the seams, which often causes disorder by ignorance or negligence in this particular. If the other parts are properly united, this method will be found to exceed in nicety any other practice for delicacy and compleat fitting.

We need not say any thing of the mode of measuring in any of the future matters we have to treat of, as the same instructions already given on previous cases , will answer in every point for these breeches, etc.

We shall not wonder if our pupils are a little astonished at the appearance of the Figure * in the Plate for those Breeches; however fancifully it may strike him, we assure him this is a true resemblance, and the genuine way to cut them.

When you have the stuff before you, as * stocking, kerseymere, etc. which runs but half a yard wide, it is impossible to make them without some of the seams; for if a seam more runs up to the seat, that behind will be but of little consequence, being quite out of sight. You must understand that nothing but broad cloth will answer to make them with one seam, to run up the back-side of each thigh. If you are about making * stocking, or corderoy, or any materials of the same width, having your measure ready, mark down about * four inches from the edge for the side seam, and leave that to turn over to make part of the inside; afterwards mark your leg-seam, as if you wanted to cut it at the chalk, and add as much stuff beyond that as may be necessary to turn over to meet the other part for the inside, and that will make the seams under the thigh all the way up. What is wanting to make the seat, you must piece to, till your seat is as compleat, as if you had made both leg and side seams.

There is this difference in those sort of Breeches from other, that when you mark your knee-slit after the manner of the Figure in the Plate, you must leave your inside much longer, that in the turning over to put a piece down the ham to set the buttons on to, it will require the same as the knee:

Q&L delete "afterwards fold it down" through "Let your waistband be as" in Taylor, and substitute:

"as from figure I, to figure I, on the plate, and from letter c to letter f and down to letter d, as those points command the power of the seat, they are left to give room to the elasticity of the seat. — For when figure I, is put to figure I, although they point downwards, yet the seat requires it, for the draft lies in the hip and stride, consequently there must be room left somewhere, and likewise when seamed up you will find that it exactly makes the hollowing of the ham true. Therefore, we aver that this maxim will answer. Cut the parts for the waistband, no longer than the measure, in any sort of materials: if of the elastic kind, less by two inches on the double; when you cut the falldown, let it be as long as from letter b to letter f, then begin to turn up for the fork at letter d. And remember that the length of the waistband will mostly answer from letter c at the hip bone, to letter d at the fork. When you cut the fall let it be as long as from letter a to letter a, and put your side welts and fall bearers to, putting a stay at the lower part to sew in with both seams. — And let your fall bearer extend as far from the spare seam, as is described in the plate. As this piece must answer for the front of the waistbands, and ought to be as far"

Q&L at the end of the text in Taylor, for this chapter, add:

"Finally, it will be necessary to leave a regular outlet, as upon the plate at letter e and letter e and letters ab and b at the top, for the waistband part all round.

N.B. Of the different letters described upon the plate; letter c at the hip bone, to letter d at the knee. Letters bb the two points centre of the ham. Letters ff on a straight line from the top of the falldown to letter f at the thigh, and letter f on the line at the spare seam signifies where it ought to turn up to the fork at letter d. At the letters a and a signifies the cut in for the side welts and fallbearers. The lines designated through the whole, will be a guide how to form the upper side thigh upon the cloth, in the piece. The different lines, such as from the knee to the fork and round to the side seam, signifies the certainly of itching the fork, and is described fully in chapters preceding this."

Re: Chapter XI
Q&L p. 65

slit that up as if you were cutting a slit in a sleeve, and put a catch under; but suppose it must want a very large one, as the trimming up for the seat always draws a very open place; * afterwards fold it down as the Plate directs in Fig. 4 on Fig. 4; Fig. 5 on Fig. 5; Fig. 2 on Fig. 2, and Fig 3. on Fig. 3, and down at No. 7: that point must be particularly noticed, as this part commands the power of the seat.

This point is left to give room to the seat for when Fig. 7 is put over Fig. 7, you will find the point very long; the seat requires it, for the draft lies in the hip and stride; consequently there must be room left somewhere: therefore we aver that this maxim will answer the same purpose as putting in a large quantity down the hip. Let your waistband part be cut no longer than the measure in any sort of materials; if of the elastic kind less; as much as is directed in the chapter of stocking breeches.

When you cut your fall-down, let it be long as from Fig. 8 to Fig. 8, then down to Fig. 9, and at that place put a welt all round, and under it put the canvas, and seam it in to the waistband; do the pockets the same way. If it is a cash welt, let it be in the same manner as all the others, viz. cut a slit and seam on a welt bit. * Let your waistband be as forward as we have in appearance drawn them in the plate; for on this principle depends the very certainly of the fall-down's sitting clear.

If a waistband is not forward enough, the fall down must be disordered; this is an evil complained of too frequently, resulting entirely from bad practice, which Taylors are as reprehensible for as bad cutting. When Breeches are not well cut, they are sure to lose their situation upon the breech, either in the act of sitting down or walking; when badly made, they are as sure to be drawn from their natural position, which causes distortion and disagreeable wrinkles.

This verifies an old trite proverb amongst the Trade, that let some men have ever such favorable incitements to study, or opportunities for practice and instruction, still the dung-fork is in their hands, and would much better become them, than either the needle or the Taylor's shears.

Chapter XI

Of the Patent Riding Habit

This matter we have most minutely observed, and given it our best attention, and sincerely think the invention deserves every notice that the warmth of panegyric can bestow upon it. For it is not only capital in the execution, but beneficial in the institution; the very fine materials of which the habit clothes are manufactured required the invention, and must have been judiciously and seriously considered by the patentee, for the Dye of many of the most elegant colours is so delicate that the press of the hot iron upon the seams too frequently changes the colour of the cloth, which carries a disagreeable appearance, but is totally done away by making the body of one entire piece, and cutting the sleeves so ingeniously that both front and back seams of the arm are eradicated, and only one seam fine drawn quite under the arm, imperceptible to either wearer or observer.

We think seams should always be dispensed with especially where they are more a prejudice than a use. When Ladies Habit sleeves are made without the usual seams, this surely prevents a great deal of dust from lodging which if caught by a shower of rain, can never have that clean and regular

Q&L delete " number of Ladies" to the end of the paragraph, in Taylor, and substitute: "hundreds"

Q&L delete "Fig. 2 to the top of the shoulder" through "the point down before;" in Taylor, and substitute:
"letter a, to the top of the shoulder at letter d, to be of the same length, as it is from the bottom of the back at letter b, and at the bottom of the fore part at letter d,"

Q&L delete the paragraph starting "Here is a distinguishing preference" in Taylor.

appearance as the inside of the arm brushed without the seam the same as any other part of the body.

Even in Gentlemen's coats, how frequently do we see disagreeable appearances in the inside seams by the lodging of powder, dust, etc. which by constant severe brushing the sewing is soon wore [sic] and the sleeves become faded and shabby before the knap is worn off the rest of the coat.

From the forementioned premises the Patent Riding Habit has greatly the advantage, not only for the great merit of cutting and making the sleeves, but also the body, being made without seams, either on the side or the back; and to shew that our opinions are not singular we have seen them upon the back of * numbers of Ladies of the first distinction, made by the patentee; and what is more, we are credibly informed it has received the sanction of our amiable Queen, the Princesses, and all the Royal Family.

There will very singular advantages result to mantua-makers, who may think proper to consult the instruction we shall adduce for the execution of this nice piece of practice, which will be full as beneficial to them as professed Habit-makers.

There is but little difference between making Habits of fine broad cloth and Cotton, the same maxims must be used; in either a strict observation must be indispensably paid to the delineations we have laid down in the Plate. When you have paid a due application to the manner of it, and are about to cut out one of those Habits without seams in the back or sides, first lay the stuff double straight down from the part where the back seam is usually made; cut the waist to point down before, after the matter of the Fig. in the Plate, and hollow it in the very same form, from the bottom of the back across to the forepart; the scheme of this maxim will be obvious, when we inform our pupil that when the shoulders are closed together, it will drag it up before, which makes an essential difference between cutting one of this sort and one with seams; for if the learner will but try, he will find from the top of the back at * Fig. 2 to the top of the shoulder at Fig. 3 to be of the same length as it is from the bottom of the back at the seam place across to the point down before; that when the shoulders are seamed together, the body part at the bottom will be straight and level all round, and the fore part no longer than the back.

There are the symptoms that produce such admirable effects, giving room in every part, yet compels the back and body to fit clean and clear from wrinkles when put on, which even astonishes experienced Taylors, though grounded in the cause that effects it.

* Here is a distinguishing preference between these and such as are made with seams; for the patent one will wear much neater and keep their place all the time they are in wear.

We have been told of many who have imagined it was a point of easy practice to make one of those Patent Habit Bodies, who for want of experience have failed as often as they attempted it, and must ever do so till they follow the rules here laid down. Such practitioners will make a better shift with habits that are made with seams, for they may have the advantage of alterations to bring them in point; in the other the merit is in the cutting; and must be achieved by the first effort with a little consideration of seaming the parts properly together. But we hope those, and the other with seams, are so clear both in detail and definition in the Figures in the Plates, that with a little practice, no professor in the business will be long in ignorance either about the practice of habits, or any other part of the business.

Q&L for "world" in Taylor, substitute: "continent"

Q&L delete "Fig. 2" in Taylor

Re: Chapter XII
Q&L does not have this chapter.

Descant -to discourse fully.
Risible - to laugh.

Very pretentious put down of other tailors

We must further observe that in making Habits with seams, one of the principal errors arises from the different parts not working well together; for to manage this matter properly, the back seam must be cut so as a kind of elasticity will result from it; the sides almost the same.

The fore parts are cut in a different direction, and run a contrary way, which if not duly observed, will cause one part not to work with the other, owing chiefly to uniting places that are cut elastic, with such as will not stretch. This results from the ignorance of those who seam them together. There are men who are so confident as to bear on the back in some places, and on the fore parts in others, and affirm that the body requires it; but we totally contradict this. They must not be fulled on in any part, nothing can be so puerile or childish as to bear on in one part of the cloth more than the other, they must be all equal. To suppose that fulling any particular part of a Riding Habit could assist the fitting of it, is a most ridiculous conceit, and unworthy the attention of any man possessed of the least scientific knowledge in the Trade.

We hope shortly to see all such monstrous incongruities banished, and that the strong will assist the weak, that a kind of sympathetic union may be maintained in every shop throughout the * world.

The previous observation with the * Fig. 2, of the separated parts in the Plate, we hope will be sufficient to define the whole method of making the Patent Habit. The sleeve, which is most peculiar to the practice, will appear so plain to every Taylor by the drawing, that a further detail will be unnecessary; his own reason will tell him, that from the front and back seams of the arms in the usual places, marked on the cloth, that a surplus both of the inside and the outside must be left on the cloth in width, to make as much as will turn round the arm to be rantered or fine drawn underneath; and that in bending, after the sleeve is marked and nicked in the hollow part of the arm, and the cloth is turned down to the under-side, that a gusset piece must be taken out of the inside, and then fine drawn to complete the bend of the sleeve; the same of the outside.

These observations might be reduced to practice by the student before his first attempt (if he is doubtful) by cutting a sleeve or two out of paper, and turning them down, as is above observed.

Chapter XII

Of Occurrences that may happen in Fat Men's Coats, made by self-sufficient Pretenders

We wish not to descant upon any Pretender to the art, further than may be serviceable to our present purpose; in order to lead our pupils from the thorny way of error and uncertainly, into the genuine flowery path of science and proficiency.

A few of the following hints, we hope will be serviceable, relative to the misfitting of a fat man's coat; for it is with great uneasiness we are obliged to declare that it is very irksome to us either to meet or follow any of those full figured gentlemen, for their garments are generally so preposterously cut, that it is almost impossible to keep the risible faculties in subjection, let the object that wear

them be ever so engaging and respectable. This we attribute in a great measure to weakness and the self-sufficiency of pride; for certain it is we have known several masters who might have been greatly assisted in these matters, after clothes have been returned for misfitting, by their own men; but instead of confessing an error, instantly falls on the whimsical unsatisfied temper of the employer, rather than candidly acknowledge a defect of their own abilities in the face of their men.

A circumstance of this kind once happened in the presence of one of the society: A Taylor of no little consequence having measured for, and made a superfine coat for a noted public preacher, it was returned upon his hands, with a list of the following faults:

First, it wrinkled under the arm, and all across the back, and likewise pinched under the arm, wrinkled across the breast, and bound in the neck; the sleeve at the bend of the elbow was out of its place, and greatly twisted.

The Taylor was so irritated that he instantly ordered one of the men to unrip it; and taking it to his cutting-board, tried it with his measure, and found it answer as to length and width in every part. This so surprised him, that he was quite uncertain how to proceed: his wife seeing his distress said,

"My dear Mr. Twist, what is the matter?" — "I wish I could tell you Mrs. Twist; I have got a Coat returned here from the great Doctor Testament, that makes such a noise in the world." — "I am sorry for that indeed," says the kind loving wife, "because the doctor has such an extensive connexion, and being such a public character, his clothes are more noticed than almost any person's." — "That's the thing," says Mr. Twist, "that hurts me so much." — "Adad," replies Mrs. Twist, "my dear, I'll tell you what you shall do; you know there is Mr. Artist, at the corner of the street, that teaches young men to cut clothes, and Ladies' Habits of every sort, he has a great name, I will myself step for him, he is a very civil man, and you shall submit the case to him." — "But consider my dear, how that will look, for a man of my note to want instructions. I have several good workmen, but I cannot submit to ask the advice of such idle drunken fellows."

The good sense of Mrs. Twist, however got the better of her husband's pride, and our friend Artist was sent for and consulted, who informed Mr. Twist, that wrinkling across the breast was an error from the scye being cut too deep, which presented it lying close under the arm; for the least extension or lifting of the arm draws it from the body, and causes the wrinkles across the breast; but the wrinkling across the back is principally from the fore part being too short from the bottom of the scye to the top of the shoulder. The method to rectify it, must be by moving the back as much lower as the wrinkles appear.

Having taken the back from the fore part, lay the top of the back within one inch of the shoulder point next the scye, pull down the back quite tight, you will find the hip drop two inches below the fore part, which must be taken off. This occasioned the above wrinkling across the back, as well as the tightness under the arm, and also the twisting of the sleeve, as well as the binding of the neck.

These little inaccuracies being rectified, Mr. Twist waited on the Doctor himself with the Coat, which fitted extremely well, and gave him great satisfaction.

FINIS

Sections that are in Queen & Lapsley, but are not in Taylor.

Chapter VI:
Theory of Cutting a Coast without Seams, Etc.

Chapter VII:
Of Regimentals [uniforms], viz. dress Infantry,
Navy, and Light Dragoons, with practical observations.

Conclusion
There is a long (18 page) conclusion at the end of Queen & Lapsley (but not in Taylor) that reads like a Book Review. The "authors" are referred to in the third person and it sort of boils down to a dissertation on how good this book is, and any tailor should be able to follow it, and the patterns are wonderful — the best ever done anywhere, etc. It seems pointless to include all of this text as it does not help with either the tailoring or give any information on the fashions of the period.

Pl. III

Plate III   Q&L   Coat Without Seams

1. coat body
2. center back

N.B. use sleeve: #4 on
   Plate II, page 91.

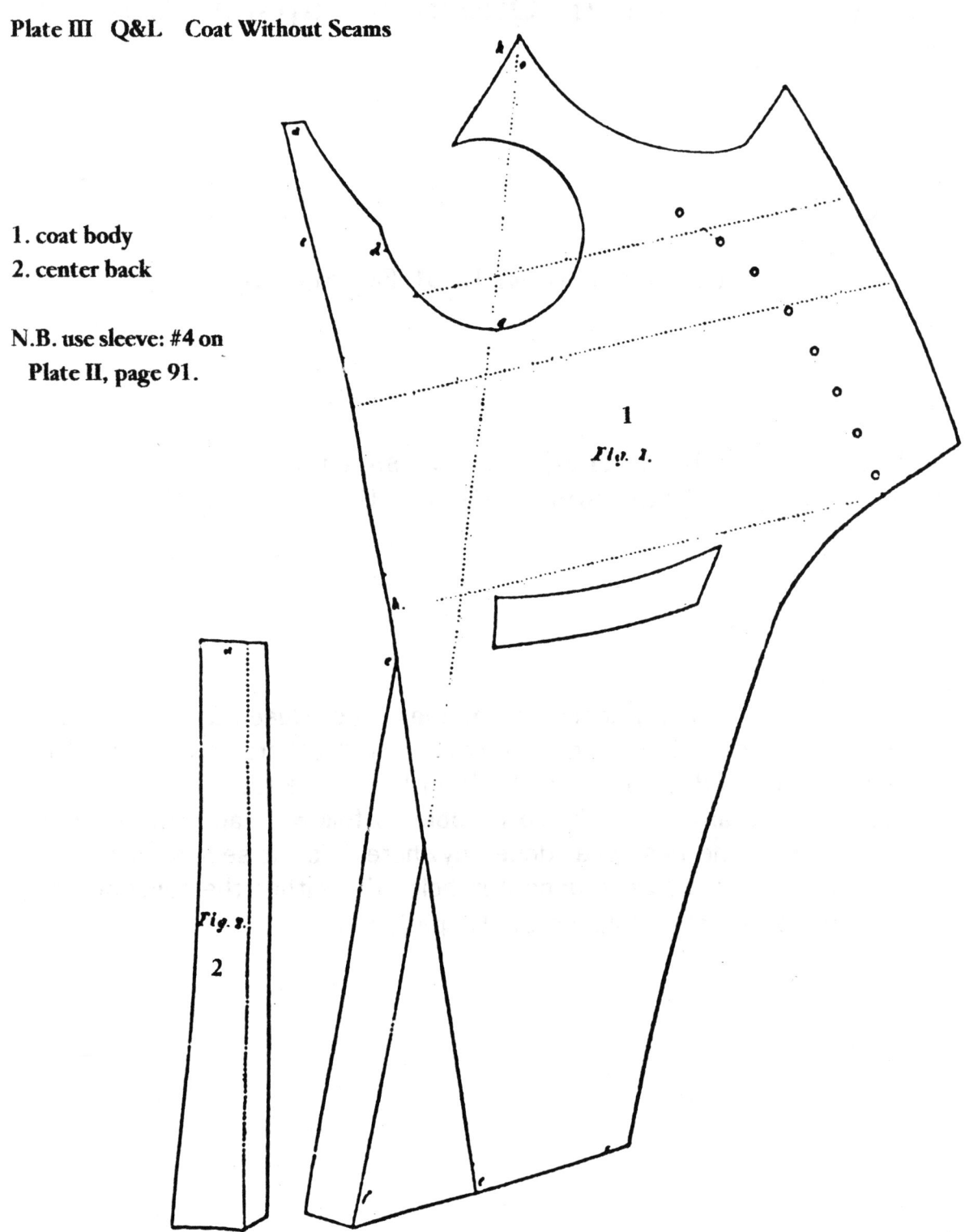

1

Fig. 1.

Fig. 2.

2

Chapter VI

Theory of cutting a Coat without Seams, Etc.

THERE is not any garment in the whole system that needs more diligent application than this one. Almost every other garment can be considerably improved, if necessary, by alteration; but if the proportion of the parts of this coat be disorganized, it destroys the whole symmetry of the garment, and leaves no room for amendment. This invention made its appearance in France, at the city of Paris, and met with merited approbation, among the nobility, not only for its novelty, but for the mechanical skill displayed in its invention; although the author did not bring it to the perfection that it has since arrived at, yet from its originality, it reflects the highest credit and praise upon the inventor. In our description the learner must pay the greatest attention to the symmetry in plate III, and digest with care and application its parts, and lines, as this is one of the truest models that can be drawn of it in miniature. You begin by measuring your customer in the manner heretofore described, for coats, with the addition of two measures more, which is rarely followed, but which cannot be dispensed with, in this garment. The first is from the top of your back at letter a, down to the lower point of your back scye, the next is from the top of your back at the seam, extending over the shoulder down to the length your customer wants his lapell, as at letter f on the plate — in beginning to cut your cloth, keep the crease of the cloth on the side opposite to you, so that you may have the breast of the coat next to you in drawing your lines. Begin by marking the top of your back at letter a, extending your measure to letter b at the waist, then down to letter e at the bottom, making a deduction of a quarter of an inch for your sweep in the wheelpiece, at the back skirts, and it must have the exact length measured for. You will readily perceive the propriety of this precaution by the examination of your place, where you will find at the bottom that your wheelpiece takes in about half of your forepart plain — you proceed by extending your measure half across the back, viz. from the seam at letter e to you breadth across at letter d— then down from the top of your back at letter a, to the lower pint of your back scye at the mark; — this will be a certain criterion for the pitch of your sleeve, and a sure method of ascertaining the height of your side seam. The next thing you have to attend to, is drawing a straight line across your cloth at fig. I, letter b, at the waist, and the same at the top of the side seam; then you may begin and form your scye, as described in the plate, observing the lowering of the scye below the line, and pitching the shoulder-strap well back, as this, if not attended to, might materially hurt the spring of the forepart,and make it wrinkle across the back and scye. Be very particular in ascertaining whether your back and forepart be of a length to correspond to each other. In order to find this out, you must lay your back over on the double at the side-seam, then bring the top of the back to the shoulder-seam at letter b, very little above the centre of the shoulder-seam; this you will find an invariable rule, if you keep by the form of the scye, as described in the plate. You next proceed by drawing a straight line, nearly from what you might calculate to be the half breadth between the hip button, opposite letter b at the waist, and let your line run straight upwards through the centre of the scye at letter g, then to letter e at the shoulder point of the gorge; next from the waist down to the length of your coat, and exactly what this line falls at, is the mark for the rise of the forepart plaits; these points being truly attended in the plate, it will undoubtedly prevent the power of any false system from injuring the exact symmetry of your coat.

There is nothing particular, but what has been discussed in the preceding pages,on the analysis of coats. Only remember to have your wheelpiece neatly fine drawn, as it will always extend to with in two or three inches of the top at the cut-in for the back at letter e, the back skirt must likewise be fine drawn or stotted [sic] across at letter b, after this is neatly executed, plait it up according to letter b at the bottom of the wheelpiece. We cannot dismiss this Chapter without recommending the patent sleeve,without fore or back-arm seam, as they look extremely well in all coats they are worn in, if neatly cut according to fig. 4, in plate II. This coat,if well examined, will excite the curiosity of the spectator,and will gain great applause from your customers, which will be more satisfactory, though not more useful, than the price.

Notes on Uniforms

Queen & Lapsley added this section for the 1809 book (it is not in the English book), thus it becomes a primary source for uniforms for the War of 1812. We actually do not have a lot of information about uniforms of that time in the U.S., aside from a few written documents. The good illustrations that we do have were all based on regulations and done much later, the other ones are stylized Victorian paintings of battle scenes.

On first sight these uniforms look as if they were British, and indeed they probably are in so far as all uniforms of that day were pretty much the same. Planche says that armour was abandoned at the commencement of the 18th century and regular uniforms adopted for every arm of the service, Prussia setting the fashion in military costume for every nation west of the Danube. American uniforms were modeled after the English, aside from differences in insignia, color of the facings, and some decoration. Reportedly Washington bought some uniforms from the French in 1779, but he did not like them and asked when he later bought some more that they be modeled after the British.

Bill Brown of the National Park Service says that the NPS made Light Calvary Uniforms from the Q&L plate of Light Dragoon Jackets. He says that this is the best thing we have for the period from 1808 to 1819.

Mike McAfee of West Point says that: "the plate, since it is of the era it is of great interest for the War of 1812, but it does not depict any pattern appropriate to enlisted uniforms on either side, although the cavalry jacket was the style used by soldiers of both sides."

There are a number of interesting, modern reference books available: *Uniforms and Equipment of the United Stated Forces in the War of 1812*, by René Chartrand (which just went out of print); *American Military Dress, War of 1812*, Journal American Military Institute: Vol III #3; *Military Uniforms of America: Years of Growth 1796-1851*, John Etting (ed); and others listed in the bibliography.

But the fact remains that we do not have good primary source illustrations for these uniforms, and people today, comparing the original period patterns from Q&L to the written information surviving from that time, cannot really come to terms with some of them.

N.B. Information on British uniforms can be found as follows:
insignia, page 174; illustrations, pages 146, 205, 206, 208.

Plate IV   Q&L   Regimentals (uniforms)

1, Navy - collar

2. Infantry & Heavy Dragoons
   - coat front

3. Infantry - collar

4. Navy & Engineers
   - coat front

5. Infantry - coat back

6. Navy - sleeve & cuff

7. Infantry - sleeve & cuff

8. Light Dragoons - sleeve

9. Light Dragoons
   - coat front (Hussar Jacket)

10. Light Dragoons
    - coat back

11. Light Dragoons - collar

1,4,6, Navy & Engineers

2,3,5,7, Infantry & Heavy Dragoons

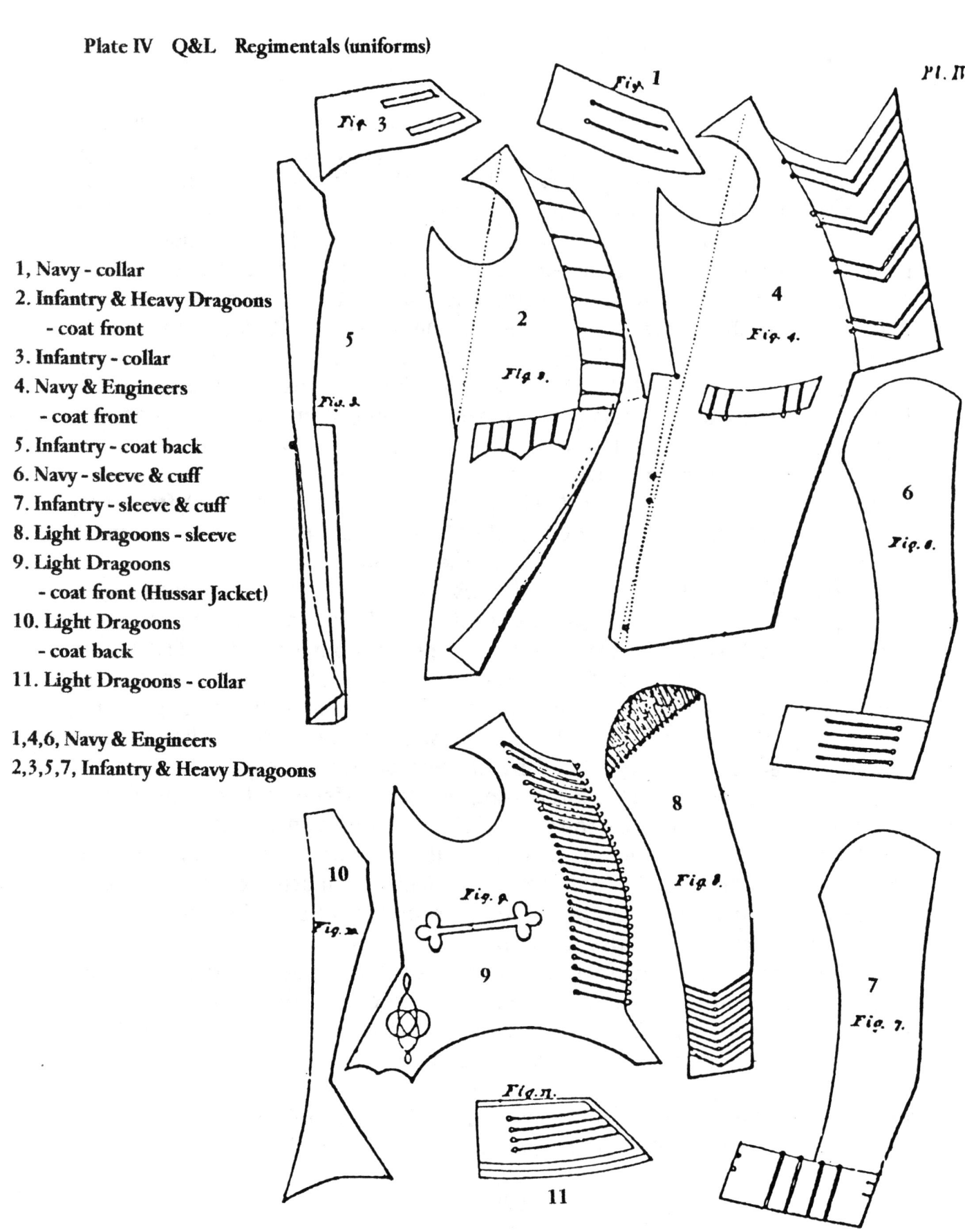

Chapter VII

Of Regimentals, viz. Full dress Infantry, Navy, and Light Dragoons, with practical observations.

REGIMENTALS, the wonder of the last century, comes next under our observations; and, from the noise and bustle made about them, claims a share in our animadversions. But, suffice it to say, there is nothing in the cutting of those articles of dress, but what is clearly solved, and judiciously illustrated, in the preceeding chapters on body coats, Notwithstanding this is the case, we frequently hear remarks made respecting them, by a few who imagine they have arrived at the *Jammun bonum,* of this part of the trade, and that all others are as unacquainted therewith as if it was not part of the business. It is true there are some Taylors, who never have had an opportunity of either making up garments of this kind themselves, or seeing it done by others; and it is for the benefit of such we write. We proceed by observing that the theory in measuring and fitting the body is exactly the same as other clothes; there is nothing which makes the distinction, but the different shapes, contours, and facing, which form Regimental Order. We know it has been the *puff* of the day, that a selection of a few in each city, should be allotted to execute the principal part of this business, from what cause we know not; perhaps it is owing to their acquaintance with the different uniforms now is use, more than their superior talents in carrying on the business. The various uniforms belonging to the crown is so diversified, that it would be puerile to discant upon all of them, as all regiments, from the guards down to the first Regiment, has different forms and facings, according to the procedure and regulations of the war department, all regular troops are subordinate to this restriction; we know also, that the volunteers, and yeomanry of the united Kingdoms, who have to clothe themselves independent of government, inasmuch as they must always have their uniform to comport with those established by the crown, yet they have a great advantage in the diversity of cloth, and the mechanical skill displayed on the facings and trimmings of many of the corps, which enables some of them to outvie the regulars, in the brilliancy of appearance, an instance of this kind may be here adduced. The lawyers' corps of Light Dragoons, in the city of Dublin, is not surpassed in point of military grandeur by any under the crown, and Henry Dundas, has adopted an imitation thereof, in the light Dragoons belonging to the standing army. You will find just a resemblance of this uniform in plate IV. fig. 9, the facings are scarlet, upon blue, with three rows of convex buttons, and the lace extending on both sides as far back as the plate describes, the lace is silver, and the rounding is done with a broader kind, staytape breadth, the buttons close together on the breast, and the round lace only leaving a light of the blue to be seen, which upon the whole makes it appear most rich and brilliant. There are three rows put round the lower part of the collar, the broad in the centre, and the round along each side, leaving a light of blue and scarlet edging, the cuffs at the top, has in like manner three rows, and at the vents must be a large bullet-hole left at the tacking, and four at the fore corners of the back, between the shoulders, and laced down the side seam with the broad lace, then forming itself into a loop below the hip button, such as is described on the plate, there is no welt sewed on at the packet, but one row of the broad lace round the slit as described in plate IV. fig. 9. forming itself into a crow's foot (as it is called) and the buttons on the sleeve put on as shown on plate IV. fig. 8. The v made with the same lace as is on the breast — there is four rows on the collar, extending as far back in gradation as those on the forepart, the wing on the shoulder is braided silver and gold lace, with a mixed fringe, and this is put on so as to occasionally take off, and their place supplied with the ring plate ones, which are made after the manner if a horse's curb but broader in the plate. This looks very elegant when properly fixed on, and makes the exact shape of the shoulder joint. This uniform as to its originality took its rise from the Hessians, hence the name of Hussar jackets. This uniform is in our military arrangement, and has received the war department sanction, whereas before this, all dragoons used to wear long skirted coats, as in plate IV. fig. 2. only with this difference of v holes laced on the sleeves, and forepart skirts down from the hip button to within five inches of the bottom; there is generally six holes formed on each, three and three together, and a button in the centre of each hole; these coats are still in vogue, and worn by the heavy dragoons, the only difference between heavy and light dragoons, arises from the one continuing the long skirts, and the other adopting the Hussar jackets. Nothing more need be remarked with respect to the heavy dragoons' coats, only keep in mind the form of the cut in plate IV. fig. 2. of infantry coats, as they must be cut exactly after this form, for the only thing that makes the difference is in the matter of the lacings and facings; and making the skirt turn-ups, there must be an inch of space between the v holes and them; this being attended to, and the measurements truly taken, you will find handles enough for exercising your ideas and genius upon. There is one or two practical remarks which may not be amiss before we close on this subject; — first, the lace that is put on for the dragoons, is flat on one side, and round or convex on the side that appears, it must be sewed on in mechanical order, for in the making there is great diversity for the journeyman to exercise his abilities on, as the cutting is the easiest, so the workman has ten chances to one, over his employer, to show his judgement. As we have said before there is nothing in those garments out of the theory and practice of the business, in fitting the body, only in the different order of the shapes, which is truly miniaturised in the plate at fig. 2. But the man who marks it off with taste, and makes it up with judgement, gives proof to his employer that more depends upon him in the execution, than on the merits of cutting it. And when left to the discrimination of the beholders, or customer, will gain applause to the shop, and carrier on of the trade, where the garment was made. It is always a good plan for employers to keep good workmen, as much depends upon them.

Having finished our observations on the regimentals worn by heavy and light dragoons, we proceed to define the infantry coats, as displayed in plate IV. figures 2,3,5, and 7. which is a true model of an infantry officer's coat, from a general to the lowest subaltern. Notwithstanding there are many marks of distinction in the faceings, buttonholes, and number of buttons, etc. For instance, a general's full dress uniform is scarlet, faced with blue, ten holes on the lapell, and two on the collar, of gold vellum lace, four buttons and holes on the sleeve, or rather cuffs, according to fig. 7. in plate IV. These holes are put on at a regular distance from each other, as on the breast, not in pairs, there is no holes on the flaps of a general's coat; just put on four buttons in such a manner that the half of the button will appear below the edge of the flap. The buttons are always round, topped with the crown and mace thereon. There are seldom more that two buttons on the plaits, in as much as the turn-ups cover the place where the buttons should be placed. But there are now many of the field officers' coats made with a single plait, consequently must have the four buttons, and the back cut in the same manner as a plain coat. The caseing runs across from the edge of the forepart to the back fly, and the corners are fastened together with a hook and eye. His Royal Highness the Duke of York, was the first who brought up the fashion of single plaits, and of the caseing being the same as the turn-ups, hence arose the fashion of single plaits in plain coats, and answers every purpose when a coat is cut with a good spring, for all extra work should be avoided when it comports with reason and common sense. We hope that the observations that have been made will enable our students to proceed in due form, should they have any of the general officers' coats to make. The lower rank of field officers, commissioned, and non-commissioned officers' coats, are made in the same shape as in plate IV. fig. 2 (with the exception of the general's) and even sometimes they will choose them made in this manner, without the skirts being broad and hooked over, the lace on officers' coats below the rank of general is silver, and only eight buttons on the breast, a colonel and major wears two epaulets, the lieutenant colonel, and adjutant one. Remember that in all military officers' coats, put the pocket inside, whether the lining be cassimere, white silk, or ratinet, and let it be all of a piece, as this looks much neater than having the back and forepart skirt lined separate. Take care that you put the bridle for fastening the epaulet, within two inches of the shoulder seam, so that the cushion may produce the desired effect, in the manly appearance, of being broad between the shoulder, for as all military characters ought to have a straight and lively appearance. The epaulets put on in this manner, makes the back appear as if there was a hollow between the shoulders, and adds much to the appearance of the figure. Let the four small buttons on the collar be put on a range very little above the collar, we mean the buttons for the gorget plate, which hangs opposite the chest, and the two for the epaulets. One remark it will be proper to make in this place, that as all those coats have no back fly, nor any forepart plait, so of course the turn-ups of the back and forepart proceed from nothing at the top, down to the bottom, and form themselves as on plate IV. fig. 2, and 5. and on the centre of the X which they form there is a horn or star placed very little larger than a button. We recommend the lapells to be fastened down to the forepart, although we see a great many regimentals, where the lapells are left loose, but this ought never to be the case, except in undress coats on engineers' full dress, and all navy coats, etc. But we recommend all infantry coats that has lace only on the lapells to be fastened to the forepart and the buttons sewed through. Keep in mind continually the form of the fig. 2. in plate IV. where you will perceive that the gorge is cut short, and the backs something broader than in other coats between the shoulders, the shoulder seam shorter than customary, and the strap not so far back, yet still adhering to the system theretofore laid down, so that the top may command the bottom in all cases, let the figure be what it may. We now come to investigate engineers' coats, as they ought not to be neglected in general order. The principle upon which they are generally made is nearly similar to the navy officers' coats, the collar is a stand-up and embroidered with gold twist, and four button holes, two on each end of the collar, done in a frame, the lapells are done in like manner on the turn-up side. Their undress generally has wrought holes with twist, the colour of the cloth which is blue, there is nothing particular in the cut of these coats, only attend to the forth described in fig. 4. plate IV. after the embroidery is on there is little more trouble in making this than a plain coat.

We shall wind up our remarks upon regimentals by describing the manner of cutting and making up navy officers' uniforms, which is illustrated in plate IV. fig. 1, 4, and 6. After having taken the measure, proceed according to the theory heretofore described, only cut your gorget pretty short, so that the collar will just hook at the seam, when made up. The back is cut with a fly as other coats, and the forepart cut full; your lapells must be exactly the form as on plate IV. fig. 4. there must be herring bone holes on both sides of the lapells: the navy buttons have their motto to designate their meaning, such as the anchor, etc. The holes on the flaps and sleeves exactly as pourtrayed upon the plates, and the buttons below the flaps, and eight buttons on the plaits, the two on the centre the same distance from each other as those on the plaits. Many of those coats are made with fall-down collars, and the holes made on the fall-down; but this is generally as undress, and cannot with propriety be called so complete a uniform. Let those garments be put into the hands of the best workmen, as there is a large scope for exercising their abilities both in marking off, and in working the notched holes. There is much depends upon the skill and judgment of the workman; for those coats, when badly made up, look truly ridiculous, and cast an odium on both master and man; whereas if they are done completely, they will justify the employer's talents, and those whose lot it is to make them up.

Thus have we given a few practical and theoretical hints upon the different kinds of regimentals now in vogue, and even traced by analogy, the systems of whose which differ but very little from the figures delineated on the plate. It would be useless to have given more forms of regimentals, when those will answer every purpose which are set forth as exact models of their kind, yet will still leave room for the student to exercise his genius upon in his day and generation. And as we have paved the way, we hope those who are to follow, upon the new beaten road, will improve upon our boasted system, and leave to posterity still farther proof, that nothing has arrived at that state of perfection, but it can be improved.

THE

Lady's Magazine

OR

ENTERTAINING COMPANION

for the

FAIR SEX

Appropriated folely to their

USE and AMUSEMENT.

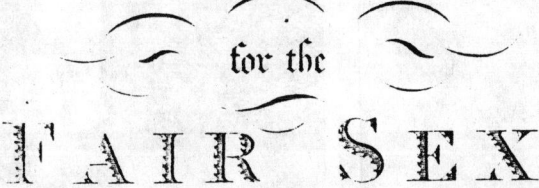

Vol. XXVII for the YEAR 1796

LONDON.
Printed for G.G & J. ROBINSON
No 25 Pater nofter Row.

Descriptions of the Ladies' Dresses on her Majesty's [Queen Charlotte] Birthday. THE QUEEN. — Her majesty was drest with her usual plainness on this day, that is, without many diamonds. A crape petticoat, richly embroidered in vandykes of purple velvet, covered with gold net, a quillery of blond round the bottom, the train of purple and black striped velvet, vandyked round the edge with gold net; a festoon trimmed with rich blond. THE PRINCESS ROYAL. — A crape petticoat superbly embroidered with gold foil, the train a most beautiful gold brocaded tissue. We cannot help remarking the extreme richness and brilliancy of the various tints displayed in this superb dress, which, we understand, is of Persian manufacture, being part of the presents from the Ottoman ambassador. PRINCESS AUGUSTA. — The petticoat crape embroidered with gold, train gold tissue. PRINCESS ELIZABETH. — The petticoat crape, with oblique stripes of sable intermixed with gold; train gold tissue. PRINCESS MARY. — Petticoat crape, embroidered with gold and silver foil; train rich tissue. PRINCESS AMELIA.— The same. THE DUCHESS OF YORK. — A white satin petticoat trimmed with a drapery of rich embroidered crape in stars, bordered with a rich vandyke, and edged with a beautiful sable, banded with rich embroidery across, and a rich gold and silver Mosaic fringe; the gown of a superb gold silk trimmed with sable, and the sleeves richly drawn up with diamonds. THE PRINCESS OF ORANGE. — A white satin petticoat trimmed with a rich embroidered crape in Greek pattern, a drapery thrown over, embroidered in coloured foils, and edged with a handsome gold plate fringe. THE HEREDITARY PRINCESS OF ORANGE. — Body and train of gold tissue; petticoat of crape parsemé [sprinkled] with gold, and fancifully ornamented with festoons of laurel, rich cord and tassels. COUNTESS CHOLMONDELEY. — A petticoat of crape, covered with ziz-zag stripes of silver spangles, a border round the bottom, of coquelicot and black velvet. COUNTESS OF BUTE. — Petticoat crape, embroidered with gold foil; a superb drapery of white satin, covered with an embroidery of gold intermixed with foil-stones and peacocks' feathers. COUNTESS OF CHESTERFIELD. — A white satin petticoat, trimmed with a crape richly embroidered in gold, in festoons, upon a beautiful painted ribbon and gold tassels. COUNTESS OF FAUCONBERG. — A rich embroidered crape petticoat in coquelicot velvet and stones; the gown gold and white. LADY ANN FITZROY. — Body and train of white satin, trimmed with maroon velvet, and gold at bottom. The *tout ensemble* of this dress was more simply elegant than any other that appeared at court. LADY CHARLOTTE CAMPBELL. — A white satin petticoat, puckered with a net richly embroidered in Mosaic, relieved by a drapery thrown over, and edged with a rich gold fillet; the whole banded with maroon and wreaths in gold plate, and wreaths of gold laurel to edge the whole. LADY AUGUSTA CLAVERLAG. — A white satin petticoat, puckered with a crape embroidered in gold feathers, tied up with green foil leaves; a loose drapery over an under drapery of rich gold fringe; the gown violet stripe stuff. MRS. HOPE. — Body and train of royal purple, with a crape petticoat embroidered in gold, and most elegantly ornamented, with a drapery purple embroidered crescents, and a rich border at bottom; gold cord and tassels.

The petticoats were mostly of embroidered crape, with velvet trains. The most fashionable colours was [sic] maroon and black. Tippets were generally worn, trimmed with fine blond, and some with silver. The caps were in the turban fashion, with profusion of high ostrich feathers, and gold ornaments. Many ladies' wore embroidered *bandeaus,* and bunches of leaves intermixed with silver. The hair was dressed rather high, turned up quite close behind, and the ends falling down the neck in curls. The waists were so short, that the ladies had hardly room to move their arms. Pearl ear-rings and necklaces were worn as usual, mixed with matted gold in various forms; but coral and cornelian ear-rings and necklaces were the most in fashion, in the form of acorns and had a very pretty appearance.

Fashions for February. MORNING DRESS. — Night-Cap of spotted muslin, trimmed with a double border of lace in whole plaits, bound round with a narrow maroon ribband, tied into a small bow in front; hat covered with blue satin, tied under the chin, and trimmed with blue and maroon stripped ribbands. Round gown of salmon-colour flowered chintz; long sleeves; gold ear-rings; blue morocco slippers; fur muff. AFTERNOON DRESSES. — I. the hair dressed in light curls and ringlets. Armenian turban, made of white and York flame-colored satin, crossed in the front with two strings of pearls, and the end trimmed with gold fringe. A white ostrich and a blue esprit feather on the left side. Armenian robe of embroidered muslin, the train with a broad hem; full short sleeves; trimming of blond round the neck, and at the top of the sleeves. Tucker of blond. Gold cord, with two large tassels round the waist, tied at the left side. Two strings of pearls and a festoon gold chain, with a medallion round the neck. Diamond ear-rings. White shoes and gloves. — I I. The hair combed straight upon the forehead, the side hair in light curls and ringlets, plain chignon. Russia bonnet of blue satin, trimmed with sable, and tied behind with gold cords and tassels. Lawn petticoat with a broad embroidered border. Russian robe of blue satin, trimmed with sable; short sleeves, trimmed with the same. Close tucker of double plaited lace. Small handkerchief within the belt, drawn together in the front with a diamond slider. Collar of sable round the neck. Diamond ear-rings. White shoes and gloves.

Fashions for March . MORNING DRESSES. — I. The hair in small curls, plain chignon; cottage cap, of fine muslin, tied under the chin, trimmed with lace, and white satin ribbands; petticoat of muslin richly embroidered at the bottom; spencer of maroon satin, plain or blue cape, trimmed with lace; muslin neck handkerchief; fur muff; red morocco slippers. _ I I. The front hair combed short upon the forehead, the side hair dressed in curls, and the hind hair turned up plain. Highland bonnet made of gold foil and carmelite-coloured satin, the ends trimmed with a gold fringe; two carmelite-coloured, and five, six, or seven black feathers, placed in the front, and at the top; plain muslin petticoat; straw-coloured chintz gown; cape and lapels of carmelite-coloured satin; long sleeves; muslin neck-handkerchief, trimmed with lace; double ruff of lace round the neck; gold ear-rings; jonquille gloves and shoes. EVENING-DRESS. — Turban of orange-coloured satin; gold and silver spangled bandeau; the hair (with or without powder) drawn through in different parts of the turban; the hind hair turned up short and plain; the ends returned and formed into a large curl at the top of the head; one salmon-coloured, and one white ostrich feather, with several diamonds placed in the front; white satin petticoat; robe of orange-coloured crape, scalloped and trimmed round the neck with lace; short sleeves, equally scalloped; sash of white satin ribband, tied at the right side, the ends trimmed with gold and silver fringe; large pearl ear-rings; diamond necklace; large gold upper bracelets; white gloves and shoes.

Female Fashions in Paris [June 1796]. The following are the raging fashions in Paris at the present time. *Robe à la Lydie.* — This dress is made to come from the neck to the ground in a long train. The waist can be made short or long at pleasure; the sleeves are so contrived that they can be either worn down to the wrists, or tucked up above the elbow. The arms are ornamented with a bracelet *à la Turque*; and the robe forms a drapery on the breast in the shape of a heart. Sometimes a waistcoat *à la Sultane* is worn over the waist, and forms a girdle at bottom; - this dress is very new, and very elegant. *Robe à la Thesée.* — This is a dress very much admired for its simplicity; it is open at the neck; the waist is formed by a lacing made with great art, and gives an infinite grace and elegance to the shape; a light mantle is worn on the back, which can be taken up, or flow loose, at pleasure. *Riding Coat à la Pallas.* — This dress makes the waist appear very neat and elegant; the lapel *à la Minerve* is made to go round the breast and shoulders in a drapery, and fastens with buttons at the throat. *Chemise à l'Indienne.* — This is a beautiful undress, the waist is formed by plaits artfully arranged, and by bows of ribband; the train falls to the ground in an elegant drapery; it is made of delicate clear lawn. *Robe Economique* — forming at pleasure three kind of dresses, - a half dress, a dress for the country, and a riding dress.

Description of the Dresses of the Ladies who appeared at Court on his Majesty's [George III] Birthday. THE QUEEN. — A royal purple coat, covered with beautiful fine blond, drawn up in festoons, with rich diamond bands and stars; a purple and silver body and train, trimmed with fine blond; a diamond stomacher, with a beautiful diamond bouquet. — Head-dress, a find blond cap ornamented with a diamond crown. PRINCESS OF WALES. — A white crape net, ornamented with silver stars and spangles, lilac body and train, trimmed with silver fringe and tassels; her head dress, a cap composed of lilac and purple foil, and the Prince's plume, set with diamonds in the front, with three beautiful feathers. PRINCESS ROYAL. — A purple and silver embroidery. PRINCESS AUGUSTA. — A white crape petticoat, richly ornamented with lilac and silver in medallion stripes, in very rich border. — Body and train of green silver gauze. PRINCESS ELIZABETH. — A white crape petticoat richly embroidered with silver chain, and ornamented with beautiful wreaths of roses. PRINCESS MARY. — The same as Princess Augusta. PRINCESS SOPHIA. — The same in pink and silver. PRINCESS AMALIA. — A rich silver embroidery, ornamented with lilac crape and silver chains, tied up in festoons with branches of lilac fancy flowers; body and train of green and silver gauze. COUNTESS OF CHOLMONDELEY. — A petticoat entirely of silver ribbon, interwoven with shaded pink stripes, with a rich drapery of Italian silver net, elegantly embroidered in silver spangles, tied up with wreaths of roses and jessamine, broad silver tassel fringe; the train spotted silver gauze, shaded with pink and silver, as the petticoat, full sleeves of Italian silver net. LADY CHARLES SOMERSET. — A petticoat entirely of Italian silver net, with crape drapery, with stripes of shaded yellow ribbon, the stripes covered with costly blond lace, a double drapery of silver net, tied up with silver fringe and tassels. LADY E. MANK. — White crape petticoat, with gold fringe, and drapery embroidered with gold, and tied with gold cord and tassels. LADY G. LEVESON. — Lilac crape petticoat, richly ornamented with silver chains, with a drapery of lilac and silver crape, tied up, large bunches of yellow flowers, and ornamented with a silver rope and tassels. LADY RANDCLIFFE. — Lilac crape petticoat, ornamented with chains of silver, fastened in festoons with bunches of hops intermixed with silver vine, a rich silver fringe round the bottom, the picket-holes ornamented with silver and lilac, tied with silver voilo [voile] and tassels; the robe lilac crape, ornamented with silver; ruffles ornamented with lilac blond; her ladyship's head-dress consisted of a green and black cottage cap, ornamented with silver net, and a plume of black feathers entwined. LADY NEWBURY — White crape petticoat, with silver fringe at the bottom, and a drapery tastefully embroidered with silver rings, fastened up with a sash richly edged with silver fringe, and tied up with silver tassels, white crape train, ornamented with silver; her head-dress white and silver.

Very little powder was worn by the ladies. Bouquets and festoons were general. The head-dresses universally turbans in different forms, with silver netting over, and feathers variegated or corresponding to the train.

Fashions for December. MORNING DRESS. — The front hair combed straight upon the forehead, the sides in small ringlets, and the hind hair in a loose chignon. Travelling cap of rose-coloured satin, trimmed with white fur. Amazon dress of lady's green cloth, lined with rose-coloured satin; cape/cuffs, and lapels with the same. Small plain muslin handkerchief - Full stock. Square pierced gold ear-rings. Fox tippet. Puff-coloured gloves. Blue striped shoes. HALF MOURNING DRESS. — Bandeau of white muslin, embroidered in black; toupee and sides in large loose curls; chignon turned up plain, and the ends returned over the bandeau in ringlets; two black brush feathers in front. Round gown of thick plain muslin, embroidered in black; short close sleeves, trimmed with black lace. Small muslin shawl, the border embroidered in black. Black and white striped sash, pinned together behind.- White enamelled hoop ear-rings. - One sting of pearls round the neck. Grey gloves and shoes. Sliver fox muff. MOURNING DRESS. — Toupee in loose curls; black ribbon mixed with the curls; black enamelled crescent, and black *plumes de coq* in the front; the hind hair turned up plain, the ends returned in ringlets on the neck. - Dress of black muslin; the petticoat with a broad pointed belt over the body; short sleeves in small plaits, trimmed with black lace; epaulettes of the same; scarf trimming round the neck, looped on the shoulders and behind, the whole trimmed with black fringe. One string of black beads round the neck; black enamelled ear-rings; black gloves and shoes; white swan-down muff.

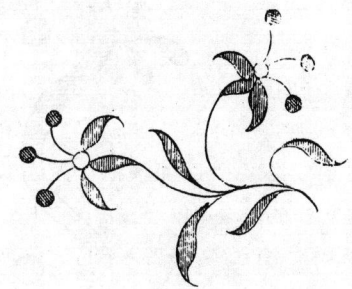

Pattern for a Gown or Apron.

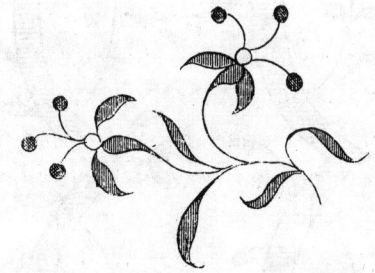

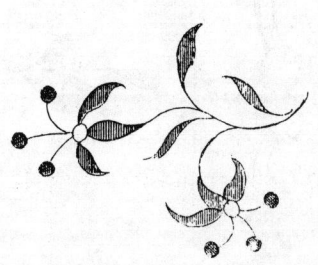

151

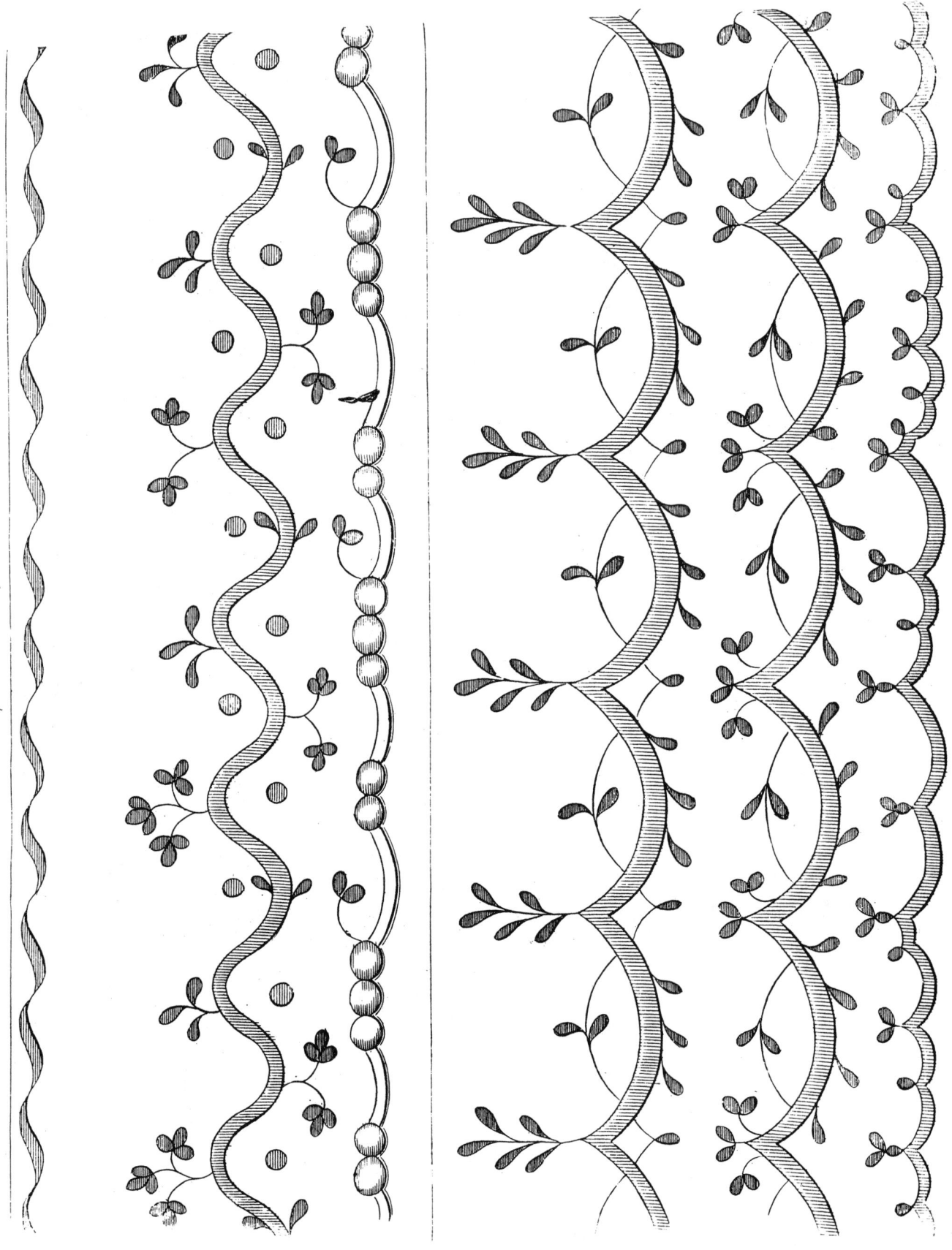

A New Pattern of Borders for Gown or Petticoat &c. — Engraved for the Lady's Magazine.

Borders for Gown or Petticoat.

Pattern of Sprigs for a Gown or Apron.

A New Pattern for a Winter Shawl &c. — Engraved for the Ladies Magazine.

Pattern for a Winter Shawl.

A New Pattern of Sprigs for a Gown &c &c

Pattern of Sprigs for a Gown.

A New Pattern for Apron or Handkerchief. — *Engraved for the Ladies Magazine.*

Pattern for Apron or Handkerchief.

LE

BEAU MONDE,

OR,

LITERARY AND FASHIONABLE

MAGAZINE.

The Fourth Number.

FOR THE MONTH OF FEBRUARY, 1807.

TO BE CONTINUED MONTHLY; PRICE HALF-A-CROWN.

LONDON:

PRINTED FOR J. B. BELL & CO.
11, Catherine St. Strand.

Fig. No. 1 — Morning Dress

Fig. No. 2 — Evening Dress

Fashions for November 1806. Fig. No. 1 — Morning Dress is a plain single-breasted frock of brown or olive with metal buttons; the waistcoat, of stripped toilinette, any colour, is rather longer than formerly; pantaloons, drabs of all degrees, in general worn with hussar boots; the hat is somewhat broader in the brim, and the hair, though less affecting the antique, is still much dressed out before. Fig. 2 — Evening Dress is almost universally of dark bottle green double-breasted coat with buttons of the same colour, covered or basket; the sleeves wide, but to fit at the shoulders, and the shirt reaching down to the hollow of the knee. The waistcoat white, and the breeches a light drab. The hair is invariable powdered, dressed high in front, and somewhat over the forehead in curls. Buckles or strings at the knees and in the shoes are equally worn, but buckles are decidedly the most dressed.

GENERAL OBSERVATIONS, For the Present Month. Fashion, tasteful yet fantastic, merciless yet idolized, seats herself in her weather-cock throne, on the dome of elevated pleasure, and dictates her unappealable injunctions to the votaries of the enchantress within. The neckcloth should, by no means be too greatly puffed out; but should be neatly united in front with a large unspread bow. Dark bottle green coats will be generally worn this season, as those of brown colours were last winter. For a morning-dress frock-coats will be prevalent; those of an olive-green hue, with a black velvet collar, will be the most universal. Fancied waistcoats of all manufacturers may be worn with this kind of coat; but fashion ordains the invariable use of dark blue or light-coloured kerseymere pantaloons, and half-boots. The boots must rise somewhat higher than the leg than has lately been the custom, and the toes of them should be formed into a perfect semi-circle. Full-dress coats will likewise be made of dark green cloth, double-breasted, and will posses the similar ornament of a black velvet collar. Single breasted white waistcoats, and light-coloured kerseymere breeches will be in much estimation. Either fleck-coloured or snow-white silk stockings, fashion now considers as elegant. The hair, for morning dress, should be a *à la Titus;* for full dress, it should be powdered. Buckles for the shoes are employed in full dress; but ribbands are allowed in afternoon or dinner dress.

GENERAL OBSERVATIONS, For December 1806. Were our Magazine published daily instead of monthly, it would be insufficient to trace the restless veerings of fashion. The finger which indicates the colour of a fashionable dress-coat is now wavering between olive-green, dark chocolate, and dark brown. The buttons must now be covered with cloth similar to the coat, which they must unite over a white waistcoat. Full-dress requires the assistance of either light-brown or white kerseymere breeches, and white silk stockings. The hair should still be powdered. For a riding dress, fashion will not be disobeyed by the use of a blue frock-coat, with metal buttons; the waistcoat to be worn under this coat Fashion leaves to her sister Fancy. The leathers to be worn with this riding dress, are to be made much tighter than has lately been the custom; and the whole boots, which are here equally necessary, must be particularly attended to. The tops should be of a glossy dark brown, and should be made somewhat longer than they have lately been worn; the toe of the boot should be broad and

Fig. No. 1 — Evening Dress   Fig. No. 2 — Morning Dress

perfectly square. Coats of all descriptions should be cut so as to shew one button only of the waistcoat. The hair continues to be dressed *à la Titus* in the morning. The bosom of the shirt now presents an air peculiar neatness;and the shirt itself is plaited, and is without a frill, the opening being united with three or four linen buttons. This improvement for a morning dress promises to be very generally adopted. In addition to these observations, we have to remark, that the style in which gentlemen have of late years worn their dress, although it does not exhibit the variety of taste which that of the ladies so eminently displays, requires equal skill in the manufacturer who adopts it to the minds of our men of fashion; and that as the variations are more minute so the formation of the becomes more difficult. Dark greens are very frequently worn as a change of dress; but black is very little seen at present, and blues are equally so. They will, however, at all times be considered genteel, although they cannot be called strictly fashionable. Gilt or plated buttons, of the basket kind, have been attempted to be introduced by many taylors of the first celebrity, but they have had very little success, having disappeared almost as suddenly as they came. The waistcoats come rather high in the neck, so as to appear a little above the coat; and the morning waistcoats are universally bound. As to the great-coats, the mildness of the season has prevented much occasion for them; and electioneering business having lately kept gentlemen too actively employed to give them time to think of fashions in those articles, we can say only,that so far as they have come under our observation, they do not seem to have suffered any alteration since the last winter, being generally made of dark-coloured cloths, and entirely plain, hanging three or four inches longer than the close coats.

Fashions for December 1806.
Fig. No. 1 — Evening Dress — For this dress are used the various shades of dark chocolate, brown, and olive coats, which are made in much the same manner as they were last month, both in regard to the collar and lapelle; but the waist is somewhat lengthened, and the hip buttons are rather farther apart than they were at that time. The length of the coat remains the same, and the buttons are either covered with the same cloth as the coat, or are formed of basket-worked twist to match. Velvet collars are still worn. White marseilles, quilting, waistcoats, continue to be the only fashionable wear with coloured clothes. The breeches we offer as before. They are made of the various shades of light drab colours; they descent comfortably below the knee, and are there tied with a silk string. Silk stockings of the natural colour are more prevalent than those of pink. Fig. No. 2 — Morning Dress — The morning coats are generally worn of the same colours and make as those of the evening; and are distinguished from them only by having a plated button, which is now worn much larger that it was formerly. — But the most gentlemanly dress is a single-breasted coat (according to the engraving) buttoning comfortably over the body, and cut away to shew the breeches. The most genteel colours are darkish green mixtures, or nut-coloured, coats of which are equally fashionable with or without a black velvet collar. Plain plated buttons are exclusively worn on these coats. — The coat itself is about two inches shorter than the evening coat, and has no pocket flaps at the sides. The waistcoats for this dress are almost exclusively of stripped toilinets, which are worn in rather broader stripes than formerly was the fashion; and the stripe is now beginning to be perpendicular with the body instead of horizontal. The breeches are made of drab-coloured milled kerseymeres,with gilt buttons at the knees, and made sufficiently long to come into the whole boot; but the most general dress are pantaloons of much the same colours as the breeches. These are frequently made of ribbed kerseymeres, and are worn with Hessian boots.

Fig. No. 1 — Morning Walking Dress   Fig. No. 2 — Elegant Walking Dress

FASHIONS for March 1807. Fig. No. 1 — A Morning Walking Dress for Gentlemen, is composed of a dark brown superfine cloth great coat, ends of the collar in the front cut into a heart; dark blue under coat only visible in front; toilinette waistcoat blue stripped with a white and yellow ground, fawn coloured pantaloons, and half boots. **Fig. No. 2** — An Elegant Walking Dress is a straw gypsy hat, tied down with a white silk or rich half lace handkerchief; a muslin gown, ornamented with knotted work crossing the shoulder to correspond with the bottom of the dress. The body is made quite plain to draw round the bosom, and fulled in the back to imitate the frock waist, with a light yellow sarsnet or camel hair scarf, richly drapered at the ends with various colours; the scarf is worn so that the dress may be exposed, tastefully tied with a careless knot in front. Lilac gloves and half boots made of kid, a beautiful white down muff, adds much to the elegance and splendour of this much admired Walking Spring Dress.

GENERAL OBSERVATIONS on Gentlemen's Dress for March. An evening suit if attempted to be described in colours, would be literally a repetition of what was laid down in our last number, as the approach of Lent necessarily prevented much alteration in coloured clothes by its customary introduction of black, which of course will ever be considered the most appropriate dress during that season; we can therefore only say, that kerseymere waistcoats and small clothes are much more prevalent than silk, which, though most assuredly more of a dress, has been gradually reducing in consumption for these many years; and satins, which were so essentially necessary to compleat the dress of a gentleman a few years back, are now totally exploded, and a pair of satin breeches would attract the observation of every beholder almost as much as a maroon coloured coat. In addition to observations of Morning Dress, we have noticed many gentlemen in plain buff kerseymere waistcoats of a very pale colour, and which certainly have a neat appearance, particularly such as we have seen with an edging of the same stuff; some few waistcoats have also been introduced of a sort of pearl colour, and also some scarlet kerseymeres, which after being rejected for several years seem to be again coming into notice; but as they do not correspond with coats usually worn, nor afford a pleasant contrast, they are not likely to become by any means general; indeed, blue or dark brown or corbeau colour coats are the only ones that can well be worn with a scarlet waistcoat. — Brown top boots seem to be somewhat more worn than they have been for some time past, and which are almost constantly accompanied by kerseymere breeches; leather being now almost exploded from the thigh of a man of fashion, and scarcely maintains the preference even in the chase. We have also observed that many gentlemen in their morning walks have attempted to introduce a sort of shooting dress, by parading in a short coat of any light colour, and with drab colour cloth or kerseymere gaiters to come up to the knees; but, however well such a dress may suit a watering place, or a walk over the grounds of an estate, we do not think it adapted to the promenade of Bond-street.

MORNING WALKING DRESSES. for April 1807.

Fig. No. 1 — Morning Walking Dress   Fig. No. 4 — Half-Dress for Gentlemen

FASHIONS for April 1807. Fig. No. 4 — MORNING WALKING DRESS, a *Manteline à la Castilliane;* a short mantle of orange and purple velvet, made to fasten on the right shoulder, and, crossing the bosom, is confined with rich cords and tassels under the left arm; rounded gradually to the bottom of the right side in a regular point; a body of the same, with sleeves and high full collar; the back and skirt are cut in one, with only one armhole; the whole trimmed entirely round with spotted leopard fur. A *chapeau à la Diane* of velvet; the right side of the crown, under the brim is intermixed with white fur. A straw hat of this shape has a much lighter and more elegant effect, which is made a Millard's at the corner of Southampton-street, Strand. The Straw Hat is worn trimmed with a quilling of French net round the side of the face, and may be worn tied down with a silk handkerchief. A train petticoat of clear India muslin, made full and quite plain, without ornament of work whatever, is worn with this dress; white kid gloves, and shoes of the same colour as the mantle. Fig. No. 4 — An **Half-Full Dress for Gentlemen** is composed of a light olive double breasted coat, buttoned close up, with covered buttons of the same cloth as the coat; yellow striped toilinette waistcoat; light brown Angola pantaloons, and half-boots; the hair cropped *à la Titus.*

GENERAL OBSERVATIONS on Gentlemen's Dresses for April. Blue coats, with black velvet collars, are quite the rage. Velvet collars are now not only general on blue coats, but on olive and dark green coats, which are likewise becoming extremely prevalent; these are, however, the only colours on which the velvet collars are used for evening coats; the blue coat has, of course a flat gilt button, (of what is termed the standard colour gold) but all other evening coats have covered buttons. The morning dress is fluctuating; scarlet waistcoats are on the increase; and, we doubt not, will obtain some preference during the present month. Coats, breeches, and pantaloons, seem to continue much the same; indeed the severity of the weather renders a great coat more and more necessary, which does away the opportunity of displaying any particular taste in the close coat. Olive brown greatcoats, are still the most in favour, and the silk skirt lining is generally adopted. Velvet collars and lappel facings do not, however, keep pace with the silk skirts, as every great coat sports that ornament, which, we believe, arises principally from the velvet being soon deprived of its appearance after suffering a few showers of rain, and also as it so soon changes its colour.

Fig. No. 3 — Barouche Dress   Fig. No. 4 — Morning Dress for Gentlemen

FASHIONS for June 1807. Fig. No. 3 — A Barouche Dress. — A compleat shell of thin white muslin, worn over a white sarsnet slip, made quite short, open behind and tied with small cords and tassels down the back; the muslin dress is made to the size of the throat, and the sarsnet slip, with a high standing collar, trimmed round the edge with a French lace; long sleeves of white sarsnet, and short full muslin sleeves worn over the sarsnet. Long square mantelet of primrose silk, embroidered with a dark rich border of embossed ribband; the two ends are tied with a knot on the front of the bosom; a rich lace cap lined with the same colour as the mantelet, made with a point, and worn very deep on the left side of the face, and exposes the whole of the right. A small bunch of primrose is fixed on the center of the cap; long streamers of primrose satin ribband at the top of the crown. The front of the cap is trimmed with puffings of lace. Primrose gloves and shoes. **fig. No. 4** — Morning Dresses for Gentlemen. — A mixed coat, single breasted, cut off in the front, and made of light greenish mixture, or pepper and salt kind, with covered or plated buttons, and collars of the same cloth; the skirts rather shorter than the dress coats, and the pockets in plaits behind. — Waistcoats of printed quilting, made single breasted, of dark brown or olive stripes, as also the gold coloured stripe, shaded with black, are most prevalent, and are made without any bindings. — Lightish drab kerseymere, or stocking pantaloons, with Hessian boots; ribbed kerseymere pantaloons are still worn; as also drab kerseymere breeches with gilt buttons and brown top boots. Nankeen pantaloons and trowsers are becoming very prevalent, and are frequently attended by nankeen gaiters. EVENING DRESS FOR GENTLEMEN. — Blue coats, lappeled, with a flat gilt button of rather a large size, continue to be very prevalent, and very frequently with black velvet collars; next to them are dark greens and dark olive browns; the green coats have, occasionally, a gilt or plated button; but the browns are constantly worn with a button covered with cloth, and a collar of the same. White Marsailles quilting waistcoats, made single breasted, are the most general, as well as the most genteel waistcoats for evening. — Kerseymere breeches of very light drabs, either of the pearl shade, or the clear stone drabs, with silk strings to the knee, and Nankin breeches, with a silk string, are almost the only breeches worn for evening dress.

GENERAL OBSERVATIONS on Gentlemen's Dresses. We observe that evening coats are lately made rather longer in the lapels than for some time past; and the waistcoats also in the same proportion; the skirts of the coat are cut a little away, but not by any means shorter. Breeches continue much the same as last month. Morning coats are cut rather light in the skirts, and rather shorter than the evening coats; but both come up tolerably high in the neck, and fall rather low and open in front. Although the kerseymere breeches and pantaloons with boots continue to be much worn at present, we doubt not but, if the warm weather continues, gentlemen will very readily leave them off for the lighter dress of Nankin pantaloons and trowsers, with gaiters to match.

Fig. No. 1 — Elegant Calypso Robe   Fig. No. 2 — Dress   Fig No. 3 — Evening Dress

FASHIONS for September 1807. Fig. No. 1 — An Elegant Calypso Robe made of rich imperial muslin of beautiful light yellow, finished at the extreme edge in a line of embossed silver and gold, worked in light open flowers, ornamented down the front, and round each side of the train, which is sloping off from the bend of the knee, with stars worked in small pearls, fastened in the centre with a gold stud; the front and back is made all in one; the waist unusually long, and tight to the form, though cut in various shapes; this robe is worn over a rich white satin train petticoat worked round the bottom with stars of pearls and dead gold, to correspond with the dress; the sleeves are white satin, made tight across the shoulders, and hangs in small folds down the arm, inlet from the bottom of the sleeve, and crosses to the back part of the shoulder with a wreath of embossed gold and silver in open needle-work. A small white Calypso cap, embroidered with gold. The hair is worn, parted in waves over the forehead, and in small ringlets down each side of the face. Over the head is thrown, in graceful negligence a long drapery of white Parisian net, tastefully embroidered into a pheasant's eye. Ear-rings and necklace of diamonds; shoes white satin, spotted with gold. Fig. No. 2 --- A dress and train petticoat of rich white Italian sarsnet, with an embroidery of grape vine and leaves, worked very light in gold thread, made open behind, and fastened with gold buttons down to the bottom of the train. The dress is made about a quarter and a half shorter than the petticoat, which is embroidered all round with gold lace about an inch in breadth; the back is made quite plain and laced in the middle with gold cord. Sleeves of white lace over white satin, made tight to the form of the shoulder; the bosom is made entirely straight, drawn tight in the centre to the busk, ornamented with a wreath of small gold leaves. Head-dress entirely of hair, combed straight on the right side of the head, formed into knots at the top of the head, fastened with a diamond comb, and is finished with a profusion of small curls, down the front of the head. Bracelets of dead gold and diamonds round the thick part of the arm. Neck-lace and ear-rings of the same. Straw coloured kid gloves; white kid shoes trimmed with gold lace. **Fig. No. 3 — An Evening Dress for Gentlemen,** is composed of double-breasted dark blue coats [sic] with large yellow double gilt buttons; white quilting Marsailles waistcoat; light brown kerseymere breeches, with strings to the knees; white silk stocking; shoes in buckles.

GENERAL OBSERVATIONS on Gentlemen's Dress. Morning coats of various mixtures are worn; the parsley mixture is decidedly the most fashionable, and that made single-breasted, with a collar of the same cloth, largish size plated buttons, and without pocket flaps. Striped Marseilles quilting waistcoats, single-breasted, or plain buff kerseymere waistcoats, of a pale colour, single-breasted, but not bound. Drab colour kerseymere pantaloons with Hessian boots, or India Nankin trowsers and gaiters. Dark olives, with covered buttons, retain their full share of the field, although the dark forest green has entered into competition against it, and is most ably supported by the blue, which, with a gilt button, is likely to retain a preference. White quilting Marseilles waistcoats, single-breasted, are still considered the most genteel, and very light drabs or nankin for breeches.

Fig. No. 1 — Morning Walking Dress   Fig. No. 2 — Opera Dress

Gentlemen's Morning Dress

FASHIONS for February 1808. LADIES' DRESSES. Fig. No. 1 — Morning Walking Dress. — The Hindu coat and hat made of dove or bright grey coloured sarsnet, of fine cloth trimmed all round with a rich fur trimming of a fancy colour; the coat is made straight over the bosom, square across the shoulder, and continues with a small peak in the centre of the back; is brought tight round the waist to the form of the shape, a high collar with long peaks in front to fall all over on the neck, ornamented with small silk tassels fastened to each corner. A rich cord and tassel are confined in the back, and hang carelessly in the hand; the coat is lined all through with white sarsnet, and confined together down the front; gloves white Woodstock, and shoes of the same colour as the coat. Fig. No. 2 — Opera Dress — The most distinguished full dress is composed of a magnificent cloth of a deep pink, worn over a white satin slip; the dress is made round and short, with a square back on the top and at the bottom of the waist, which is rather increased in length; the skirt is made entirely plain, and is laced down the back with small pink beads, in the form of diamonds; the honey-comb front, made to the form of the bosom, short sleeves straight over the shoulders, and at the back; broad Vandyke at the bottom of the sleeves of white satin, ornamented round the neck, and in different parts in the Kolana style; the dress caught up and fastened with a bunch of silver roses and green foil on the back of the left side above the knee, and hangs in loose folds round the bottom, about a quarter of a yard distant from the bottom of the petticoat, on the right side. The hair is combed straight from the crown of the head behind, and is formed into a thick twist, which is confined with a rich diamond comb, on the top of which three gold crowns are placed; the ends of the hind hair are seen in pendant ringlets falling over the left side of the head; on the front of the forehead the hair is divided, and lays smooth over the right temple, and is kept back by the Kolana crescent. Necklace and ear-rings of diamonds; gloves white kid; and shoes white satin.

GENTLEMEN'S DRESSES. Morning Dress consist of olive or green mixtures; and though doubled [sic] breasted coats are worn by many, the single breasted coats are the most fashionable; either of them, however, has a collar of the same cloth, is made without pocket flaps at the sides, and with full sized plated buttons. — Scarlet kerseymere, or striped toilinet waistcoats, single breasted; and drab kerseymere breeches or pantaloons. — Blue pantaloons are again coming much into wear, and will be generally worn during the winter season, but they have no kind of ornament or trimming on the front. — Hussar boots are, of course, worn with pantaloons; and brown top boots, with riding breeches. Dark blue great coats trimmed with fur, or darkish olive brown cloth great coats are generally worn. — Under waistcoats are considered fashionable; white is worn in Evening Dress, and scarlet or Maroon colour in the Morning, although many gentlemen prefer small spotted patterns for that purpose. There is not the smallest alteration in Evening Dress; therefore the description we gave in our last Number may be referred to.

Fig. No. 1 — Morning Walking Dress   Fig. No. 1 & 2 — Kensington Garden
Dresses

FASHIONS for June 1808. Fig. No. 1 — Kensington Garden Dresses. — A rich India muslin dress, with a superb embossed border, worked in floss silk, white or coloured, made short, walking length; high in the neck, and drawn full round the throat with a turban collar falling over; the sleeves are long and full, and confined tight round the wrist; whilst the back of the dress is loose and drawn into the shape. The Arabian Tunic worn with this dress is composed of India shawl-work of a bright primrose, elegantly relieved with a turban trimming wreathed with green sarsnet. The Arabian hat is a graceful *melange* of the turban and gipsey [sic] forms, of a delicate straw or chip, confined under the chin with a bow and tassels of green sarsnet. Gloves straw colour, and half boots of green jane. Fig. No. 2 — A short train dress of white net, bound with white satin round the bottom; the back of the dress is made square and low as also the front to match, with a deep rich lace falling over; a French body of pink satin, confined close under the bosom; the sleeves are short and full, and bound with white satin to correspond with the bottom; the Catalani tippet of white lace drapery, finished at one end with a rich white lace tassel, is thrown negligently across the shoulder, whilst the other end hangs down plain, and without ornament. The Flora bonnet is made of white chip, trimmed with pink sarsnet and ornamented in front with a bunch of various coloured flowers. Necklaces of emeralds, or imitations of the same, are much worn with this dress; the gloves and shoes are of white kid. Fig. No. 1 — [Gentlemen's] Morning Walking Dress. — A dark blue double-breasted coat, with large gilt basket buttons; white India dimity waistcoat and trowsers, and white silk stocking with a narrow clock; shoes with strings.

GENERAL OBSERVATIONS on Gentlemen's Dresses. The most fashionable coats for Evening still remain dark blues, with full size gilt buttons, and black velvet collars; or forest greens, with buttons covered with cloth, and collars of the same; white waistcoats, and clear light drab kerseymere breeches, with silk strings at the knee. Light coloured mixtures or drab coats are again resuming their station for Morning Dress, and these are made single-breasted, and, after buttoning on the breast, slope regularly away to the skirts, they are also something shorter in the skirt than the evening coat, have flat plated buttons, and collars of the same; quilting Marseilles waistcoats, single-breasted, in a variety of small stripes on a white ground; white corduroy breeches, made rather long, with pearl buttons at the knees; and boots with brown tops. — White India dimity trowsers; also Nankin trowsers and gaiters. Some few striped trowsers we have seen worn, but they are considered as only adapted for dirty weather, or for wearing at the watering places.

MISCELLANEOUS Notes on Gentlemen's Fashions: Court Dress - 1807. — Dark-green, or other dark colour, coat and small cloaths [sic] of silk, velvet, or fine cloth, covered with a small spot somewhat lighter of the same kind of colour, edged with silver lace, and embroidered with any kind of wildflower of acknowledged British growth; waistcoat of white satin, embroidered in a very light pattern of gold thread. Silk stockings perfectly white. **Gentlemen's Dresses worn on Her Majesty's Birthday, 1807.** — The most striking of the dresses, with the exception of the uniforms, were, A purple velvet coat and small clothes; embroidered waistcoat. A dark green coat with elegant cut-steel buttons; a satin waistcoat richly embroidered. An elegant olive coat, richly embroidered; a richly embroidered satin waistcoat. A brown cut velvet coat, nearly black, most brilliantly embroidered with silver and colours, and lined with white satin; waistcoat of white satin, embroidered like the coat. — This suit was distinguished for taste and elegance.

Dresses of the Army, 1808. The following changes are spoken of in the dress of military officers, whereby each rank will be distinguished, as in the Continental armies, and in our navy; so that on actual service each rank maybe known, though the officers are unacquainted with each other: — **Ensign** — An epaulette of gold or silver fringe on the right shoulder, and white plume with red bottom. **Lieutenant** — Epaulette of fringe and bullion right shoulder; plume as above. **Captains** — Epaulette, with bullion and fringe, right shoulder; and one of fringe on left shoulder; plume as above. **Majors** — Epaulette on each shoulder of bullion and fringe; plume white, with red top. **Lieutenant-Colonels** — Epaulettes as above; white plume, with black top. **Colonels** — Epaulettes as above, black plume, with white top. **Generals** — Epaulettes as at present, and white plumes. Their different ranks are already distinguished by buttons. N.B. **Ensigns and Second Lieutenants of Highland and Fuzileer regiments** to wear two epaulettes as formerly, but of gold or silver fringe only. **Lieutenants of Fuzileers** — An epaulette, with fringe and bullion, left shoulder; and one of fringe on right shoulder, being the reverse of Captains.

GENTLEMEN'S DRESSES for April 1808.

Morning Dress — In this we are scarcely at present able to point out any variety, as the coldness of the weather still renders a good great coat indispensable, and this far precludes the opportunity of exhibiting the motley changes of fashion and taste, to any advantage. We are, however, justified in saying that light colours will certainly take the lead in the *ton* for coats. Waistcoats of striped Marsailles quilting will of course resume their stations as soon as the mildness of the weather will permit; and drab kerseymere or leather breeches, with brown top boots, will be as much the rage as ever. **Evening Dress** — The most prevailing at present is a dark blue coat with large sized flat gilt buttons, with velvet collar, or collar of the same cloth, according to fancy; with this we see single breasted white Marsailles quilting waistcoats, black silk breeches and stockings; some few sport drab coloured kerseymere breeches and white stockings.

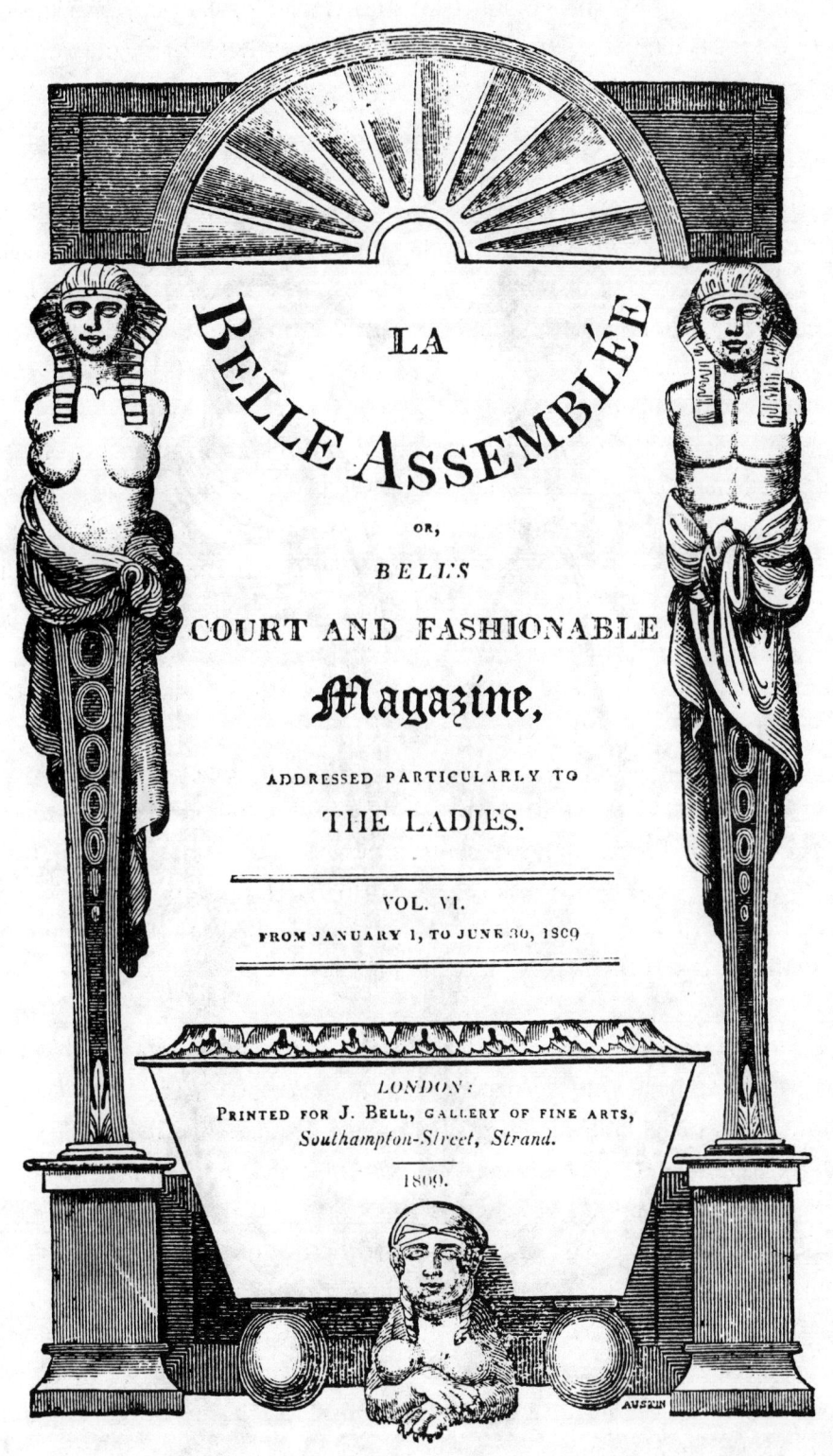

LA

BELLE ASSEMBLÉE

OR,

BELL'S

COURT AND FASHIONABLE

Magazine,

ADDRESSED PARTICULARLY TO

THE LADIES.

VOL. VI.

FROM JANUARY 1, TO JUNE 30, 1809

LONDON:
PRINTED FOR J. BELL, GALLERY OF FINE ARTS,
Southampton-Street, Strand.

1809.

No. 2 — Full Dress   No. 1 — New Spencer Walking Dress

No. 3 — Madame Catalani

No. 4 — Parisian Walking Dress

Fashions for February. ENGLISH COSTUME. No. 1. — A New Spencer Walking Dress. Incognita hat of French grey, or pigeon's wing, formed of sarsnet, velvet, or the Georgiana cloth. Tassels and trimming of *chenile,* velvet, or Trafalgar, contrasted agreeably to the taste of the wearer. A Tuscan spenser, the same colour, formed with a round lappel, continued from the back, and round the bosom on one side, with a full flowing robin on the other; descending a little below the knee, and terminated with a rich tassel. A chemisette, with a high standing collar, fastened with a brooch at the throat the whole trimmed to correspond with the hat. The hair in loose curls; gold hoop earrings; York tan gloves; and shoes the colour of the spenser. The hat, as worn by Miss Duncan, is of pink sarsnet, trimmed with black but the colour is necessarily changed by those fair fashionables who have selected it for a walking dress, to shades of less conspicuous attraction, amidst which the most esteemed are those mentioned in the above description. No. 2 — Full Dress. A Roxborough jacket of soft white satin, flowing open in front, and down each side the figure, in regular pointed drapery. A plain full sleeve, and short jacket flaps; black and gold Turkish riband down the back; trimming and tassels of gold. A round train dress of the finest India muslin over a sattin [sic.] petticoat, embroidered round the bottom, in a light pattern of gold. The hair twisted in a fanciful form, and short corkscrew curls flowing at the temples, and in various directions from the crown of the head; a tiara of fine pearl blended with the hair, and placed rather towards the left side. One row of fine pearls forms the necklace, which is fastened in front with a diamond brooch. An armlet of hair, in the new patent plait, with a row of the finest pearl on each side; bracelets to correspond. Earrings of pearl, with a diamond in the centre. White satin shoes, with gold trimming. Fan of Italian grape [crape?], with gold spangles, and devices in transparencies. French kid gloves. PARISIAN COSTUME. No. 3. — **Madame Catalani.** A long flowing *veste* and drapery of crimson velvet, lined with white sarsnet, and richly ornamented with a Turkish border, in gold; the drapery drawn through a *cestus,* formed of gold and sapphire, and terminated with a large gold tassel; confined in front of the right shoulder with a brooch to correspond, from whence flows another point of the vest, finished with a similar tassel. A double *tunique,* or under dress, of French net, with loose long sleeves, and round bosom, cut low, spotted, and most splendidly embroidered in gold at the bottom. White satin petticoat embroidered to correspond. A Grecian diadem, of gold, and brilliants. A square Brussels veil of the most transparent texture, lightly embroidered in gold, fixed at the back of the diadem, and flowing negligently over the left arm. Hair close cropt behind, falling in irregular corkscrew ringlets in front and on the sides. The necklace, one row of fine brilliants, set transparent, and fastened in the centre with a long square brooch of sapphire and gold; earrings to correspond. White satin shoes, trimmed, and embroidered at the toes, in gold. No 4. — **Parisian Walking Dress.** A fine milled kerseymere Opera coat, of a silver grey; wrapt plain round the figure in front, and buttoned down the left side; square lappels, and rolled collar, of black velvet; deep cape *à la pelerine;* belt buttoned in front; double erect, Vandyke frill, plaited *à la Queen Elizabeth.* Hunting bonnet similar with the coat, bound with black velvet, bows and ends in front trimmed to correspond. Hair in confined curls; amber earrings. Ridicule of crimson velvet, with gold-coloured silk fringe and tassels. Crimson velvet shoes.

OBSERVATIONS ON THE FASHIONS FOR FEBRUARY. The fawn colour, so universally exhibited in mantles, bonnets, and pelises, is now too common to be chosen by our first order of females; and the dove brown, or shaded morone velvet, trimmed with swansdown, Indian mole, or grey squirrel very happily supplies its place. They are chiefly formed in large Opera coats, or Cardinal cloaks with long sleeves, and a deep coachman's cape. When composed of sarsnet, the back and collar are made to sit close to the form; and the robins to flow loose from the shoulders; which are invariably trimmed with skin. Velvet bonnets of silver-grey, have been the distinguishing ornaments of many modern *belles.* The Russian helmet, or bonnet of sarsnet, or velvet, trimmed with skin, and entirely concealing one side of the face, is a new and very tasteful article; and the pointed turban is of the same novel standard. The African robe, of grey velvet, trimmed with silver, in Vandykes, is a most elegant habiliment; with this most attractive robe is worn a tiara of silver frost-work, finished at the edge with Trafalgar trimming in silver. The apron dress, is also very elegant; it is formed of silver, or gold crape, and worn over a satin round-dress. Short frocks are seen on very young women, richly embroidered, or trimmed with lace at the bottom. Gold and silver net is worn as a drapery over white satin dresses; and the hair is confined with the same. It is impossible to conceive a costume which exhibits at once more richness and elegance. The Spanish vest of satin, or velvet, like that given in out Mourning Dress of last Month, is much esteemed by our females of rank and fashion. It is usually worn with a petticoat of silver, gold, or embroidered muslin. Round dresses of clear muslin over white satin, trimmed round the bottom, bosom, and sleeves with a satin ribband, laid flat, representing the leopards skin, has a truly grand effect. With this dress is commonly worn a tiara of similar skin, frosted, or thickly scattered with small gold spots. Brown muslin robes, with silver or gold stars, and diamonds to correspond. Shawl dresses trimmed with Vandyke thread-lace. The Spanish spenser, of velvet, flowing in pointed drapery from the waist, trimmed with narrow gold or silver Trafalgar, and small Tekeli cap to correspond, have each their share of fashionable distinction. The long sleeve, is very generally introduced in evening dress, but is ever composed of the clearest materials. Sometimes of lace, patent, or spider-net, and embroidered book muslin. Several females of taste and fashion have re-introduced the curled crop; but the general mode of wearing the hair is in loose curls in front, divided so as to discover the forehead; some form of hind tresses in several small braids, and then twist them in the form of a cable, and bring them round the temple, confining them on the right side, in a knot, with an ornamental comb; others form it in one large braid, and curl the ends, which is mode to flow in irregular ringlets on the opposite side. The most distinguishing ornaments for the head are, diadems and tiaras of silver, gold, fur, or bugles. The shawl veil *à la Parisian,* is also adopted within this last fortnight, forming at once the head-dress and drapery. The passion flower, of diamonds, pearls, or foil, is a most chaste and elegant ornament. The Madona front is entirely exploded amidst females of taste and fashion, they are now only worn by the obscure individual. We observe that the bosom of dresses are cut much lower of late, and worn with a square tucker of lace or embroidery; the back and shoulders are as much exposed as ever. The short sleeve varies little from our last; the twisted, or rucked sleeve, is also much admired for its simplicity. Morning dresses are universally composed of cambric, or jaconot muslin, and are either made high towards the throat, with Vandyke frills of lace, or embroidered muslin, or cut low with a frock back and Flemish front; a border of needlework at the feet, and shirt to correspond. The full plaited, or surplice sleeve, is a new and distinguishing appendage to the morning costume. The veil, or cloister cap, the flurry mob, and the cap *à la rustique,* as given in our last, very inconsistently forms a part of this habiliment.

No. 1 — Walking Dress   No. 2 — Evening Dress

No. 3 — Ball Dress   No. 4 — Parisian Winter Dress

Fashions for March. ENGLISH COSTUME. No. 1 — Walking Dress. A Polish robe of purple velvet, flowing open in front, rounded gradually from the bottom towards the lappels, which are continued across the shoulder, and finished in regular points on the back. A *chemisette* of the same, with high full collar; the whole trimmed entirely round with the red fox, mole, leopard spot, or grey squirrel. A rich cord and tassel fastened in the centre of the back, which occasionally confines the robe. The back and skirt cut in one; and the sleeve nearly to fit the arm. Polish cap of the same material, trimmed round the edge, and across the crown, with correspondent skin; a cord and tassels suspended in irregular lengths from the right side of the crown. York tan gloves; and primrose, or purple shoes. No. 2 — An Evening Dress. A round train dress of soft white satin, buttoned simply down the left side; the back very low, and quite plain. High, and double puffed sleeves, with wrap front. Military sash of cobweb muslin, embroidered in gold spots, commencing from the back of the right shoulder, crossing the waist behind, and passing under the right side of the bosom, gathered into a pearl brooch at the opposite corner, and flowing within a quarter of a yard to the bottom of the dress, where it is finished with a rich gold tassel. Hair brought to a point on the forehead, irregularly curled at the ears and on the crown of the head, where it is confined with a coronet, or diadem of pearl. Pearl necklace, earrings, and bracelets; gold armlet. White kid gloves. Shoes of white satin, embroidered with gold. Fan of white crape, with gold spangled border. No. 3 — A Ball Dress. Of plain crape, over a white satin slip, made a dancing length; plain back and sleeve, with quartered front, trimmed round the bottom, on the waist and sleeves, with a white velvet ribband thickly spangled with gold. A white satin sash, tied in long bows and ends on the right side, terminated with splendid gold tassels. High gathered tucker of Brussels lace, Hair in dishevelled curls, confined with a white velvet band similar with the trimming of the dress; bow of the same blended with the hair, and placed over the left eye. India shawl, a deep amber colour, with a rich and variegated fringe and border, negligently drawn through each arm, so as to form a flowing drapery on the right side of the figure. Necklace composed of bright topaz, set transparent, fastened with a diamond stud in the centre. Topaz earrings of the fashionable shell form; gold elastic bracelets. French kid gloves. White satin shoes, with gold roses. Fan of amber crape, with devices in purple and gold. PARISIAN COSTUME. No. 4 — Parisian Winter Dress. A promenade coat of soft Circassian cloth, a pale olive colour, buttoned down the front, and formed high in the back, with open round lappels at the bosom, double roll trimming round the arm-hole and wrist; full lace tucker, and double *demi* ruff *à la Queen Elizabeth,* plaited in vandyke. Sash of pale salmon colour, or pink sarsnet, tied in small bows, and long ends on the right side. Equestrian hat, composed with similar materials with the coat, projecting leaves in front of the same. Hair close cropt behind, divided on the forehead, and curled on the sides. Shawl of pale salmon colour, with blue and crimson border, carelessly thrown over the left arm. Necklace, two rows of fine pearl; earrings of gold; and fan of white tiffany, embroidered in blue and gold. Straw-coloured gloves and shoes.

General Observations on the most Prevailing Fashions. We are enabled to give a description of a species of Pelice equally new. This most graceful habit is styled the Hibernian vest, and is formed of velvet, the colour pigeon's breast; it is formed as a flowing robe in front, so as occasionally to wrap round the figure; the back is cut round in form of a high gown, without cape or collar, and is trimmed entirely round with a full waving skin of grey squirrel. The vest is formed by a width of velvet fastened down on the inside of the waist, brought across the bosom, and gathered into a brooch on the left shoulder; it is hemmed on the edge next the throat with the same skin. The back in formed very broad, and is drawn loosely at the bottom with a band, which is brought through the lining and confined in the centre of the waist with large topaz clasps, leaving the sides flowing open. The Hibernian hat worn with this pelice, is of the Spanish form, perfectly flat in the rim, and trimmed round the edge, on the inside, with a skin the same as the pelice; it is turned up directly in front, and over the edge waves two short brush feathers of the same colour. The chastity and elegance of this habiliment stand almost unrivalled. The Cottage cloak, of scarlet kerseymere, is another very attractive covering; it is made with a hood, or cape, and ties immediately on one side of the throat, leaving the shoulder occasionally exposed. The front end of the cloak is pointed, the other rounded; and the whole is terminated with a Turkish ribband, or fur, happily contrasted as to colour. With this cloak is worn a Jockey cap, or Cottage bonnet, composed of the same material. Some females of fashionable celebrity have sported lately silk stockings the colour of the pelice, with open-wove ankles. We have lately been favoured with the sight of a most elegant round robe, formed of a delicate white Italian crape, embroidered all over in small silver stars. This dress was made with a train, and worn over a white satin slip; the bosom sharply rounded at the corners, with a fall of Mechlin lace round, and a drawn tucker above it; the sleeve a plain wrap, trimmed at the edge with silver *à la corkscrew.* From the left shoulder flowed the Peruvian scarf, of a deep salmon colour, with Indian border. The round apron of lace, or patent net, in white, or morone, with light border in silver, gold, or coloured foil, is considered as very elegant; it is generally worn with a round dress of white satin, or sarsnet, and is confined tight round the figure, the fullness being thrown quite behind, where it is tied with bows of white ribband, or tassels to correspond with the border; it usually reaches within a quarter of a yard the bottom of the dress, and is invariably trimmed with a lace at the bottom, put on easily full. The sleeves of this dress are of the same materials as the apron. Some of our *elegantes* only shade the bosom by a simple drawn tucker of lace. The front of dresses are rather lowered of late, in compliment, we presume, to the back and shoulders, which still continue their public exhibition. The short sleeve, worn in full puckers on the shoulder, confined at the bottom with a broad armlet corresponding with the other ornaments, is considered as elegant in full dress; while some, on the contrary, wear the short sleeve nearly plain, trimmed a the edge similar with the dress, and crossed to a point in the centre of the arm. The simple frock sleeve, with a cuff of lace, is much esteemed, with dress of coloured Italian crape. We think the waist a little increased in length of late; and the square and round bosom, plaited or gored with lace, have an equal portion of celebrity.

183

No. 1 — Half Dress   No. 2 — Lady in Her Opera Box

No. 3 — Mounted Parisian Lady

Fashions for April. ENGLISH COSTUME. No. 1 — A Half Dress. As prepared for the Duchess of Roxburgh, under the immediate direction of Her Grace — A petticoat and tunic of the clearest French cambric, vandyked all round with the same; the tunic cut in the form of a crescent in front, closed on the left side with a tassel, and continued in a point nearly to reach the bottom of the petticoat, where it finishes with a tassel as above. Long sleeves, vandyked at the wrist, with full tops terminated with a band of open-hems, or lace; front of the waist wrapt to the left side, where the tunic closes. Imperial chip hat, of a light lead-colour, turned up in the form on an arch over the left eye; a band of shaded velvet, with waving brush feather of correspondent hues. Necklace of pearl, linked with dead gold. The unique, and much admired muff and tippet, formed entirely of shaded Turkish feathers, patronized and adopted by the Princesses, and now the distinguishing appendage of all ladies of rank and elegance. This very novel, tasteful, and ingenious ornament is to be obtained at the celebrated shop, late Dyde's and Scribe's, Pall-Mall. No. 2 — A Lady in Her Opera Box. Her dress a round robe of pliant white satin, made to sit close to the form; trimmed round the bottom, bosom, and sleeves, with gold brocade ribband. The Curacao turban, of white satin, embroidered in spots of raised gold; confined on the forehead with Indian bandeau of the same composition. Necklace one row of fine brilliants, from whence is suspended a most curious Egyptian amulet. Earrings and bracelets to correspond. Hair closely confined under the turban behind, and worn in irregular curls in front, divided over the left eyebrow, so as to discover the temple. Rose-wood Opera fan, with mount composed of military trophies in transparencies. White kid gloves and shoes. PARISIAN COSTUME. No. 3. Represents a Parisian lady, mounted in the most fashionable style, for the *Long Champs* and *Elysées,* at Paris. — An equestrian habit of fine seal-wool cloth, with elastic strap; the colour blue (but olive, or puce, are equally esteemed), with convex buttons of dead gold. The habit to sit high in the neck behind, lapelled in front, and buttoned twice at the small of the waist; a high plaited frill of cambric, uniting at the bosom where the habit closes. A jockey bonnet of the same materials as composes the habit, finished with a band and tuft in front. Hair in dishevelled crop. York tan gloves; and demi-boots of purple kid, laced with jonquille chord.

General Observations on Most Prevailing Fashions. Since the introduction of the Polish pelise, we have remarked nothing particularly new in the formation of this article of attire. The texture of which they are now composed, is almost exclusively of twill sarsnet; but various alterations have taken place in the ornamental part of them. The long flowing robbin is laid aside; the high collar is seldom seen; and the simple folded vest has banished (amidst the most distinguished females) the chimesette of antecedent date. The loose flowing opera coat, with deep pelerine cape, the Polish robe, and the Hibernian vest, as given in our last Number, are selected by the most fashionable fair; but these are chiefly formed of sarsnets, quite plain, the skin trimming being on the decline. The colours commonly chosen are shaded dove browns, lined with persians, tastefully contrasted. We have lately seen one of silver-dove sarsnet, lined throughout with pale pink, and another of light brown, shot with amber, and lined with a Persian of the latter colour. Hats and bonnets are still worn of correspondent materials; not do we know of any other at this season, which could be adopted so consistent, and unobtrusively elegant. With females of rank and taste, these articles are generally confined to the three following orders; the Bereford hat, the peasant's bonnet, and equestrian hat. The latter is given in one of our prints of fashion for the last month. The two former are more novel, but not more distinguishable. The throat is now universally covered in the morning costume; and those who have not yet adopted the high Parisian chemise, (or morning wrap) wear the new habit shirt, which is sometimes formed to unite in front, with a high-rounded collar, richly embroidered, and trimmed at the edge with very narrow net; at others, the shirt is finished with buttons on the shoulder, and the collar cut so as to sit close round the chin, and high at the ears; but in either case, lace and work is let in at all points; and in caps, bottoms of dresses, petticoats, and sleeves, this ornament is always seen. Indeed, we never recollect a period when needle-work was so universally fashionable; and lamenting (as must every considerate individual) on the few occupations left for the female of fallen fortune, we cannot but give credit to our amiable countrywomen, who thus judiciously unite *humanity* with elegance and taste. Short dresses of crape, of clear muslin, with long sleeves of lace, are now admitted in the evening costume; and, strange to say, are often seen in full dress! We cannot by any means subscribe to a fashion which destroys that distinguished uniformity, the acknowledged attendant on a correct taste. A short shirt in full dress must ever be a marked inconsistency; except expressly designed for dancing. The *train,* however inconvenient, and inimical to the approach of surrounding *beaus,* gives much dignity and grace to the figure; if banished from the drawing-room, the *coup d'aeil* is destroyed. The exposition of the back and shoulders is still universal in the evening costume; but we think the bosom of dresses are a little advanced of late. The simple wrapt fronts, commencing immediately at the corner of the bosom, and finished at the edge with a trimming, corresponding with that of the dress, is again revived, and is remarkable amidst the peasant's waist, and square-gored front, which contend with it for popularity. Those whose judgment reject the long sleeve for the evening, for full dress, wear the sleeve very short; sometimes we observe a plain frock sleeve of satin, with a high cuff of lace, trimmed at the edge with plaited net, beads, bugles, foil, or silver, as may best unite with the dress. The Spanish or slashed sleeve, is also very new, and a sleeve, formed in shell-scollops, over white satin, has a chaste and elegant effect. A dress of white crape, ornamented with steel beads, and the Russian hussar cap, with Polish plume, scattered with steel dust, is amidst the splendid novelties of the season. This dress attracted universal attention at the Marchioness of H——'s last grand assembly. The shawl dress is a most select and tasteful attire, and is usually worn with a white satin or sarsnet slip; muslin, or crape round dresses, trimmed with silver or gold velvet ribbons, in white, or colours, has a most animated appearance. We observed one of these dresses, with the ribbon laid in waved stripes, at regular distances from the bottom of the waist; the effect was attractive and elegant. The home costume, or half-dress, (on relinquishing the morning attire) is usually composed of muslin, of divers kinds; plain and coloured sarsnets, or Italian crapes. They are chiefly formed in simple round dresses, with wrap fronts; or the peasant's jacket and petticoat, with trimmings of needle-work or ribbon. The hair exhibits little variety since our last communication. The Grecian style continues as yet unrivalled; but ringlets are often seen flowing irregularly from various points, but chiefly from the left temple; bands are partially admitted. The plait is too general to be ranked with a select delineation; and no female now wears her hair without ornaments.

No. 1 — Evening or Ball Dress   No. 2 — Walking or Carriage Costume

Fashionable party at the Frescati in Paris

189

Fashions for May. ENGLISH COSTUME. No. 1 — An Evening, or Ball Dress. A round dress of soft white satin, with short train, slashed sleeve, and square bosom, made to sit close to the form; embroidered round the bottom and bosom with a delicate border in silver. The shawl drapery, formed of a large square of pink patent net, embroidered in correspondent border of silver; which, by crossing the back, and being confined with a brooch on the left shoulder, forms the tunic drapery (now so much in esteem) by the aid of a single pin only. Silver cord and tassels, suspended from one side of the figure. Large diamond brooch in the centre of the bosom, continued in a chain to the bottom of the waist. Drawn tucker of Mechlin lace. Hair in dishevelled curls on the crown of the head, flowing in ringlets towards the left ear. Bandeau of diamonds finished in the centre in the form of a cockle-shell. Earrings of a similar form; armlets and bracelets of blended pearl and hair. Pink satin shoes, trimmed with silver fringe. White kid gloves, rucked. No. 2 — Walking, or Carriage Costume. A French coat of imperial satin, or twill sarsnet, of a lavender-blossom, or light lilac colour; bordered at the wrist, and entirely round the coat, with a brocade ribband of the shaded jonquille colour. A plain walking dress of the finest French cambric, or jaconet muslin, scolloped at the feet in the form of shells; two rows of open hems, or work, at regular distances, immediately above it. Habit shirt of similar material, let in with rich point lace in front; with treble high collars of lace and embroidery. A small brooch of bright amber confines the shirt at the throat, and one of a larger size ornaments the gown in the centre of the bosom. A sash, the colour of the coat, tied immediately in front. Indian turban cap, or bonnet of correspondent materials, worn generally with a veil of Brussels lace. Hair cropt behind, and in simple curls in front. White sarsnet parasol, with kid shoes, the colour of the coat. A FASHIONABLE PARTY: at the Frescati in Paris. First Lady. In a round dress of Italian crape, of a bright lemon colour, over a white sarsnet slip. A short full sleeve, and round bosom, cut low, with a tucker of French net. Conversation bonnet of chip, ornamented with lilac ribband. Hair curled on the forehead; and in ringlets on the shoulders. Second Lady. A round dress of plain India mull muslin; with long waist, full sleeve, and frock back. A deep fall of Mechlin lace quite round the bosom. A short sash, of bright morone tied behind, A turban hat, of morone, satin, shaded in checks, and ornamented with field flowers in front. Necklace and earrings of mocho-stone linked with gold. Hair cropted close behind, and in dishevelled curls in front. Long Angola shawl, of a bright amber colour, with a rich and variegated border. White kid gloves.

General Intelligence of the Most Elegant Spring Fashions. We have seldom witnessed an article more tasteful then the French coat and vest; this habiliment is also formed of coloured sarsnet, or imperial satin. The one which attracted us in particular, was composed of a celestial blue twill sarsnet, and is formed nearly like the last new Opera coats, not a single gather being seen to unity the waist to the skirt, which sits close to the form behind, and flows open in front, discovering the graceful vest, which is composed of a width of the sarsnet near three yards long, is passed through the left shoulder-seam, crosses the back, and is brought through the bottom of the waist on the opposite side, where it meets the adverse end, and is simply tied so as to resemble a military sash. The coat and vest are trimmed entirely round with a brocade ribband of shaded purple, which has a novel and attractive contract with the pale blue of which this elegant habit is composed. Spensers are formed in similar style, except that the lappel is much smaller, and encroaches but little on the vest, which completely finishes the spenser in front. With these articles are chiefly worn the chip or straw Gipsy hat, with correspondent trimming; or the porcupine hat, of straw, with deep tiara front. Several cloaks are seen of the cottage form, with deep pointed capes, finished with a cone, or barrel tassel; these are formed also of sarsnets. Indeed the season is not yet so far advanced as to admit of a slighter covering. The Woodman's hat, of figured sarsnet, in celestial blue, olive, dove-colour, or lilac, is an ornament where much taste and whim is united; on the youthful countenance it has a becoming and unstudied effect; for walking, however, we recommend the Cottage bonnet, or Gypsy hat of imperial straw, tied across the crown with a silk or patent-net handkerchief. There is in these articles a sort of retired elegance at once appropriate and distinguishing. Dress gown are worn much ornamented, chiefly with lace or needle-work; and for occasions of public display we have witnessed coloured borders on crape, or India muslin; either in painting, embroidery, or foil; we have seen a border of ivy, of liburnium, and of the geranium leaves, have a most attractive effect. White satin jackets, trimmed with chenille, with short Spanish sleeve, and two rows of Vandyke lace plaited thick, and continued round the back, finishing at each shoulder, and terminated in front with a long white satin sash, are much worn with a round train dress of Moravian muslin; this is one of those intermediate habiliments which attracts by its simplicity and elegance. The general style of forming dresses is very high in the bosom, so as to preclude the necessity of the neckerchief; plain fronts, uniting in the centre with a clasp, and a demi wrap over it, finished on the left side, where the dress closes, are uncommonly elegant. We observed a dress of this formation at the Duchess of G——'s assembly, let in all round, and up the left side, with the most delicate Mechlin lace, and tied with tassels of cut steel; the back is a little advanced of late. The short sleeves is almost universal in full dress; and the evening short dress in confined to the ball costume. Morning dresses are formed with the large full sleeve, high collar, with a single fall of French lace, or a double plaiting of Vandyke; they are laced, or buttoned down the back, and so constituted as to sit close to the bosom. The Parisian chemise is trimmed round with plain French net; and the Turkish wrap is formed like the flowing pelisse, and composed chiefly of striped coloured muslin, plain jaconet. French cambric, or Indian long cloth. The Spanish hood, the Parisian night-cap, the Curacao turban, the long lace veil, forming both cloak and head-dress, are variously adopted. The hair is chiefly worn in dishevelled curls, exhibiting much of the forehead. Bandeaus of diamonds, garnets, or emeralds, are considered elegant; and the rainbow coronet, formed of diverse precious stones, worn by the Marchioness of E—— on a late splendid occasion, excited universal admiration, from its singularity, brilliancy, and beauty. It should be remembered that the morning costume, according to the present standard of fashion, is considered vulgarly deficient without a cap. Shirts, as an intermediate article, are as much in esteem as ever; they are often made without a collar, and worn with a double frill of Vandyke lace, sometimes with a fall of Mechlin lace; and those who cover the throat in public, have adopted (instead of a collar) a buffooned net, which is gathered into a large brooch of various compositions, in the centre.

No. 1 — Morning Walking Dress   No. 2 — Full Dress

No. 3. — Parisian Full Dress   No. 4 — Walking or Carriage Costume

Fashions for June.

ENGLISH COSTUME. No. 1- Morning Walking Dress. A plain round gown of French cambric, or jaconot muslin; long sleeve, wrapt front, and spenser back. Open shirt, frilled round the neck with scolloped lace. Mountain hat of straw, or Imperial chip, trimmed with jonquille ribband. Shoes and gloves to correspond. Flemish mantle of twill sarsnet. Gold hoop earrings; and patent parasol of shaded green. No. 2 - Full Dress. A round robe of white Italian crape over white sarsnet; with frock back, plain sleeve, and pointed front; trimmed round the bottom, bosom, and sleeves with an elegant border, composed of the pearl bead, blended with green foil and gold. The robe confined at the centre of the bosom with a brooch formed of a single pearl. One row of the same forms the necklace, which is fastened with an emerald snap. Hoop earrings, and bracelets to correspond. Hair *à la Madona* on the forehead, twisted behind, and flowing in full curls on the crown of the head; a bunch of white roses in front, inclining towards the right side. Gloves of French kid; shoes of white satin, with silver trimming. Square shawl of Chinese silk, with a rich pointed border; finished at each point with correspondent tassels. The style of wearing this graceful ornament is, simply giving it a twist from the cross corners, and flinging it negligently over the left shoulder; thus one point ornaments the figure behind, while the others, falling irregularly, form a drapery on the left side, and gracefully occupy the right hand. Chinese fan of frosted crape, with ivory sticks, carved in Egyptian characters. No. 3 - Parisian Full Dress. A round train dress of India muslin of the clearest texture, worn over a white satin slip, ornamented round the bottom, and up the front, with a rich border composed of ruby foil, and gold embroidery; long waist and stiff stay; the dress formed with a round bosom, and cut so low as greatly to expose the bust; the back simply drawn to a point at the extremity of the waist behind, and finished with a short sash of white satin. A full sleeve, ornamented towards the bottom with a roll and tuft of satin, finished at the extreme edge, round, and across the bosom with a full trimming of the same, or with plaitings of French net. Hair in the Eastern style, formed of the cable braid, bound and twisted on the forehead in alternate bands and knots, confined in a similar style behind with a caul of gold net. Earrings and necklace of rubies, set transparent, and linked with gold bracelets to correspond. White kid gloves; and white satin shoes, with gold roses. No. 4 - Walking, or Carriage Costume. A Cossack spenser and cap of lilac twill sarsnet, ornamented with silk frogs, cords, and tassels of the same colour; high collar, and sleeve with full tops. A plain round dress of cambric, or simply open-hemmed at the bottom, or let in with work of lace. Straw-coloured kid gloves, and shoes the colour of the spenser. Large parasol of the Eastern form.

Select Delineations of the Most Prevailing Fashions.

The out-door costume of our fashionable females, was never more tastefully selected — it is at once various and attractive. We shall endeavour to delineate such as appeared to us most novel and striking. And amidst these we must remark the Hungarian vest, the Spanish mantle, Cossack spenser, Grecian scarf, and French coat. The later article is particularly described in our last Number; but the Hungarian vest is perhaps the most graceful and elegant ornament of the kind that was ever offered at the shrine of taste and fashion. It is to too fanciful a formation to allow of a minute representation, but we offer to our readers such a description as its fanciful structure will best afford. The one which attracted our notice was formed of a silver lilac, or shot sarsnet, and the effect in front is somewhat resembling the spenser, having a high collar and long sleeve; but a mantle, or scarf, is suspended from the left shoulder with a few gathers, crossing the back plain behind, and flowing in the form of the hood worn by our Masters of Arts, except that it wraps over the adverse side, is fastened with a belt of a gathered silk across the bosom; and the whole of the mantle is trimmed round with a border of silk in reversed gathers. On a tall and elegant figure, nothing can out vie the very distinguishing effect of this article. The bonnet worn with it was the Foley poke, formed of the same material as the vest. The Spanish mantle is a species of the Gipsy, or Spanish cloak of established celebrity; but is much shorter, is formed of sarsnet, cut to a point behind, and sloped square on each side, till it meets the bend of the elbow; it is formed with pointed capes, nearly resembling those of the Polish pelice given in our winter Prints of Fashion; the cape and cloak are trimmed entirely round with a border of the same material in reversed gathers. This very neat and ingenious trimming is the most novel and select finish for all kinds of coats, spensers, and mantles that has come within our observation for a length of time. Before we quit this article of attire, we will give to our fair correspondents the only ornament in the style of a scarf which has struck us as worthy of notice. — It is composed of a simple width of muslin, coloured or white, is two yards and a quarter long, and one yard wide; it is doubled in form of a roll at the edge, and immediately above is placed a ribband of correspondent hue with the scarf, laid flat all round, and at each corner is fixed a tassel in form of an acorn. This scarf is thrown over the left shoulder, crosses the back, and passing under the left arm, is brought over the bosom, and meets at the opposite corner, where it is confined with a diamond pin. — Thus disposed, the ends on the left side nearly reach the feet in irregular folds, and the right constitutes a short pointed tunic. Many of our fashionable *belles* have this scarf formed of lace, or crape, embroidered tastefully at the edge, and placed as above, over a white satin under-dress; this forms a most elegant drawing-room costume. Little alteration has taken place in the style of full dress since our last communication. French aprons over sarsnet gowns, ornamented with natural flowers, are still considered fancifully elegant. Robes of jonquille Italian crape over white satin, and frocks of lilac muslin, with white sarsnet or satin slips, are the distinguishing selection of the fashionable and youthful female. The bosoms of full dresses are universally made so high as to ask no aid from the neckerchief; but we still look in vain for a modes veil to shade the back and shoulders. We cannot conceive how the sex can so degenerate from their wonted ideas of taste, judgment, and delicacy, as to continue this unbecoming display. We lament the more exceedingly this impolite and gross custom; as in other instances the taste and elegance of our English *Belles* stand at this moment unrivalled. The costume *à la Mary Queen of Scots,* is at this moment selected by a few individuals whose rank and fortunes give them a title to that singularity, which in a more obscure situation, would be out of place and unbecoming. But as this style of decoration can never be consistently adopted by the many, we recommend the simple frill of double vandyke lace, gathered easily full round the back and terminating at the corner of each shoulder in front. With either muslin or coloured crape dresses, this embellishment is highly advantageous to the figure.

No. 1 — Her Royal Highness the Princess of Wales

No. 2 — Parisian Fashions, the Frescati in Paris

Fashions for July. ENGLISH COSTUME. No. 1 - Her Royal Highness the Princess of Wales in her Court Dress, as worn on the Birth-Day. This dress, for taste and magnificence, stood unrivalled amidst the splendour and elegance displayed on the Birth-Day of our justly revered Sovereign; and we consider ourselves fortunate in having it in our power to procure a representation of it for our fair correspondents. The body and ground of the drapery was formed of a rich silver and lilac tissue; with a most superb border, composed of emeralds, topazes, and amethysts, to represent the vine-leaf and grapes. The train and petticoat of silver tissue; bordered all round like the drapery; and each terminated with a most brilliant silver fringe of a strikingly novel formation. Rich silver laurel and arrow on the left side, to loop up the train. Head-dress of diamonds and amethysts, tastefully disposed; with high plume of ostrich feather. Neck-dress, the winged ruff, *à la Mary Queen of Scots;* sleeve ornaments to correspond. Amethyst necklace and earrings, with Maltese cross; diamond armlets and bracelets. White satin shoes, with silver rosettes. French kid gloves, above the elbow. Fan of Imperial crape, studded with amethysts and topazes. No. 2 - Parisian Fashions, Taken from a Group of Conversation Figures at the Frescati, in Paris. Ladies Dress. A white Italian crape robe over a white satin slip, ornamented round the bottom and drapery with a border of shells, painted to nature. Plain scolloped bosom cut very low, and made to sit close to the form. Waved sleeves, easily full, formed of alternate stripes of crape and pink satin. Hair, bound in smooth bands, confined, on the forehead, and ornamented behind with wreaths of wild roses. Earrings and necklace of pearls. Shoes, pink satin, trimmed with silver. White kid gloves, rucked.

Birth-Day [George III] Dresses. Her Majesty [the queen]. — A lilac and silver tissue petticoat, trimmed with draperies of point Brussels lace, with point lace of the same description, flowered round the pocket holes; the front of the draperies superbly ornamented with large diamond rosettes, from which were suspended diamond bows and tassels. The under drapery fancifully ornamented with diamonds in diagonal stripes. The mantle to correspond with the drapery. **Her Royal Highness the Princess of Wales [Caroline]. [see above].** Her Royal Highness the Princess Charlotte of Wales [the future George IV and Caroline's daughter]. — A pink and silver slip, with a beautiful Brussels lace frock to wear over it, and a pink and silver girdle. Her Royal Highness the Princess Augusta. — A yellow crape petticoat richly embroidered with silver; a sash across with a border of honeysuckles, and rich pointed embroidered draperies. Body and train to correspond. **Her Royal Highness Princess Elizabeth.** — A superb dress of apricot and silver tissue. The right side of the dress a magnificent drapery, composed of an Etruscan net of large silver beads, tastefully divided at distances by a thick bullion of beads, chains of beads in dead silver relieved with bright bullion, elegantly ornamented with massy wreaths of laurel in silver foil, and bouquets of chestnut blossoms, with the kernel bursting from the shell, formed the *tout ensemble* of this strikingly novel and elegant dress, which, for taste and effect, surpassed any dress of the kind we have observed. The bottom finished with a wreath of laurel in raised foil and beads. The whole looped up with large silver cords and tassels. Robe of apricot and silver tissue trimmed with broad Vandyke silver fringe, point lace and diamonds. **Her Royal Highness Princess Mary.** — Wore a magnificent dress of brown crape, embroidered with silver and pink roses over a petticoat of royal purple; oval draperies, richly spangled all over, and terminated with marking borders of dead and bright foil in vandykes, with roses beautifully interspersed lightly in the embroidery, the whole completed with elegant cords and tassels. Robe of brown, purple and silver tissue, trimmed with broad vandyke fringe, point lace, and diamonds. **Her Royal Highness the Princess Sophia.** — A pea-green petticoat, over which an elegant scarf drapery of the same colour, most magnificently embroidered in silver pines and branches; on the right side a wing of scale embroidery of uncommon richness, and on the left a richly spangled drapery, most tastefully hung round the bottom of the petticoat. The robe of green and silver tissue, most elegantly trimmed with silver, and looped on the sleeves with silver chains and acorns. Head-dress, an elegant plume of green and white feathers, with a profusion of diamonds. **Her Royal Highness Princess Amelia.** — Petticoat of white crape richly spangled, and border a mosaic pattern. Draperies of purple Albany net with silver acorns; pockets formed with rich springs of laurel; train of handsomely embroidered purple tissue; on the left, a beautiful formed drapery of shell-work, ornamented with Parisian trimming. The whole in appearance truly elegant and becoming to her Royal Highness, and we think it one of the handsomest dresses at Court. **Her Royal Highness the Duchess of York.** — A white sarsnet petticoat, richly embroidered with an Etruscan border in silver draperies, a silver tissue drawn up and ornamented with a wreath of silver hoops, which had a very novel and elegant appearance. Train, silver tissue trimmed round with the wreaths of hop leaves; Brussels lace sleeves, with diamond armlets and broaches. Head-dress, diamonds and feathers. **Her Royal Highness Princess Sophia of Gloucester.** — Wore a splendid dress of white and silver superbly embroidered, and was much admired for taste and effect, the whole finished with a massy border at the bottom. Her Royal Highness wore a robe of lilac and silver tissue, with rich embroidered sleeves and fronts. **Princess Castelcicala.** — An elegant dress of lavender-coloured crape, fluted in divisions, trimmed with broad black lace, and ornamented with wreaths of fancy flowers, same colour and the dress, and bows of ribband; robe of black lace trimmed all round with flowers. **Duchess of Northumberland.** — A white crape petticoat, richly spangled in silver, and ornamented with silver grapes; train to correspond. **The Duchess of Rutland.** — Was elegantly dressed in a beautiful petticoat and train of straw coloured crape, with rich silver vine-leaves, and ropes of silver arrows. **Duchess of Dorset.** — A rich embroidered silver crape, ornamented with lilac crape and silver tassels; train lilac crape. **Duchess of Montrose.** — A yellow crape petticoat, with a rich painted Grecian border; train yellow crape. **Duchess of Athol.** — A white satin petticoat, with a lace drapery of Reine Marguerite flowers, appliqued on white satin; lace train. **Duchess of Buccleugh.** — A very rich dress of brown and silver, superbly embroidered; brown train, elegantly ornamented with silver; head-dress brown and silver, with a profusion of diamonds. **Marchioness Dowager of Bath.** — A petticoat of violet crape, embroidered in rich silver draperies, with a silver foil border, pocket holes richly trimmed, silver cords and tassels; body and train to correspond.

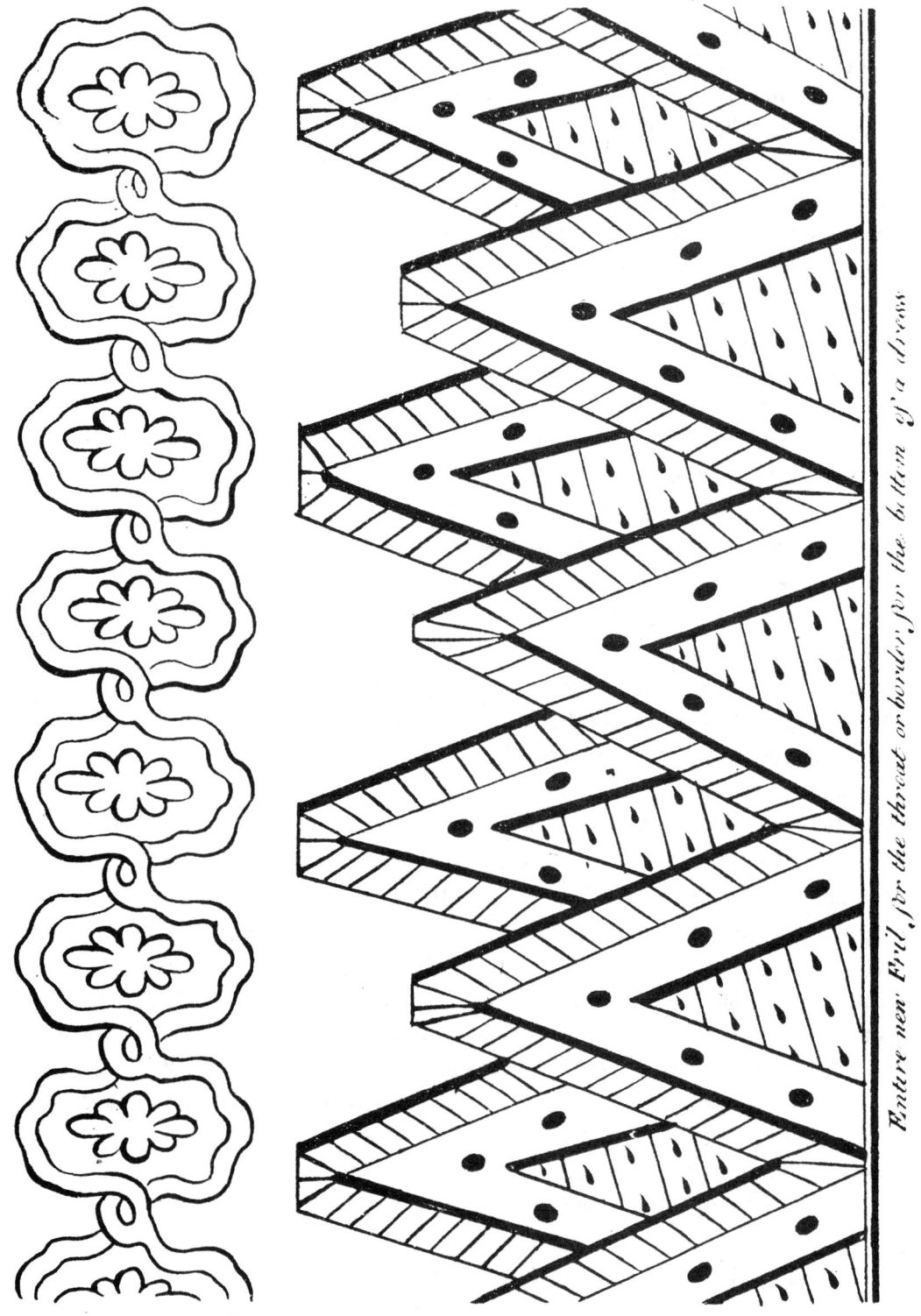

Entere new Fril for the throat or border for the bottom of a dress

Engraven for La Belle Assemblée February 1. 1807.

Fril for throat or border for bottom of a Dress.

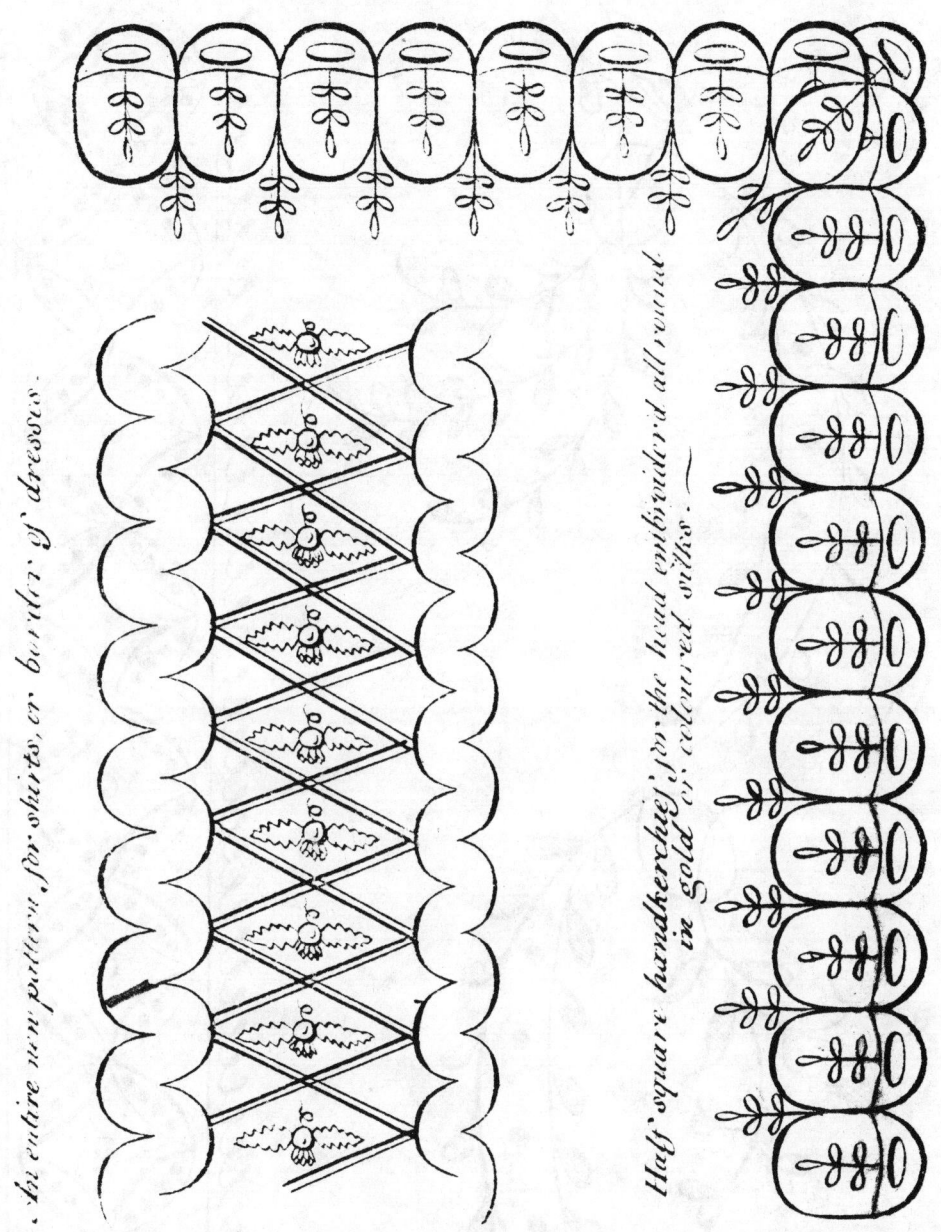

An entire new pattern for shirts, or border of dresses.

Half square handkerchief, for the head embroider'd all round in gold or coloured silks.

Designed & printed for La Belle Assemblée N.º 14 March 1.1807

Pattern for shirts, or border of a dress +
pattern for head-kerchief.

New pattern for Needlework, designed and printed for La Belle Assemblée Nº 15 April 1807.

Needlework Pattern.

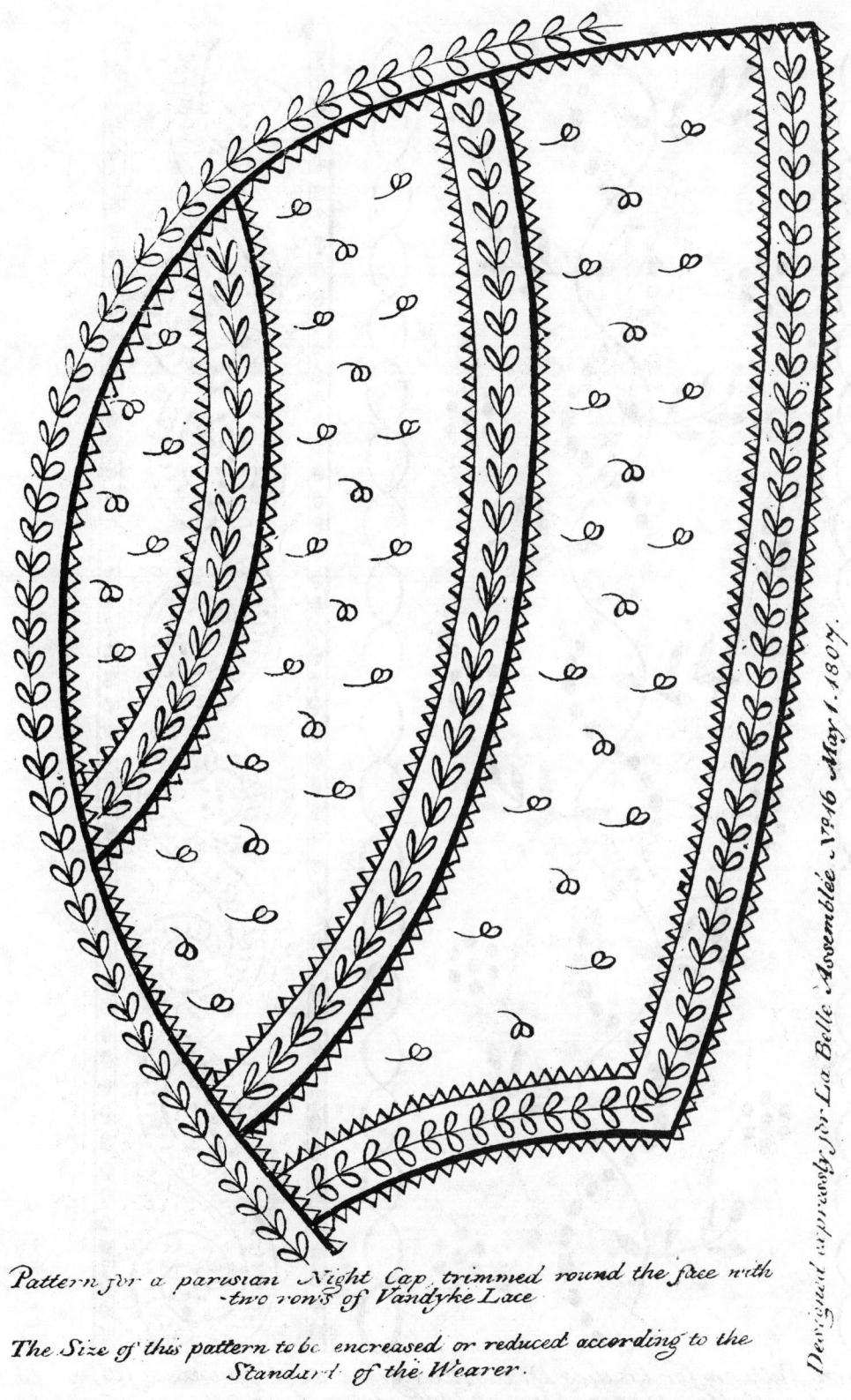

Pattern for a parisian Night Cap, trimmed round the face with two rows of Vandyke Lace

The Size of this pattern to be encreased or reduced according to the Standard of the Wearer.

Designed expressly for La Belle Assemblée. Nᵒ 16. May 1. 1807.

Pattern for Parisian Night Cap.

New Pattern for Ladies Dress, designed and printed for La Belle Assemblée Nº 17, June 1, 1807.

Pattern for Ladies Dress.

1789 - Duke of Richmond & Lennox

1792

The Evening Walk

1796
Gallery of fashion, London

1792, Juni
Journal des Dames

1796 - Lord Adam Gordon & Comte d'Artois
(later Charles X of France)

1810
The Repository, London

A ce soir!
La Mésangère, Paris; um 1800

1816
The Repository, London

1816
The Repository, London

1817

PARISIAN HOME COSTUME.

Engraved for N⁰ 98 of La Belle Assemblée. Jan.ʸ 1817.

Glossary of Terms – Men and Women

Amazon Dress, Amazone Dress - riding habit.

Angola, Angora - fine wool woven with a silk, wool or cotton warp.

Apron Dress - having an apron-like skirt, tied at the waist and open in back.

Armenian Turban - small, of tulle and satin, trimmed with feathers.

Armlet - like a bracelet, but worn on the upper arm.

Bandeaus - a woman's wig or hairstyle with high slanting and hanging curls.

Barouche - a four wheeled carriage with a folding top.

Bear on - to distort the fabric, either stretching or shrinking, usually through stitching and the use of an iron.

Blond, Blonde - cream colored silk bobbin lace, Chantilly type but with more densely worked pattern areas.

Book muslin - muslin with a hard finish.

Breeches - pants or outercoverings for legs that ended just above or just below the knee, closing snugly with buttons.

Brown Holland - plain, wide linen cloth, but slightly thickened.

Brussels lace - a point lace.

Busk - the center front stiffening of a bodice, often bone or whalebone.

Cape à la Pelerine - waist length in back with long pointed ends in front.

Carmelite coloured - yellow/green.

Cassimere, Cassimir, Chassimere - patented 1766 by Francis Yerbury; thin woollen cloth, pattern loom produced, the term often used interchangeably with Kerseymere.

Cestus - a girdle, narrow cord or belt tied and the end hanging down in front.

Chemise Dress, Gown, Robe - thin muslin, cambric or colored silk, short sleeves and buttoned down the front.

Chemisette - white muslin or cambric "fill-in" for the bodice of a day dress.

Chenile - fine silk cord with plush surface used for trim; silk honey-combed lace.

Chignon - the mass of hair at the back or top of the head.

Chip - wood or palm split into thin strips for making hats and bonnets.

Circassian cloth - fabric of wool, cotton, or mohair with a diagonal weave.

Coachman's Box Coat - a gig coat or driving coat heavily caped overcoat, the capes often multiple, worn by coachmen, travellers, etc.

Coatee, skirted coatee - a short coat or spencer (in this case worn by a child)

Conversation Bonnet - poke bonnet with one side of the brim projecting beyond the cheek, and the other side turned back from the cheek.

Coquilicot - a stiff bunch of cock's feathers.

Corbeau - black, with greenish reflections.

Corduroy - a heavy, pile-woven cotton fabric

Cottage Bonnet - straw, fitting the head closely and with a brim.

Cottage Cloak - hooded and tied under the chin.

Crape, Crepe - transparent crimped silk, or silk and wool gauze.

Dimity - fine cotton fabric having a stripe or figure raised like seersucker on the face and depressed on the back. Usually white, with or without a colored pattern.

Dragoons - mounted soldiers or calvary with light or heavy equipment.

Fall Down, Falls, Broad Falls - a buttoned flap in the front of breeches, pants, etc. A Broad Fall extends from side-seam to side-seam.

Flaps - pocket flaps covering the opening and extending down.

Flash Flaps - by 1790 usually decorative, placed on the sleeve on top of a formed cuff.

Festoon - decorative trim arranged in loops.

Fine drawn - like rantering used to butt two cut edges together with a ladder stitch

Florentine - a heavy expensive silk fabric (for breeches), figured or twilled, for waistcoats; or a worsted waistcoating material; or a twilled cotton fabric for trousers.

Fork - the crotch.

French net - for evening frocks, similar to Brussels net.

Frock, Frock Coat - a formal coat, at this time it was a coat with tails and a turned-down collar, in 1816 it changed to have a skirt in front - but both types continued to be worn. there is always some confusion about terms amongst Frock, Frac, and Frock Coat and often historically they were not used in the way we would today.

Frog - ornamental cloak or coat button made of braided silk or wool.

Frogmouths, Frog Pocket - a pocket opening made in front of the side seam of breeches, and cut with a rectangular flap, the point secured by a button.

Fulled - to thickened wool by heating, moistening, or pressing. Also the term may be used to mean easing, gathering or ruffling (trim being fulled onto the front of a dress).

Fustian - cloth with a linen warp and a thick cotton woof.

Gaiters - covering the ankle and often small of the leg, spreading out over the top of the shoe or boot, and fastened underneath; worn with trousers.

Georgina, Georgian cloth - light weight broad cloth from 1806 on.

Glazing - a glossing process effected by steam heated steel rollers.

Gorge - that part of a coat or vest encircling the neck, where the collar, if any, is joined.

Gorget - ornamental neckband, full and broad in front.

Great Coat - any heavy overcoat, particularly a skirted overcoat.

Gypsy Hat, Gipsey Hat - plain hat tied carelessly under the chin with a ribbon.

Habit - riding habit.

Habit Shirt - worn as a "fill-in" for a day dress.

Hair à la Titus - brushed forward on the forehead.

Hair Cloth, Hair Shag - Elastic resilient material woven with a cotton or linen warp and a weft of hair from horses manes or tails.

Ham - the region behind the knee joint.

Hessians - soft leather boots which curved up to a point in front to below the knee-cap and decorated there with a tassel.

Hibernian vest- a short jacket or spencer of velvet with fur trim, 1807.

Hollowed out - cut concave.

Hussar Jacket - a short military jacket, braided and frogged.

Jockey Cap - peaked cap of black velvet.

Jaconot, Jaconet - a cotton textile between muslin and cambric.

Kerseymere - similar to Cassimir, possibly introduced as a rival to Cassimir which was patented.

Knap-Kneed, Knock-Kneed - knees turned inwards or rubbing against each other.

Lappell - lapel.

Lawn - a very fine semi-transparent linen cloth.

Levett Coat - for women. Levetes, or Levite gowns had long undraped skirts, therefore this type coat would follow the same lines.

Mantelet - half shawl or cape, often with wide sleeves.

Mantua Maker - dressmaker.

Marsailles, Marseilles - reversible fabric with raised pattern; a hand quilted cotton or cotton woven to resemble quilting.

Massy - massive.

Mechlin lace - fragile bobbin lace with ornamental designs outlined with shiny chord or thread.

Mob cap - white indoor cap of cambric or muslin having a frilled border and high crown.

Morone - maroon (?)

Mosaic - fabric designed in a geometric pattern.

Nankeen - naturally yellow colored cloth imported from China, or cotton made to imitate it.

Patent Thread - cotton thread gassed to scorch off fine fibers, used for net and lace.

Pantaloons - close fitting tights, shaped to the leg and ending just below the calf.

Petticoat - also called a "Lingerie gown," sometimes this is revealed when the skirt of the gown or robe is pulled back, and sometimes it is worn by itself with a spencer jacket or a tunic. In the case of a riding-habit the skirt part, which is separate from the jacket.

Phaeton - a light four-wheeled carriage having no sidepieces in front of the seat or (two) seats.

Plush - fabric having a longer pile than velvet when made of silk, or a type of woolen velvet used for garments and upholstery.

Police or Pelisse Coats - 18th c., a 3/4 length cloak with shoulder-cape or hood and armhole slits. 1800-1810 progressed to sleeves and then ankle length, sleeved, figure fitting often with one or more capes.

Post-chaise - carriage having a closed body on four wheels and seating two to four.

Privately, Private Stitches - preliminary stitches.

Quillery - pleated lace or ribbon giving flute like folds, dress trim.

Quilting - ready made padding usually of satin inter-lined with cotton.

Rantered - much like reweaving, sewing separate ravellings of the fabric and darning partway through the thickness, either from the front or the back, to bring the cut edges of thick fabrics together in a butt join.

Ratinet - a thin form of rateen (a class of coarse woolens) also commonly used as a lining fabric.

Ribband - narrow border of silk or decorative material.

Robe, Gown - a woman's dress with the skirt open in the front and usually long behind (1790s).

Robin, Robings - broad flat trimming decorating a gown round the neck and down the front of the bodice.

Round-about Jacket - short, single-breasted, cutaway sack coat or jacket worn by boys.

Round Dress - dress with joined bodice and skirt, closed all around.

Rucked - puckered.

Sarsnet, Sarcenet - silk fabric in a plain, twill or taffeta weave.

Scye - tailoring term for the curved lower segment of the arm-hole of a coat.

Shag - heavy woolen cloth with a long nap.

Shamie, Chamie, Chamois - soft pliable leather. Chamois Fiber: a stout crinkled paper fabric for interlining.

Slops - cheap, ready-made clothes.

Small Clothes - a polite way of saying: breeches (at this time).

Spanish Sleeve - short puffed sleeve for evening dress, slashed on the sides over a silk lining.

Spencer - (female) a short jacket ending at the waist level (outdoors); evening wear, very ornamental and often without sleeves (inside).

Sprung - a belled or flared effect.

Stock - high neck cloth.

Stocking Frame - any knitting machine.

Stockinet - a heavy, elastic, close woven material, usually white, from which breeches are made.

Stomacher - long ornate panel forming the front of an open low-necked bodice.

Stride - the crotch seam.

Stuff - material.

Surplice sleeve - a long loose sleeve.

Surtout - an overcoat made in the style of a frock coat.

Tabby - coarse kind of taffeta, glossy and watered.

Thickset - a coarse usually napped, fustian (linen warp & thick cotton woof).

Tiffany - transparent silk gauze.

Tippets - short shoulder cape.

Toilinette, Toilinets - fine woolen cloth with a silk &/or cotton warp - plain, stripped, or checked; somewhat like merino or cassimere.

Toupe, Toupee - false hair, a small wig.

Trafalgar Dress - evening gown of white satin, trimmed with silver.

Trowsers, trousers - long unshaped leg coverings. Worn by boys, sailors, and workmen. Became fashionable for men in general from 1807 on.

Tucker - a white edging to a low-necked bodice.

Tunique, Tunic Dress - dress with an over-skirt, closed all around.

Under waistcoats - sleeveless, shorter than the over waistcoat, but showing at the top.

Undress - Common Dress, un-ceremonial attire such as worn for everyday purposes, especially morning dress.

Vandykes - a dentate border either in lace or material.

Velveteen - silk or cotton pile, the pile formed by the weft on a cotton back.

Vest - a short sleeveless bodice for women.

Voile - sheer dress material in silk, cotton or wool; also commonly used to line men's summer coats.

Wheelpiece, Wealpiece - an extra piece patched onto the plait-side of the skirt of a frock coat (because of the inability to cut the pattern whole from narrow-width materials).

Woodstock gloves - fawn skin leather.

Worsted - fabric of combed wool, hard woven.

York Tan Gloves - fawn colored soft leather of undressed kid.

Bibliography

American Heritage (eds) **The Revolution.**, 1958

Ashdown, Mrs. Charles **British Costume during 19 Centuries.**,

Baker, William Henry **Dictionary of Men's Wear.**, 1908

Batterberry, Michael & Arane **Mirror, Mirror: Social History of Fashion.**, 1977

Baumgarten,Linda **18th Century Clothing at Williamsburg**, 1986

Boucher, François **20,000 Years of Fashion**

Bradley, Carolyn **Western World Costume.**, 1954

Buck, Anne **Dress in 18th C. England.**, 1979

Byrde, Penelope **Male Image: 1300-1970.**, 1992

Calasibetta, Charlotte **Fairchild's Dictionary of Fashion**, 1975

Calkins, Carroll (ed) **The Story of America.**, 1975

Chartrand, Rene **Uniforms & Equipment: U.S. Forces, War of 1812.**, 1992

Contini, Mila **Fashion: Ancient Egpyt to present Day.**, 1965

Cunnington, C.w. & P.E. & Chrles Beard **A Dictionary of English Costume 900-1900**, 1976

Earle, Alice Morse **Costume of Colonial Times.**, 1894

Earle, Alice Morse **Two Centuries of Costume in America.**, 1974

Elting, John (ed) **Military Uniforms America: American Revolution**

Elting, John (ed) **Military Uniforms America: Years of Growth 1796-1851.**,

Evans, Mary **Costume Throughout the Ages.**, 1938

Giles, Edward R **Art of Cutting & History English Costume (1887).**, 1987

Gorsline, Douglas **What People Wore.**, 1952

Grafton, John **The American Revolution**, 1975

Hill, Margot & Bucknell, Peter **Evolution of Fashion: 1066-1930.**, 1987

Jounal American Military Inst. **American Military Dress, War of 1812.**, Vol III #3, 1939

Katcher, Philip **The American Soldier: Uniforms 1755 to present. **, 1990

Kemper, Rachel **A History of Costume**, 1977

Kidwell, Caludia & Christman, Margaret **Suiting Everyone.**, 1974

Kidwell, Claudia **Cutting A Fashionable Fit.**, 1979

Kohler,Karl **History of Costume.**, 1963

Kredel, Fritz **Soldiers of the American Army: 1775-1854.**, 1954

Kybalova, Ludmila **Pictorial Encyclopedia of Fashion.**, 1968

Laver, James **Costume Illustration: 17th & 18th C.**, 1951

Laver, James **Dandies**, 1968

le Bourhis, Katell (ed) **Age of Napoleon: Costume 1789-1815.**, 1989

McClellan, Elizabeth **Historic Dress in America 1607-1870**, 1977

Nystrom, Paul **Economics of Fashion.**, 1928

Payne, Blanche **History of Costume.**, 1965

Picken, Mary Brooks **The Language of Fashion**, 1939

Planche, James R. **Cyclopedia of Costume or Dictionary of Dress.**, 1876

Riberio, Aileen **Art of Dress: Fashion England & France 1700-1820.**, 1995

Rigby, Janet **Life & Work of a Rural Taylor: Stephen Powell 1771-1844**

Ruppert, Jacques **Le Costume IV: Louis XVI - Directoire**, 1931

Ruppert, Jacques **Le Costume V: Consulat - Napoleon III**, 1931

Russell. Douglas **Costume History and Style.**, 1983

Shep, R.L. (ed) **Late Georgian Costume.**, 1991

Uzanne, Octave **Fashion in Paris: Revolution to end of 19th C.**, 1901

V & A Museum **Nineteenth Century Costume**, 1947

von Boehn, Max **Die Mode: Menschen und Moden 1790-1817**, 1905

Warwick, Pitz & Wychoff **Early American Dress.**, 1965

Waugh, Nora **The Cut of Men's Clothes 1600-1900.**, 1964

Waugh, Nora **The Cut of Women's Clothes 1600-1930**, 1969

Wilcox, R. Turner **Mode in Costume.**, 1948

TITLES PUBLISHED BY R.L. SHEP

ART OF CUTTING & HISTORY OF ENGLISH COSTUME (1887) by Edward Giles

THE BOOK OF COSTUME: or Annals of Fashion (1846) by The Countess of Wilton. ANNOTATED EDITION.

CIVIL WAR ERA ETIQUETTE: Martine's Handbook & Vulgarisms in Conversation

CIVIL WAR LADIES: Fashions & Needle-Arts of the Early 1860s from Peterson's Magazine, 1861 & 1864 plus hair styles & hair jewelry from Campbell's Self-Instructor in the Art of Hair Work, 1867

DRESS & CLOAK CUTTER: Women's Costumes 1877–1882 by Charles Hecklinger. Revised & Enlarged Edition

THE HANDBOOK OF PRACTICAL CUTTING on the Centre Point System (1866) by Louis Devere

THE LADIES' GUIDE TO NEEDLE WORK (1877) by S. Annie Frost

THE LADIES' SELF INSTRUCTOR in Millinery & Mantua Making, Embroidery & Applique (1853)

EDWARDIAN LADIES' TAILORING: The Twentieth Century System of Ladies' Garment Cutting (1910) by J.D. Hopkins

TAILORING OF THE BELLE EPOQUE: Vincent's Systems of Cutting all Kinds of Tailor-Made Garments (1903) by W.D.F. Vincent.

LATE GEORGIAN COSTUME: The Tailor's Friendly Instructor (1822) by J. Wyatt + The Art of Tying the Cravat (1828) by H. Le Blanc

THE LADIES' HAND BOOK OF FANCY & ORNAMENTAL WORK—Civil War Era by Florence Hartley

EDWARDIAN HATS: The Art of Millinery (1909) by Mme. Anna Ben-Yusuf

CIVIL WAR COOKING: The Housekeeper's Encyclopedia by Mrs. E.F. Haskell

THE COMPLETE GUIDE TO PRACTICAL CUTTING (1853) by Edward Minister

FREAKS OF FASHION: The Corset & The Crinoline (1868) by W.B. Lord

ART IN DRESS (1922) by P. Clement Brown

CORSETS: A Visual History

VICTORIAN NEEDLE-CRAFT: Artistic & Practical

CIVIL WAR GENTLEMEN: 1860s Apparel Arts & Uniforms

LATE VICTORIAN WOMEN'S TAILORING: The Direct System of Ladies' Cutting (1897) by T.H. Holding

REGENCY ETIQUETTE: The Mirror of Graces (1811) by a Lady of Distinction

FEDERALIST AND REGENCY COSTUME: 1790–1819

For more information write to:

R.L. SHEP PUBLICATIONS
P.O. Box 2706, Fort Bragg, CA 95437